# HOOT 'n GIN

## write to recovery

Virginia N. & Michael N.

ISBN 978-1-958128-10-7 (softcover)
ISBN 978-1-958128-11-4 (hardcover)
ISBN 978-1-958128-12-1 (ebook)
Library of Congress Control Number: 2022906695



Printed in the United States of America.

Book Vine Press
2516 Highland Dr.
Palatine, IL 60067

# Disclaimer

# Acknowledgment

Thanks to Jan McGrath for her encouragement and especially for her editing skills as she helped carve this book from a tome. Also thanks to Kathie Spiss for further encouragement and refinement of the text.

To Marc and John and all the mirrors
who helped us see yet could not see
themselves.

# Contents

# Preface

More than a love story, this collection of letters is a chronicle of our first five years of recovery from alcoholism and co-dependency. It is an intimate study of how incorporating the Twelve Steps of Al-Anon and Alcoholics Anonymous in our convoluted lives helped us to grow up, face reality, and find joy in living.

For us, the initial physical recovery from the compulsion to drink came quite swiftly. Then the real work began. As our heads cleared, we began to see the wreckage alcoholism has caused our families and us. No longer anesthetized, feelings returned and with them came guilt, anger and resentment. The concept of "rigorous honesty," proposed by Alcoholics Anonymous as the prime ingredient for successful sobriety, posed a problem for us. We had come to view our relationship as a means to survival and its life depended on the deception of others. Consequently, we avoided the moral inventory and admission of wrongs (Fourth and Fifth Steps) that A.A. and Al-Anon offer as a way to address guilt and resentments, fearing their threat to our relationship. We also feared scrutinizing repressed childhood secrets that were just beginning to surface.

With both of our recovery programs mired in guilt, Verge on the brink of leaving an abusive marriage, and Michael beginning to experience rolling depressions, Hoot and Gin, (childhood alter-egos) spontaneously emerged in our letters. With the mobility of mental apparitions, Hoot and Gin were able to swoop into the hidden recesses of childhood, to nurture each other and to rewrite painful history. Just as easily, they were traded back and forth between us, their adult counterparts, to encourage, to model new behaviors, to broach sensitive subjects, and to teach the healing art of laughing at one's self. They moved us through the stuck places until we could give up our stubborn resistance to change. When we finally become fiercely honest about our self-serving motives, we were able to release blame, offer forgiveness, and begin the spiritual search that led us each to our personal transformation, that true sobriety and self-respect promised by the Twelve Step Program.

The intent of this project is most importantly to offer hope to anyone struggling with the disease of alcoholism, whether thinking about recovery, newly recovering, or living with someone afflicted. Complicated lives can change, "sometimes quickly, [or] sometimes slowly,"[1] as our story attests. For those who may be mystified about the practical application of Twelve Steps to a situation as complicated as alcoholism, we indicate how we, too, were skeptical, but eventually found all twelve were gifts and not punishment. *Hoot 'n Gin* offers a nostalgic trip through the Steps for those who have already "trudged" their own "road" successfully, and demonstrates how the act of letter writing itself can augment a recovery program. It can be a beneficial tool for encouraging introspection, lending support, and measuring progress.

Secondarily, in the spirit of education, the intent of this book is to give an inside view of the newly-recovering, addicted person's thinking process as it changes, to those who work with them (counselors, social workers, religious representatives, or probation officers) who may not have personally experienced the ramifications of this disease. To them we suggest that we found correspondence so beneficial, other addicts might find it an auxiliary tool in their recovery program.

1 From the Promises, *Alcoholics Anonymous*, (New York: Alcoholics Anonymous World Services, Inc., 2001) 84.

# Foreword

Some of these letters, selected from more than two thousand, written over a five-year period, are verbatim other than minor corrections of grammar or punctuation, and others are compilations of two or three letters written in the same time frame and edited to avoid redundancies. Names are changed to protect the privacy of people we love, and to honor the Eleventh Tradition of Alcoholics Anonymous that requires, "personal anonymity at the level of press, radio, and film."[2] Hoot and Gin (alter-egos) spontaneously emerged one day in our letters. At first, italics set them aside in the text, later they became incorporated into the letters as they become incorporated into our lives, and finally we merge as whole. We do not advocate divorce as the means to solving problems in alcoholic marriages. We have known many marriages made stronger through the experience of recovery. This is simply how it was for us, what happened, and what we did to become sober.

2 Alcoholics Anonymous, *Twelve Steps and Twelve Traditions,* (New York: Alcoholics Anonymous World Services, Inc., 1981) 180.

LXXI

The Moving Finger writes; and having writ,
Moves on: nor all your Piety nor Wit
Shall lure it back to cancel half a Line,
Nor all your Tears wash out a Word of it.
*Rubaiyat of Omar Khayyam*

(From the fifth edition translation by Edward Fitzgerald)

# PART 1

# Early Sobriety

**Virginia N. & Michael N.**

September 1981

Dear Michael,

I suited up and showed up, eager to teach on a Monday morning, and I was promptly sent home by the Board of Education. A water main break. Pandemonium began when the announcement came that the students were going to be released at 9:30, but teachers were expected to stay. You can imagine the insurrections plotted in the interim, before we, too, were told to go home. Ain't ever going to get these kids settled into a routine!

Volatile truth is it? So far the volatile truth is toward my own self. That is what seven months of sobriety has done for me. Have you ever been in an attic or an old unused building with dust encrusted windows? Perhaps the sun was shining on the other side, but all it succeeded in doing was brightening the window. It did not focus the diffused images on the outside; sometimes even blocked them more. That is how I feel my life was. Now that I have rubbed a little space clean, some things are nearly blinding me by their light. Truths. A lot of my life I have denied, or kept the edge off, with a muzzy brain. I am not sure I want to see everything with such clarity. Now I don't have a cushion against feelings that are sharp aches thumping around my insides. I don't know how to handle them.

You said laughingly, they might as well put you on ice until Verge comes back to Cleveland. Without the laugh I can say the same. I walk; I speak; I function; but my joy part is someplace else. Things are quiet and momentarily non-threatening here, and I can tolerate being in Eric's company for longer than five minutes at a time. I can respond in a compassionate way to his attempt at becoming human again. I can work up a clinical caring, but there is no magic in it. I will be glad for him if he can get back to owning himself, but I feel like an emotionally uninvolved bystander. Our relationship is like the shell an emerging cicada leaves, complete with legs and body—even eyes, but nobody is home. I made our marriage up in my own head. It never was about sharing or growing, it was about a son we both loved and about my obsession with trying to understand what went on in Eric's brain. I gave up my rights from the beginning when he told me he wanted his child, but did not want the other responsibilities of

marriage. Early on he told me if his book got published and he became an established author he would take his son and leave me because I was too jealous and would not fit into his lifestyle. He said that he would kill me if I contested custody. On our wedding day he exonerated himself from any claim of exclusivity by telling me if I thought he was going to bed with anyone, he probably was. As painful as his words were, I accepted them, because he was the funniest, most challenging man I knew. I loved him, I was pregnant with his child, and I had little self-esteem. Those are just some of the mental snapshots hidden behind that dusty window. No more illusions or delusions. Time to grow up.

When you look truths square in the eye, though, they no longer lurk with frightening glints of almost revealed hurts that gain ominous proportion each time you push them away, until your hill of moles becomes a mountain of moose.

Verge

9/81

My Verge,

How demoralizing it must have been, when the time, effort, and hope you have invested in Eric were washed away again with one drink. Not to mention the locked in human being, the waste, the hold of the chemical! I ponder and ponder your question, "Does one abandon hope? Turn his back on a human life, especially when there is knowledge of certain help if the sufferer will ask?" Naturally, I can't make a decision for you. That is your choice, your lonely process. I can only offer for your consideration good old AA/Al-Anon Step One,[3] "Powerless over alcohol"—including those who use it. You have extended help in every way since you have grown to understand about alcoholism, and now Eric has to make choices. But one doesn't brush those questions aside easily. Even if he were not a person we loved, to watch his indifference toward life is painful.

I only speak now with the aid of what I have learned in the past few months. Please humor me if it sounds elementary. It will help me to write it even if you have heard it before. It seems to me, life is filled with times when choices must be made, or a series of choices, carrying a person from one experience to another. Ideally this travel

[3] Alcoholics Anonymous Step One: "We admitted we were powerless over alcohol—that our lives had become unmanageable." Ibid., 21.

through experiences becomes a root system of growth. A person meets situations, weighs the alternatives, chooses the one that best suits his needs and temperament, and then acts on it. To choose not to choose is an alternative, but one that leads to non-growth. The consequences of one decision on another cannot be foreseen, sometimes causing new dilemmas, making necessary more choices and more decisions. Hopefully the struggle is ever forward. Sounds simple and mapped out, but what doesn't show is the gut and heart pain those choices entail. We have seen that in the development of our love. We like to think of it as uniquely beautiful in spite of the frustrations imposed by circumstances. Those choices a person makes are his own to stand with or to alter as he sees fit. Just be sure you stay safe.

Michael

November 15

Dearest Michael,

I am presently in the middle of a head and heart war. I am inspecting honesty and truth again—how our honesty and truthfulness to each other has created need for dishonesty and untruthfulness to others in our life. Yet that is necessary for our self-preservation while preserving our ability to go on being what others want us to be. There seems to be no black and white about honesty and truth. You and I have come as close to truth as two people can with each other, aided by the fact that we think and act much alike. It is hopelessly confusing. All I know is that I have one pure constant in my life that I will not give up, unless that constant needs to be given up for his own growth.

Truth is that I love you in a clean, pure, responsible way, and you love me in the same way. Truth is, I do not feel guilty because I no longer have a commitment to my marriage. It never has been a healthy relationship or a proper marriage. I am willing to continue it in a familial way if it is a means to Eric's mental health, but I don't trust anything about the relationship. Truth is, yours has been a proper marriage and you are both growing now in your sobriety. Perhaps if you put all your forces to the marriage it can become stronger and healthier than ever. Truth is, our relationship drains many of your forces, despite the pact we made years ago that it would never come between our families and us. Truth is, facing that makes me want to throw up. Truth is, I know of no way to un-love you. Truth is that your love makes it possible for me to do what

I am doing. Truth is that truth swirls around in one giant circle, and it seems impossible to pull out a piece and get edges around it. Truth is, perhaps a person can think too much about truth, and she would be better off being dragged along by life, not thinking so much about it. Even I didn't believe that last statement. Truth is, I'll bet you would just as soon I wouldn't bring up all this stuff. How can one take a personal inventory[4] when one cannot even figure out truth?

I'm at the point where I need a long talk with you—either that or to say, "To Hell with it," and just go to bed with you and get my revelation there. One truth is its own circle—my love for you.

Verge

12/9/81

My sweet Verge,

Here I am at work in the good old United States Post Office writing to you. I got the airline tickets off to your son last night. I put the envelope right where the Phoenix mail goes out the door to the airfield, and I enclosed instructions on how hard to flap one's arms at high altitudes. This afternoon I talked to him on the phone. He was a delight for aged ears to hear. Especially rejuvenating was his enthusiasm and anticipation of his pending visit. First flight for him, and for you, too. You will both love it.

I was going to send the invoice and itinerary on to you, but Doreen said she thought it better not to send them to the house as Eric might open it, or at least be curious. I nearly said, "I'll just send it on to the school," but I bit my tongue before it came out. Your Milo arrives in Cleveland around 4:30 P.M. on the 26th and departs at 10:30 A.M. on the 30th.

Thanks for the picture of little girl you and your pet chicken. I lap up what you tell me about your girl life, like a desert traveler does water at an oasis. Did you really jump up and down, with your braids jumping, too, when you were angry? I adore you when you get brat-of-the-yearish. You get all inside yourself and are so intense. My favorite part is when you look up and see me, and reach out and pull me into your world,

4 Refers to Alcoholic's Anonymous' Step Four: "Made a searching and fearless moral inventory of ourselves." Ibid., 42.

too, with a little grin. It makes me want to laugh my joy to the stars. Destroying your letters gets harder and harder. The pile just grows. I read one with the intent of getting rid of it, but then, I have to save this one because it talks about your chicken, and that one talks about your struggle finding a Higher Power. I can't do it.

I don't even marvel anymore at our interlocking thoughts. I, too, had some discussion at a recent meeting about the brain washing idea. Approaching it that way puts my back up, too. The Program and the Steps [*Twelve Steps of Alcoholics Anonymous*] are just good old fashioned mental health. And as you say, blind faith is necessary because folks come to The Program [*unless otherwise noted refers to the program of Alcoholics Anonymous*] in such desperate straits they can find no order other than by being shown. Analyzing and pride don't make recovery; the delusion is too great. The saving fact is that The Program works if a person tries. By the time the fog lifts, if a person finds himself immersed in the Steps, they are a healthy guideline for anyone's life. As you know, I also have a problem with the Higher Power concept.[5] But as strange happenings become more numerous, I am forced to look again at that possibility.

Hurry, 12/23,
Michael

January 3, 1982

My Sweet Michael

After being with me, do you ever feel that this is the beginning of a new chapter in the unfolding book of our life? For me it begins with the first new glimpse of you. I fall into your eyes and I am overwhelmed with such joy that nothing seems to have any particular progression. Afterwards, upon reflection, it gets an order that is always new and different.

I loved sitting in the restaurant with you and Milo. You were both laughing at me trying to gracefully down my soup. Your easiness with each other and mutual respect makes me happy. I think, of all our

5 Refers to Step Two of Alcoholics Anonymous: "Came to believe that a power greater than ourselves could restore us to sanity." Ibid., 25.

children, he most nearly intuits our relationship. I love him for not passing judgment. It has been a secret gladness in my heart that through the years you have been a stable role model for him.

Sometimes a moment is so astounding to my mind I know it will be indelible in my memory, even as I live it. I felt an overwhelming tenderness toward you when you stood in the airport so calm, and uncrowding, letting me deal with the sadness of my son's departure. In that short space of time I got rid of a whole year and a half of worry and unacknowledged sorrow at his need to get away from the craziness of his father and me. During the visit, I was reassured that he had gracefully grown into manhood with the stable support of his aunt and uncle. Despite the troubled years at home, he is going to be all right. You knew to leave me alone to cry because I needed to, and later, you were there to listen when I needed to talk. I dare not say, "I could not have loved you more," because we have found our love grows at such a mighty rate neither of us knows its bounds, but at that moment you were my heart's husband.

Even with all the separation and pain, our love is total, fulfilling, and committed. You ask if I am being hurt by our relationship the way it is. Yes, I am, just as you are. The rewards are so great that hurt is irrelevant. From someplace I find the strength to believe it will all work out in its rightful way at its rightful time. Our love is too big and too old to become a cataclysmic force in lives not ready for it. If we end up together there will be no question of guilt or destruction between us, for that would be the one wedge that would drive us apart. If we are destined to be together, it will be with benedictions, or at very least, resignation. I will not wake up some morning and see shame or regret in your eyes.

I have no fear that reality would dissipate our love, or fear that either of us would be jealous of the other needing a space in which to grow. I fear your loss of self-respect. Until that is resolved, it is unthinkable to consider the unthinkable. I have unfinished business, too. If we come together, it must be as clean and pure as our relationship has always been—not to trade one kind of sorrow for a deeper, more ugly one. I have to live by those chance words from an ordinary human being at an Al-Anon meeting: "When the time comes, you just know. You walk away and you don't even think about it."

Just don't catch me at a weak moment and ask me to flee with you. My insanity over you is such that I cannot vouch for always being so sensible. Don't ever call me and say, "Verge, I can't bear it. Please come with me." At least don't say it fast, twice in a row, unless you know you are ready.

Verge

Later:

I find you so much with me today; I can't seem to shut up. After spending the early afternoon writing to you, I went skating. It didn't seem a particularly propitious day for it, but I knew from my walk yesterday the ice was perfect. The snow stopped just as I got on the ice, and I had a joyous skate over to the cove to visit my favorite summer haunts for painting. Hungry and exhilarated, I returned and made clam chowder. On New Year's Day, Eric resolved not to drink until his birthday in April. Consequently, he is spending reclusive days recovering, so I sit here consuming my unlonely meal with you.

While I was skating, I was thinking of how I can tell you ugly things about myself and have no feeling you would condemn me for them. You accept me as I accept you—totally. I will go now to snuggle under the benediction of my mother's quilt and read for a while. Come join me? In case you were wondering, in case you maybe forgot, in case you just want to hear it one more time, I love you.

Verge

1/10/82

Sweet Michael,

I peeked each day into my school mailbox but found it empty. I had to chin up and hope for tomorrow. Friday night I had a distressed phone call from Eric's sister. Apparently while I was in Cleveland, Eric, in his cups, called her and begged her to let him come out there with them. In good alcoholic fashion, he was threatening suicide, saying she was the only one who loved him, etcetera. She and her husband tried to reason with him and finally said he could come out if he would go to treatment for his alcoholism. She said he was totally distraught, and she was afraid if she didn't offer some hope he would indeed have killed himself. After thinking it over, she was sure her offer was not a good idea. She was in the middle of writing to him, but she didn't know what to say.

I had to tell her that in all probability he was in a blackout and wouldn't remember anything that was said, as he hadn't mentioned it in our long New Year's Day talk. If he did mention it again, the best thing to do would be to tell him what she told me. We talked for an hour with me feeding her Al-Anon concepts. [*Al-Anon is a Twelve Step recovery program for people whose lives have been directly affected by people addicted to alcohol.*] It was the first time she and I ever discussed the depth of Eric's alcohol problem. She told me of her guilt feelings about being so far away, being glad that she didn't have to deal with the problem up close, and that she had known of the problem for years. His progression was evident to her through his phone calls. I am sending her the book, *Getting Them Sober*, by Toby Rice Drews, which explains better than I can some suggested approaches to dealing with the problem. She said he did seem on the edge of seeking help. She also said that everybody who sort of encouraged him to drink, including me as she sees it, seems to be abandoning him when he is most needy. I was able to understand her hurt and to explain the concept that sometimes it is necessary to give the disease back to the person, so the person realizes he needs help. She wasn't being judgmental of me *per se*—just examining the fact that she, too, was abandoning. I told her there was no reason for her to feel guilty about not wanting him to come out there and disrupt her family; besides there is Milo to consider. It would do no one any good. God, all the extended pain of this disease!

Today, I wanted to start some artistic endeavors. But it is cold, Babe! My sun porch nest was so drafty from the wind blowing off the lake that my hands were turning blue. It wasn't destined, anyway, as Eric decided to get off to a good start on his New Year's resolution with a bottle of Scotch. The specter of three dry months looming in front of him forced him right back to alcohol. If it weren't so damn tragic, he would be the best advertisement for how not to stop drinking according to AA. He has always doomed himself to failure by making wild, longrange predictions. I can remember when it was: "If I am not a success at writing by the time I am 30, I will never make it." He was 18 at the time. Programmed failure!

All day I balanced on the Al-Anon Program. With an increasing period of personal dryness, my tolerance for the nonsense gets less and less, although this time it was relatively mild, being psychological rather than physical. I have to watch my anger, because he will feed me nine lines of lucid thinking and then throw in three lines of pure alcoholic whammy. It makes my head spin. I try to just shut up and not react to any of it, but during the lucid lines I sometimes feel compelled to respond—usually just in time for the whammy part. He says things like, "Sober is better than half-drunk all the time. I'm starting to have ideas again, and I couldn't think when I was drinking. I thought I had lost that ability." He is forever throwing in little gems like: "Here's something I'll bet you have never discussed in your little Al-Anon group. Sometimes when I am drinking, just before I say something, I know I will not remember later what I am going to say. The person will say to me later, 'But you said...' and I will look that person straight in the eye and say I never said that, because I don't remember what I said, right after saying it." [*The blackout.*] Try not responding to something like that! It is the pits to live with someone who is insane most of the time, but somehow it is worse to be with someone who has been mostly sane for weeks then begins slipping in and out of insanity within minutes of ingesting something—and he knows it's going to happen!

Thanks. Writing to you was my day's best medicine. Tension is gone now, and I'll close before his next restless walkabout. Wish me luck. I'm going to enter two pieces in a juried art show next week.

Love,
Verge

1/16

My Sweet Verge,

Mmm mmm mmm, the frigids have set in heavy upon me. The only thing that makes it bearable is that the media tells me you are frigid, too. My memory says that January is the only month we have not shared. Is that right?

The "disease" certainly has a long arm. It amazes me how it is not obvious that it affects all of the family. I think back to a year ago and remember how hard a time I had getting that idea through my head. Eric's call to his sister reminds me of it. Sounds similar to a middle of the night phone call he made in a blackout to Doreen some time ago. How the spirit does cry out!

You can't possibly know there is a long mental pause before I begin to write my thought about your Sunday letter. I have to compare this pause to that one "awful pause," as you have called it, I took long ago when you told me out loud that you loved me. Then I was unable to answer immediately because a great door slid down shut behind me and simultaneously another slid open. The light and change were astounding. I can still duplicate my heart jump when I remember it, see the sun shining on the lake as we walked from the car to the house, feel the quizzical looks from the others. We both knew for years—unspoken. After we called it a name, we thought we could master it with our pact, but little did we know how it would take on a life of its own.

The pause was at how beautifully you echo my thoughts in your letters. I can only nod and nod. You dealt with the stark realities of our relationship and talked of them in a matter-of-fact way. What you tell me makes me feel that all is as it should be, and there is no other way at this point in time.

You did delight me with your invitation. Clam chowder (I have always been in awe of your culinary skills, both creative and practical) and quilt benedictions! What defense has a poor soul against such tempting? Get thee hence, Jezebel!

I love you,
Michael

Monday

Sweet Michael,

There are things that get broken—pottery, antique sculptures, paintings slashed by demented people—that when painstakingly mended are still valuable, speaking for the genius of their maker or for the history of a culture. These things are even, at times, impressive, but I weep for each missing chip, for each finger lost, for the weakened fiber of the canvas, and for the skillfully matched color that can never match the master's own stroke. I am glad they are there, but I never think of them as being entire. I can accept the value of mending such things, but I do not care to look upon them overlong, for they make me sad.

But human things that get broken, I do not know how one mends. I don't mean little sprains; I mean rent asunder. I understand alcoholism is a disease. I have come to accept that as fact. What I do not understand is, in cases where trust is broken mentally and physically, and every personal thing between two people has been besmirched and shredded, how then does the cognizant one ever feel anything again? It is all beautifully blocked from the sicker one's mind by the disease itself. That person can pick up and carry on as if nothing ever happened, because he doesn't remember. I don't mean he willfully doesn't remember; he actually doesn't remember because of being in a blackout most of the time. You cannot forgive him, for there is nothing to forgive, anymore than you can forgive a person for having any other disease. You can understand, you can have compassion, you can feel pity, but when the emotional ties are broken and the body doesn't respond anymore, what does one do?

I have asked that question of various Al-Anon people who did get it back together. In particular I have asked older ones who did not have the incentive of raising children or of being financially dependent to influence them. Those who did get back together said their partner got sober and they just pretended for a long time until feelings came back.

I'll say this as swiftly and as painlessly as possible. Should you want or need to be released from the all-surrounding force of our love to concentrate on mending your other relationships, I will do all that I can to help you. I don't know how you feel about that, for it is a very personal subject and perhaps you are not sure how you feel. As the disease is notorious for bringing most of the involved to similar experiences and feelings, I think I can understand edges of how you feel. Doreen rather staggered me at the end of Sunday's phone call with the Marriage Encounter business, so I know some pressure is being put on you. I know how you must feel, being hit at this vulnerable time. Michael, mine is not mendable. Too many pieces are missing. But yours may be, with concentration. Please know, my very dear Michael, should you need a distance I will understand.

Verge

2/22

My Darling Verge,

I can't say anything less than I feel humble in the face of what you say about giving me room to mend my relationship with Doreen. I knew that Marriage Encounter business would be a surprise to you. It came about in the course of events at church that morning. I know the super sacrifice involved in saying you would give me room. We have made that offer to each other many times. I can hardly stand the room we have now. Don't go away.

I recently re-read a letter you wrote a while ago, about my mother. It was interesting from the standpoint that I never thought about those things. I quote, "She knows about loneliness, and duty, and roads not taken." My mind has never felt there was much of a relationship between us. (I say mind because probably that is the only place where that notion exists.) I never stomped around being overtly alien or did hateful things, or consciously felt deprived or resentful. We had no big conflicts. The relationship on my side is just a tacit acceptance that I can't get along with the woman for very long. I feel nervous in her presence after a short period of time because of her ever-present attempts to control. That is as insightful as I can get for right now. I am sure there must be psychological reasons seething underneath that bubble and boil to push out, causing untold mental turmoil that manifest in aberrant behavior that if not resolved will cause my demise. But I really don't feel all that.

It must be grim to have affection for a child and feel none in return. I just never felt close to her. I guess, as a child, I believed she was someone who was supposed to be there to fill needs. Here is a person with whom I grew up, with whom I have had contact through my whole adult life, and I have to ask, "What makes her tick? Were there roads not taken? Or did she just muddle through, searching, not knowing why or for what—going on out of a sense of duty and maybe fear?" How little we know of the turns fate gives to the lives of others (or for that matter to ourselves). But now I wonder, were there broken dreams… fantasies… hopes? Does one live a life of 86 years in a straight line, ignoring all of the dreams just because that is what one must do? Does each of us carry hidden, life living dreams to our graves?

I must conclude that life is only meaningful if it is shared. I don't understand why that is so, but in our present state of mental development that seems to be a necessity. If one lives life to the fullest but harbors it all to self, there seems to be no growth or meaning to it. Is it because it is ego feeding, or is it that we need to share to survive?

It feels strange to suddenly find myself standing back and looking at life as if for the first time. I am seeing and trying to learn about things I should have when I was a pup. I thought I functioned rather normally during my drinking days, but my sponsor said that considering my daily consumption of booze, I probably never got alcohol out of my system from one day to the next. As these baby-learning experiences crop up, they seem to prove that the drug does arrest development.

I haven't had time to say half of what I want to say, but it is time to go. I have never been able to talk so much to anyone in my whole life. I say yes to the brightness.

Michael

March 16,1982

My Beautiful Michael Man,

On this day twenty years ago, just slightly more than a month pregnant, I was made an honorable woman. The choice of days I'm sure had something to do with Eric's warped sense of humor, that being sandwiched between the Ides of March and St. Patty's Day. Our witnesses were two male lovers who lived together and were friends of mine. They thought it was a lovely camp. As uncharacteristic as it might seem, we were married by a minister in a church, after being referred by a minister at another church that required some preparation for the event. I carried violets. I think that may have been my last totally selfish request. Where in God's name Eric found them this time of year, I cannot fathom. Had I realized the goose chase I was sending him on, I would probably have requested something simple... like lilacs! After the ceremony, I called my parents and told them. They were gravely kind about it, didn't beat their breast and wail or anything, but upon later reflection I realized how hurtful it must have been. My reasoning was beyond reason at the time. I didn't have room for emotionalism beyond what was transpiring between Eric and me.

In the three weeks between finding out I was pregnant, and being married, my mind blanked out the events that were good indicators of where we were headed. Eric totaled my car on the way home from asking my friends to be our witnesses. He was playing drunken games swerving back and forth in front of oncoming cars. I was terrified and screaming that I wanted to have my baby. The car finally got away from him and we swirled around hitting a guardrail—the first of many "deer" that ran in our path. Another night he put his fist through my kitchen window and cut his wrist. The blood was gushing out. There I was again, screaming, "You are going to be the father of my child. I won't allow you to bleed to death!" and running out to a neighbor to call the police. They took him to the emergency room.

Earlier, there had been another prophetic night when we came home from late night barhopping when he crawled up my outside steps saying, "Verge, help me. I really think I have a drinking problem." It was clearly diagnosed then, and many times through our marriage, but I simply did not know what that meant. I knew no drinkers before Eric, and after meeting him I found I enjoyed drinking, myself. Members of my immediate family were teetotalers, and warning references to my alcoholic grandfather had taken on a romantic flavor in my rebellious teenage years. After I met Eric, all of our friends and acquaintances drank, and of course, there was lovely you. "Having a drinking problem," meant to me, one got drunk too often or spent too much unproductive time in a bar. I certainly did not know the real ramifications. I didn't know about drug-induced psychosis that foists itself off as a "personality". You could not have told me that Eric's fine mind could turn real into unreal and vice versa. It couldn't happen! Yet it already was happening before we were even married. Even harder for me to believe was that, by then, I, too, was sick. I was denying and deluding myself, enabling and controlling, and shutting myself off from my family.

I had known and loved Eric for six years before we married, although much of that time we were apart. My romantic notion of marrying the boy poet of my dreams was shattered on our wedding night. When we got home, everyone was a bit tipsy and it had begun to snow, so of course, Eric invited the friends to stay over. My little apartment had one bed and one bear rug on the floor. I slept between the fellows and Eric slept on the bear rug. That was not and still remains not my idea of a wedding night!

There, purged! You are the only person I ever told about my wedding night. Of course, three other people know, and I'm sure it has brought gales of giggles in quarters unknown to me. That was always a hurtful memory, and somehow shameful, but now I've told you and it doesn't hurt anymore. It is just a little sad and a somewhat curious tale. I am finding that, more and more, with some fairly unpleasant memories. It seems their venom is being drained. Their magic hurting power is leaving as I begin to understand the disease of alcoholism and talk to you about them. [*A glimpse at the healing power of Step5.*][6]

Of course, one of the hardest parts about revealing this is that the person being discussed is part of your history, too. You have feelings of your own about Eric, as complicated as mine and different from mine. I hope there is the unspoken understanding that anything I say about my relationship with him is not intended to sway your thinking about a person who is an integral part of your life. Just as I had no part of the part of him that loves you, I have no part of the part of you that loves him. It was so much easier when we were all deluded or drunk. It was certainly easier to stay deluded when we were drinking! Another part

---

6 Alcoholics Anonymous Step 5: " Admitted to God, to ourselves, and to another human being the exact nature of our wrongs." Ibid., 55.

of the dilemma is, I'm not only contemplating abandoning my husband, but also a person connected to your history.

I know you will read between the lines for the love. I can trust enough to bare my soul and know it is all gathered into safekeeping, like the evening you tenderly draped my nude body from all those eyes when I returned to Greg's boat after skinny-dipping in the Hudson River the night of the sky filled, fire-struck sunset. Thank God they were all looking at the astounding sky, for had anyone looked at you holding me, or at my face, a stone statue would have to know!

I love you,
Verge

6/82

Dear Verge,

Did you hear me calling and calling you this weekend? My head must have said, "Verge!" a million times. Nothing was going right. Well, not as I thought things should go. They were just little build-up things. I expected Doreen to know this was wrong, and that wasn't going right, and to side with me, but how could she know if I didn't tell her? When I tried to voice this or that, it all came out garbled, so she could only be confused. Chalk one up for the Program; at least my head told me where the trouble originated—in me! As resentments began to bombard and little nagging urges to drink tried to creep in, I was able to dispel them. [*The so-called "dry drunk" syndrome, where, although still sober, the person's behavior reverts to drinking behavior, often accompanied by craving alcohol.*] Down deep in me a voice would say, "Verge would know." I found that very comforting.

My daughter—what do I think? No way to keep this simple. I have to go back to what you said when you were here at Easter. You told me I was cutting myself off from my family. I never consciously set out to do that. I remember being aware of a different feeling. I attributed it to growth in a different direction, but not pulling away. When you put your finger directly on it, I began to see what I was doing. I always thought it good and healthy to maintain a loving relationship throughout the family. I tried not to hide behind the Program, to use it and my illness as a cop-out for not being responsive. I believed, in time, as I healed, everything would settle back to business as usual. As things stand now, I feel that pulling away almost as a physical thing and can only stand helplessly by as it happens. Indifference is setting in of its own free will. Others seem to be struggling mightily, but I feel like a bystander, just watching. I am bothered by the reality of my withdrawal, and by the thought that it is an unhealthy situation, and most of all because I don't do enough to fight it. I try to "turn it over," but I know I keep taking it back. I would be evading reality if I were to believe our relationship had nothing to do with it, but this cutting off feeling seems to have feet of its own. It is almost with that detachment that I view my daughter's pregnancy. It is certainly not without love and fondness, but still a feeling of watching the whole episode unfold. It is like being in the middle of things, but on the sidelines, as in a dream. Weird.

I am well enough to know I have to "let go". I willingly stand by for support or succor. The rest of the family calls itself doing the same, but as you pointed out, that certainly is not the case. It does not seem to be blatant control or vicarious living, but the family is having a baby. I can only bless them and wish them well.

It is only our beautiful trust that has allowed me to put this all in writing, however hurried.

Michael

June 82

Dearest Michael,

Oowweee, those little babies have nearly gotten my last goat! One-thousand-and-one days of rain have improved no one's outlook. This is embarrassing to admit, but I begin to feel I'm out of control in my first period classroom. For the first time in my teaching career, I stand in front of a class and actually feel intense dislike. They are like a whole room full of alcoholics. Eric's behavior at his worst would be right on target with them. They would think he was normal. I have not been able to find their strength, or weakness, or fear, or anything to appeal to for control. I found out today that I have to proctor that group in their final exams. I am unabashedly praying for the strength to hang on for the next two weeks. If it weren't ending in a matter of days, I could not continue feeling this panic and stay straight!

If there is a design to things, why have I had to go through the indignity of a year such as this? I can't imagine, unless it is to get me to do something new. I didn't know that turning points came up and beat you on the head. It seems that everything of my life is broken. The strange part is that I don't feel unsure of myself. My self-esteem is at the highest point it has ever been. I feel good about the growth I have made in the last year and the emotional shackles I have pried open. I don't feel broken. You would think that back when I was daily fearing for my life and spending every other night driving around the countryside afraid to go home, getting three or four hours of sleep, would have been when I had trouble with my job. Very little seems to make sense. I am not saying there is no sense, just that my outlook is too limited to see the sense. (How is that for growth?)

Thank you for trusting me enough to talk about your feeling of detachment. Pregnancies are never convenient unless they are super planned, and those are too contrived for my taste. There should be a little wonder to them. They do make some major influences on one's life for a long time to come. You are a good loving papa. Your daughter is grown, and all you can do is to put your arm around her shoulders and let her make her own decisions, no matter how hard she tries to get someone else to decide for her. It is beautiful that your daughter trusted the family's acceptance enough to confide her problem right away.

Stay strong. We both know a drink will not solve our problems. I take your hand in mine. Time may show us the reasons.

Verge

6/19/82

Dear Verge,

I was just thinking of the look of concern on your face, that day in February last year, when I told you Doreen and I were going to stop drinking. I remember you mentioned once or twice about changes and that things would not be the same anymore. I didn't realize at the time just exactly how much was involved. I had decided to stop the booze, but I didn't know what a grip it had on me. I thought the hard part would be changing my habits. I didn't fully understand that by then you had a pretty good idea of the immensity of change and growth and pain that lay down the road. I remember thinking, "Why should Verge be so concerned? I will quit drinking. It should be a time for happiness." Well, it was, but, oh Babe, little did I know!

I am taking tomorrow and Friday night off from work to help ready the house for the party on Sunday for our two graduates—high school and college, the youngest and the oldest, where did the time go?

Two months before I turned five years old, I was sent alone by train to spend the summer with my aunt in Michigan. If I had ever met her, I did not remember the occasion. I had no fear of the trip; my memory says I relished the prospect. The trip itself and the events leading up to it are surprisingly clear. My father bought me some gum and a roll of lifesavers, which was a big deal, as money was tight those years. In the excitement of getting on the train I dropped them. I began to cry only because I figured it made him sad that I had lost them. I am sure he and my brother thought I was crying, as any kid would at that age, because they had to get off the train and leave me alone. That was not the case. I recall being full of anticipation and longing for the train to start. When I arrived, my aunt who met me looked so much like my mother I thought I hadn't gone anywhere. After the confusion was dispelled, I found she was a delightfully different person. Our relationship was cemented when she took me to the barber to get my first boy's haircut and my pesky mop of curls was finally gone.

That has remained part of how I have gone through life. I have preferred and enjoyed my own companionship when exploring or discovering new places, new thoughts, or new times. That is, until I met you. As our relationship grew, I found I could open my cocoon a little and let you peek in, and now I am comfortable coming out and letting you walk with me. Sharing jealously guarded wishes, needs, desires, and delights with you does not diminish them; rather, they are enhanced and multiplied. I don't recall ever knowing anyone else who could make me feel that way. Doreen? Different things turn her on. She does not travel down the same road. That does not make one road better than another, just different. Eric? He challenged me with life. He put it in my face and made me taste it. For that I am ever grateful. He sharpened my awareness, but he was always ready with the put down that pulled the joy rug out from under me just as I began to sail.

Thanks for telling me about your trip upstate to see your daddy. You talk of him in such a loving way. It surprises me a little, as I always thought you had conflicts with him. Speaking of traveling, are you going to come out to spend some time this summer with us? I am giving my first AA lead soon. [*Lead is a personal story of what it was like when the person was drinking, how the person got to the Program, and what the person does now to stay sober, regularly told at AA Meetings in some region of the country.]* Will you come? I'm glad you can hang in for the few remaining days left at school and that you have been able to grow with this year's disagreeable experience.

Love,
Michael

Thursday night

Dear Michael,

Guess what! I'm getting me a P.O. box! As I walked into the local post office, a lady was complaining about the position of her present mailbox and could she change to one of the new ones? If you remember when I asked before they were all taken. So I scooted around the corner, and sure enough, there was a whole bank of shiny new mailboxes. I decided right then and there, one was gonna be mine. They don't have locks yet, so it is not official, but my name is on the list.

Your last letter asked if I was going to visit this summer. At the moment, I've just had to turn that over, because I have a crimp in my plans. According to our contract, the job opening at the high school cannot be officially posted until July when the retirement takes effect. If it is not excised, I will need to be available for an interview when it is posted. I want to be in the right place, at the right time, because I am not happy where I found myself this year. Whatever else happens, I will be there for your AA lead, even if I have to come back the next week.

I didn't finish telling you on the phone how your letters are different lately. Vestiges of reserve are gone. You no longer attempt to write things so they can be taken a couple of ways, either to save face in case I might not want to hear what you have to say, or to protect me, so if I don't want to accept what you are saying I can hide in the perhaps other meaning. You have finally come to trust that it is all right to say exactly what you mean, that I want to hear you straight, and that we will both deal with whatever is said. The strange part is, after struggling to get some troubling thought into just the right words so the other will understand and not perhaps take offense, worrying it around until the need to share is stronger than the fear of not being understood, after it hangs in the air between us, the response usually is that slow warm light that builds in the other's eyes of, "I'm glad you said that, for it has ached and troubled me so." A saying from my childhood was, "She thinks the sun rises and the moon sets on him." That is how I feel. If I had never met you, I would still be wandering around wondering what driving thing it was that left me so unquiet.

You asked about my father. If you recall, most of the tales you heard of him were of Eric's telling. Eric had a problem with his own alcoholic father and immediately clashed with mine, who did not drink, and assumed for me that I had a father problem. As a girl I was excessively sheltered and protected in a clan sort of way—not allowed to date, having to fight to go to an occasional dance, not allowed to wear make-up. I was the first girl, and my father especially had a hard time letting go. (They were quite blind to a progressively unsheltered relationship, beginning when I was ten, initiated by an adult neighbor trusted by the family.) Eric was my first official boyfriend. Consequently, just learning to let me go caused conflicts. Smoking and drinking were anathema in my family, and perhaps the worry that they might be entering my life caused conflict, too.

I did love my father, and I was the apple of his eye, but I was also a symbol to him—my plans to go to college to become a teacher fed his pride in material things. That was our main point of disagreement. He had struggled to make a comfortable living for himself and was the impetus behind his whole family getting out of the poverty and disgrace caused by his alcoholic father. He was the youngest of five brothers and two sisters. He got the brothers to buy a farm jointly, started several businesses to employ them as they left to marry, took care of his ailing mother until she died, and, with my mother's help, raised a sister's two babies when she died in childbirth, plus his own five children. He was damn proud of his accomplishments. Money meant a lot to him and I didn't understand why. Position meant a lot to him. Reputation and the people with whom one associates meant a lot to him. I was contemptuous of his values as soon as I became aware of them. (I have only come to understand that part of him as I have learned what alcohol does to families.) I always played with the wrong kids. I learned to be a sneaky child because my choices were often against his principles. I always had to struggle to be me. (Strange with all that struggling to resist domination even as a small child, that I should allow myself to be so completely dominated by Eric.)

My father was an oddity among other country folks I knew. He loved to read and had a passion for history. He often took us to battlegrounds, monuments, and other historical places and told us lively stories of what had happened there. He read us poetry, drew amusing pictures for us kids and taught himself to play a variety of musical instruments.

I wonder what he would have done with a college education. My relationship with him was a paradox. I loved the sensitive side of him and hated the materialistic side.

That is my view of my father. A couple of these things I never thought out before tonight. Every letter is a fresh paean to our love and the discovery of life it encourages.

Verge

August 6

Dear Michael,

Tonight I have had to realize, after all my knowledge of Al-Anon, I am still trying to control Eric. I have measured out all money given to him since New Years for whatever immediate needs he had—going to the movies and such—telling him I would not pay for his booze. He didn't drink as much during that time except when I was away and gave him larger amounts of money to buy "whatever" while I was gone. Booze was usually his "whatever". I deluded myself that he was willingly not drinking—that he was getting his head together, as indeed he may have been—but now he has a job and his own money and I can no longer regulate it. I fear we are on a collision course with trouble again.

He went to his job and stayed dry the first two days I was back home. Tonight is his night off, and he rewarded himself with a fifth of rum and two bottles of wine. Darn it, Michael, before my sobriety I would have understood his philosophy: "I've worked all week, this is my night off and I deserve a drink." I would have considered not drinking all week marvelous restraint. We all would have sneered at a fifth. Who ever bought less than a quart? I'm sure he thinks he is doing well to control so nicely.

I had the God-given grace to not react, but what seething anger and fear that bottle's appearance evoked in me. Every piece of literature I have read on the subject, and every AA lead I have heard tells me that controlled drinking doesn't work and imminently we are going to be in the same old jackpot! I'm not sure what my approach to it should be. It doesn't seem possible that he is unaware of the fact that an alcoholic cannot become a social drinker, ever again. I guess I have to sit down and tell him what I feel about the dangers of playing games with the bottle, and then, just let go.

Now it is Sunday night. Today I fell right into Eric's game when he initiated a conversation by asking if I was going upstate to see my father. When I said I was, he asked to go with me to see a family friend. I suggested he go by himself some other time, so he could leave when he wanted to. When he kept pushing the issue, I told him I didn't want to go anyplace with him when he was drinking because it made him erratic and untrustworthy, even with just a few. I didn't say it mean, just a statement of fact. He said he wouldn't be drinking if he were with me, "Come, sit, I want to tell you my new plan."

Eric's New Plan:

1. The drinking upsets you.
2. I've just got a second chance with the book. People don't often get a second chance, and I have to get started writing a new one.
3. I cannot constitutionally stand liquor anymore. It gives me horrendous hangovers.

Therefore:

4. I will only drink on weekends and stop before I get drunk.
5. If I see one peek of *Dr. Jekyll and Mr. Hyde* coming out I will stop. All you have to do is say, "Eric, it is happening again," and I will stop.

Classic alcoholic thinking! Most classic remark was, "I'm different from those other people. You said I couldn't stop drinking without help." I couldn't refrain from saying, "You haven't stopped drinking," but it was a useless stab.

I allowed myself to think I might safely have a conversation with him. It was like a slow motion movie; I could see every alcoholic trick being conversationally played, and I could watch myself going right back to reacting to each one despite knowing better. The truth is that I can't talk to him. He sidesteps every issue or twists it around to where it sounds like I am the unreasonable one, all the time using the craziest logic to prove his point. I remained calm and simply stated my views until he got so preposterous that I reacted.

The whole situation fell apart when the sadness, futility, and frustration caused me to start crying. Nothing could have pleased him more. He said, "I didn't know you still cared enough about us to get emotional," then really started the old alcoholic, cruelest whim whams. I told him what was making me cry was the thought of him getting really sick and incompetent again, just when he was getting his head together and things were starting to go a little right for him; to blow it by thinking he can control the alcohol, when everything I have heard tells me it is impossible. That was all futile. The conversation dwindled to him ranting and browbeating, saying that I was just trying to lead him around by the nose by threatening to leave him (subject I blessedly had not brought up) and that by not backing his new plan I was being a ballbusting bitch and so forth.

After I started crying, and realized I'd never make my point sink in, I did stop trying. I could not get a lid on the sadness though, of Eric, and the overwhelming hurt of missing you (not to mention more than a little self-pity at having left you to come home to this nonsense). I ended up having a good cry for myself. It was a lesson on not becoming complacent.

I am about to go to bed now. Great gray looming clouds have filled the sky all day (that is why I was in the house talking to Eric instead of being out in the canoe.) Now, big plopping raindrops have just begun. Every other one has the Michael message of love.

Verge

8/7/82

My Sweet Honey Woman,

Let me take you with me to The Bluff. It is important because it speaks for the growth of our courage and faith. Last year, I wouldn't have been able to go back so soon after you left. The day began mostly gray, but by the time the AA Meeting was over it was bright and sunny. I was determined to go there today, although I did not dare to think about it. I moved along putting one foot in front of another, as I do so many things these days. Just take things as they come, don't stew, and don't project.

I was amused to overhear a piece of conversation among the fellows on the grassy place adjacent to the parking area, as I was gathering the blanket from the trunk of the car. They must have just seen *Victor Victoria*, because one of the men said, "I could play Victoria. I've done it many times." Involuntarily I looked around to catch your eyes—they had a large knowing smile in them. Then I turned away to cross through the trees, and caught a glimpse of the lake. I took off my sunglasses to make sure it was really that deep blue you love so well. I could feel you beside me almost dancing for joy. The fear left me and I felt quiet for you were surely with me.

A brisk north breeze had whipped up a frosting of whitecaps, a startling contrast against the dark background. Through the faint haze, I'm sure we could see to Canada. There must be a regatta cooking up for the weekend, for 'lebenty-zillion white sails were skimming along quite far out, stretching in a line as if racing. Near the shore, white gulls floated.

I soaked up sun and read. When I looked up, the gulls were all soaring on the breeze. They silently glided along for remarkable stretches of time and distance without moving a wing. Later, when I glanced up, the sails had grouped at a point closer to shore, as if the sailors were comparing scores. I was surprised to see those sails were all colors, some plain and some striped. The boats reminded me of women dressed in their Sunday finery, that I used to see as a child, congregating after Mass each week to gossip. Suddenly they separated, and their sails seemed to change back to white. (I later discovered their puffy jibs were colored and could not be seen when they turned away).

Then the ever-nagging watch said 3:15. I must be off to the store, and food, and bed. As usual we were loath to leave. We walked slowly back through the trees. Lovers were scattered here and there. We stopped at just the spot where we last stopped to kiss, a brief linger. I could feel your lips on mine, the touch of your warm body. Then you were gone. That fast. Reality formed a knot in my throat, choking me as I walked to the car. The streets were bright with sun, but that sweet joy had vapored away in the heat.

When I got home, my daughter announced that you had called. I almost dropped the bags of groceries. How could I stop that loud thumping in my chest? When I went to bed you came to tuck me in.

Michael

Friday night

My Sweet Love,

You sounded so sad today, coming from The Bluff. We have had a full range of life there—everything from tears to deep, serious talks; from dreamy gazing to nonsense; from healthy lusting to gentle loving; from just plain enjoying the way it feels to be together to laughing our fool heads off. Go there on occasional days and be sad, but other days go and remember when we laughed. It seems unfair that I, who would rather tear my limbs off than hurt you, just by the necessary act of leaving, hurt you. I just wanted to melt and ooze through the phone line to give you a hug and a mighty rocking. I'm sure rocking is not a new-to-the-universe discovery we have made (obviously the pleasure of rocking inspired the good old rocking-chair) but perhaps we have a slightly unique approach to its comfort.

Childhood memory: Country kitchen with wood stove and double porcelain sink frankly exposing all of its plumbing, large wooden worktable, roundy Philco refrigerator, and plunk, in the middle of everything, a big old rocking chair. My dad would rock in the chair when he came home from work and waited for supper, or after supper, holding whichever big or little kid wanted to pile on. He would rock and sing with my mother while she did the dishes, or on Sunday mornings while she might be stuffing a chicken or making pies. Sometimes Dad's four brothers would gather in our kitchen. They would have marvelous arguments, forgetting me, the big-eyed child on my father's lap. Dad would rock fiercer when the arguments heated up, or slowed when his point was the winning one. It was a sport that had rules, somehow agreed upon by them, and after a certain volume was reached, everyone went home convinced he was still right, but no one held a grudge. One would decide, "You are all crazy," and walk off, and the others would remember a chore that had to be done. After they were gone, Dad would remember me on his lap and give me a wink so I would know none of it was too serious. The best of all rockings was when my mother would take time out of her busy day to read to me in that rocking chair. I loved the comfort of her cushiony lap and breasts as we rocked to *Uncle Wiggly, Alice in Wonderland,* and *Robin Hood.* As you see, rocking is an old comfort to me, but the dear touching of our flesh makes our brand special.

I got distracted during our phone call and did not finish telling you how I appreciate your teases that always stop on the kind edge of torment. My brothers, even with friendly teasing, would keep it up way beyond torture. Your teases get to the essence of what needs shaking up a bit: pride, pomposity, withdrawal, or sneakily trying to hide a mistake; exposing it and making me examine things I try to hide from myself. Because you know me so well, you help me laugh at myself. It is a valuable tool between us. I never knew that dimension of teasing until you taught me. I love how nothing between us has any intentional hurt.

Verge

9/24/82

Dear Verge,

When a letter comes from you, I devour it, sucking it into me as fast as the situation allows, like a starving man. The many other times I read it are the digestive process. Anything that helps connect us is life sustaining. Now watch me getting a letter. Full of anticipation, I open it. Try to imagine my delight to see you peeking out of the envelope! Two photos of you in the canoe, two moods of you—one with your hair up and one with it free flowing—I love them both.

My son's wedding day. Marrying off the first-born. I have written some surface thoughts about that day and those approaching it, but the down deep stuff didn't surface until the deed was being performed, and then it was in bits and pieces that I didn't fully grasp. Pieces of the puzzle are still floating up, so I don't suppose I will get it fully straight for a while, but I will tell you where things are for now.

Many years ago, I asked Eric about my giving that same son too much love. I was overwhelmed with love for my babies and was concerned about smothering them with my affection. Eric's answer was something like, considering the brevity of life and the human condition, there is no such thing as too much love. I was resolved to let love take its natural way, and knew the future would take care of itself, but from then on, little by little, I found myself holding back, in spite of myself. Was it because being conscious of it made me lose spontaneity? Or is there a defect in me that makes me hold back from love? I don't mean I lost love for the boy, just that intensity. Perhaps it was a maturing process, but it became easier and easier to let go, to give him room. As he grew older and his tastes and attitudes grew away from mine, the closeness between us diminished. Again, I don't mean to imply that we became estranged or unfriendly, just not as close.

During the days leading up to the wedding, we had small passing conversations that satisfied me he was mature in his approach to the marriage and was ready for the emotional responsibilities of it. I was surprised to find his attitudes toward, and impressions of life were much like mine when I was his age and also embarking on those great traditions that adulthood thrusts upon one. Strangely, I began to feel a new affinity grow between us. Prior to this my feelings toward his marriage were: college is over; you are grown; it's time to leave. Now I feel we are two adults who have shared a beginning, each understanding and accepting the other. During the marriage ceremony, I found myself staring at the back of his head, being carried back through the years. It was a brief trip, inclusive and involuntary. In my mind I felt an urgent prayer for his life, and love, and peace. Though the regrets tried to sneak in, I felt a new bond forming. Now I miss the kid like I never thought I would.

Love,
Michael

9/30/82

Dear Michael,

Thank you for your letter about marrying off your son. I walked that day with you, in my mind, as a sort of preview of December. There is a whole space in my head around Milo marrying that I am not sure about. I guess it will take some time to work it out. Some days it feels like I never had a child. I know that is good old over-developed alcoholic defense mechanisms at work.

If I dwell on it, the one place I can still work up a black and awful hatred toward Eric is thinking about his behavior the last few weeks before Milo left. Mostly I accept my part in the disease, and understand Eric's behavior is part of his illness, but I blame him for that ugliness I can't seem to wipe from my mind. The ostrich approach is: if I feel I never had a son, I will not have to resolve that anger.

You said something when I was last out there, in a moment of annoyance, which rankles in my head because I don't know what you meant. Doreen had been complaining about wanting some closeness—some romance—that you couldn't, or just plain were not moved to give. You said to me that people are just not that demonstrative after twentyfive years of living together. We did not pursue it, but I indicated I didn't believe that you believe that. Do you? I know it was said in annoyance, and perhaps with a twinge of guilt, but in twenty-two years I haven't noticed any calming of our wanting to touch, smell, or feel each other. Granted we have not lived together, but all I know of us tells me that we would never grow tired of each other. You have not lost your desire to touch, be touched, or to feel romantic—its center has just shifted. That she should want to feel those ways should not be as surprising to you as they seemed to be.

If we choose to be physically selective, or if our bodies choose for us, or the fates, it is not realistic to presume that the persons who get shut out are going to be appeased by having owned our lovely presence for a married lifetime. If they indicate a need, they do have a right to pursue their own happiness. No, we are not responsible for another person's happiness. Faking it doesn't work unless you want to be committed. But sliding responsibility off on such a stereotypical statement (insensitive at that) is not like you. It is something I have to remind myself about, as well.

Lord knows, you and I have worked on our love over the years, but some of the brand new shiny stuff has to be getting sharper and more focused because we are getting our full senses back after years of dulling them with drink. And, wow, does it feel good! There are two other people getting reports back from their senses with no place to express them. Eric knows I don't want any physical contact, mostly because I freeze or shudder at his touch. It is involuntary. My body can't even fake ease with his body, even with a passing touch. It must be very painful for him, because a total stranger doesn't react that way to a passing touch. He occasionally makes a bitter comment like, " If you can't even stand my touch, why would you ask me to sign a card with you?" My impatient head says to self, "Why doesn't he have better sense than to even mention it?" But, I realize he does deserve compassion. I am never again, out of pity, going to do something I don't feel. That is dishonest and serves no good purpose for me or for the other person. I must, however, remind myself I'm not the only person besides you who feels things. Perhaps I shouldn't say those things to you. Well, as they say at meetings, "Take what you can use and leave the rest here."

Verge

10/82

My Dear Verge,

Even if I weren't mad, crazy about you, I would still think you were the finest person I ever met. You say just the right things to me in just the right way. What you said about the only way to hold a butterfly (regarding our brand of possessiveness) made me want to rush to you and say, "Perfect, Babe." I struggled with that thought, and just couldn't make it come out right. The way you said, "...terribly careful not to crush each other's wings...encourage each other to fly...a matching of wills so equal." I can hardly resist the temptation to write the whole thing back to you. Besides telling me pretty love things, you also tell me things that advise me, encourage me, and prod me. There have been several instances when a word or two from you has caused me to change to a more beneficial direction, or to pick myself up and start anew, or to rethink something.

I hear from my brother, through Doreen who sees him at her Monday night AA meeting, that Grammy, my mother, has had a few small attacks lately, and she is giving up her job at the end of the month. What a shirker! Quitting, at only eighty-six. Just got no spunk. I don't know what this older generation is coming to. After seeing her dancing and carrying on at the wedding, I'm surprised she wasn't in her grave the next day, or on the spot.

From what you tell me, your son certainly does write an information packed letter. He sounds like he knows just what direction he wishes to travel and is sure enough traveling it. Being married in white tails and top hat—go all the way, I say!

Michael

10/22/82

Sweet Michael,

No letter from you in my post office box! Forlornly I wander home. With the perpetual hope for a letter from Milo, I open the mailbox at home and THERE IT IS! A letter from Michael! But it isn't for me. Big breath. The handwriting, so familiar it races my heart just looking upon it, and against my fingers it seems like little kisses yet I must not acknowledge them. Casually, I lay it on the counter just as Eric comes out of his room. I keep walking out to the sun porch to make an unnecessary phone call, stretching it out.

After the phone call, Eric, who had gone back to his bedroom with the letter, returns. I inspect my plants on the porch and then walk into the living room. He walks toward me saying, "Michael says he can come out on the sixth of November. Is that weekend all right with you?"

"Sure, that will be fine." Carefully said, heart beating loud against my ribcage, but voice under control. Mentally I am willing him to commit to that date, for he has been known to change his mind and say he doesn't want to see someone, out of an alcoholic perversity that rejects the world before it rejects him.

Then, out of the blue, he asks, "How long ago did you stop wearing your wedding ring?"

I am so shocked by the question, I am not exactly sure what he says afterwards, but I answer, "About a year and a half or so."

"Has it been that long?" I reply that the jade broke off it a year ago in the summertime, finding it pointless to remind him it cracked when he was pushing me around in one of his rages.

He zings those things in quicker than scat. Beware. You must, with all your knowledge, steel your heart before you get here and not allow yourself to get sucked in. No matter how "normal" he appears, and what sense he seems to make about being able to control, he is still drinking and his attitude is still that of the alcoholic. Whenever you find yourself sliding into trusting him, remind yourself of that, or you will get zinged. Or worse, he will shake your belief in yourself.

You once said to me, when we first dared to voice a hypothetical thought of living together, that you were afraid you wouldn't be exciting enough for me. This stuff isn't exciting. It is duller than tripe; wearying and dulling to all the senses. His calm is worse to the spirit than any of the other behaviors, because it sucks on your pity and sense of fair play. It makes you think the person is working on getting better, just because he looks and sounds better. But the attitudes and sickness are just sitting there waiting to explode.

I don't know exactly how to explain this, but it seems the more I cut off the relationship—God knows, there is hardly anything left to cut off except cooking, and washing and ironing—the better he treats me. That is sick! I hate it. He refuses to acknowledge the fact that I don't care anymore. Eric is no fool and clear is clear. It seems he is making it unnecessarily cruel for himself. Deep down I know it is good old alcoholic preservation, not wanting to lose bed and bread, which makes me hate it even more.

It is unfair for me to influence your thinking about Eric. That is something you have to work through for yourself, but on the surface I think you will find the change in him so great you will at least momentarily forget the illness, so I feel I must warn you. I realize there are lands in you I must keep foreign, for they are none of my business. There is a perverseness in me that resists the idea of any part of you being foreign to me. Please give me a warning when I tread where I do not belong.

As you know, I am struggling with the dilemma of how to attend Milo's wedding without sending his father into a tailspin. Eric's behavior is too unpredictable to suggest he go with me, and I don't know what crazy thing he will do if I go without him. I called Eric's sister to find out how she thought Milo would react to my coming for a visit during spring break rather than attending the wedding in December. I said that it is so close to Christmas vacation the school will especially frown on my taking time off, so I couldn't come for more than a weekend. She understood my real reason, and said that she didn't think he had a major interest in the ceremony part of the wedding so he probably wouldn't have a major distress in our not coming. I asked her to feel him out on that subject, and she said she would.

Love,
Verge

(Now it is Saturday. I anxiously drove to the P.O., and lo, behold, my letter from you! I have just greedily read it, so I will add this little note to last night's letter.)

Earlier on, you were talking about your son moving from the house and how empty it suddenly felt. You asked if that feeling ever goes away. My situation is slightly different, because my son doesn't come back two or three times a week, so the cut is cleaner, but every once in a while THAT FEELING comes back. The first frost is always hard. On cold mornings, Milo used to write me funny messages on my frosty car windows. After he left, those first blank white windows each year shook my heart. With Eric bringing the car home pre-warmed this fall, I haven't had that reminder until this morning. I went out to go to the store and there it was—frost—and THAT FEELING welling up out of nowhere. Big obvious things I have steeled myself against; it's little things that catch me unawares. If it goes away, it goes slowly. What doesn't go away is the concern. If I don't hear from him for a couple of months I panic. Old W. W. (worry wart) strikes again! Between college and his upcoming wedding, I hadn't heard from him for a while, but his aunt assured me he is well and spending a lot of time with his fiancé apartment hunting.

At my AA meeting last night I got a chance to return to the program one of a hundred kindnesses offered me. A colleague, who has been absent from his job and would reportedly be out for a month with some illness, was there. I well remember that awful feeling of being recognized for the first time at a meeting, not thinking that the other person must be there for the same reason I was. I only had a sinking feeling that now everyone would know. I immediately went up to him and reassured him that anonymity was one of the strengths of the program, that no one there would mention seeing him. You never saw such a look of relief. I was glad to give him the same reassurance that was given me by the first couple of people I recognized in the program.

Now I really am going to stop writing, or this letter won't fit into the envelope.

V.

11/17/82

My Michael,

Coming back from driving you to LaGuardia was uneventful, other than holding up an exact change lane on the Triborough Bridge. I had to get out of the car and retrieve my dollar from the change basket to the tune of a great deal of honking. Then I had to walk across traffic to another lane, and beg an attendant for a dollar's worth of change. I didn't panic though. I just did it, and even accepted a lecture about people who cannot read a foot high sign saying things about "NO DOLLARS!" I still do not know where it says that, but I surely do know they mean it. Later, as I drove by the West Point Military Academy, I gave a nod to the sign for the Stony Lonesome Gate. Can you imagine pulling guard duty at that gate? Some kind of lonesome—um, um, umm! I've been there and I don't recommend it.

Now the weather has turned firmly around, and I will have to spend the weekend battening down the house against the winter winds. It has been bad this time since you left. I keep telling myself I must stop, but it is something I have to ride out. It feels like a giant hand in my chest squeezing my heart just enough to make me aware of my mortality and to give me a steady ache. Once, when I was a child, my father showed me a place where I could put my ear to the ground and hear a stream running underneath us. I think if one put his ear to my body, he would hear my tears flowing inward. It is crazy though. There are petals flowing with those tears. You would think we would get used to this, that our minds or hearts or bodies would find some defense against this pain. Not only does that not happen, it hurts more each time. I will take it. Pour it on! If I can have the being with you time, none of this matters in comparison.

I'm glad the weather held while you were here. Thanks for that pretty walk at Manatoga. I can comfortably do things with you that in the past I would have preferred to do alone—in this case, walk in the woods. Sometimes we walked hand in hand, sometimes I walked in front, and sometimes you did. A couple of times I lost the trail, and you found it for us again. It never mattered who was ahead and who followed; what mattered was the excitement of discovery, fern, leaf, pool, and discovery of how we are together in a new place. You have a natural respect for the outdoors that I don't believe an adult can be taught, about not trampling things or disturbing the order. To them, a leaf is just a leaf and a stone stays a stone, but you understand that a whole day can be captured in a stone—or a whole love.

Last night, to ease my ache, I went to an Al-Anon meeting that's not on my usual schedule. A young girl of eighteen was chairing the meeting. Her Dad has been in the AA Program for five years. Her leading questions were, "Why do I have to have a disease just because I live with an alcoholic? My mother and father talk as if everything about them is part of the disease. What of the person is the person? What part is me?"

Through her self-pity, I could hear the seed of a valid question. I know, since listening to hundreds of AA stories, that I attribute nearly all of Eric's behaviors—especially anything I consider bizarre—to alcoholism. You can list his symptoms: one, two, three and there is not much left that I consider essential, personal, or his own behavior. I haven't had that trouble with you, because somehow we managed to not shut each other out with our drinking, and I never thought your behavior was bizarre. I never felt you put alcohol before me, and I always knew Eric put alcohol before everything. They say an addicted person's emotional development stops when he starts drinking. I guess the purpose of the Program is to search out the essence of our self and to develop a person from the point where we stopped growing. The growing you and I have done since we got sober seems to have begun at about adolescence. Eric seems stuck at an earlier level. It makes me wonder if the age of stopped growth has anything to do with the severity of the disease? If this strikes any of your thought bones, I wish you would share.

I do have to get out of my miserables enough to tell you about a man who started out trying to string one word after another on paper so he could tell a person who loved him about himself. He was unused to telling anybody things personal. At first he was very careful to say little, in case the other person might not like it, or might not understand, or care, or might even ridicule something he said. Every now and again, though, some imp beyond his control would let slip some very personal hints of self. The man found The Other remembered those hints, and she had begun to play a serious game of stringing them together into the real person he was. Because The Other proved caring enough to do that, the man began to ease up the tight control and allowed a little more self to get out. The man began to find he was discovering things of self he didn't even know. At every turn, he found he was more than he supposed. The writing began to come easier. The Other encouraged his poetry, his humor, his hurts, and his humanness to flow. Soon the letters were not only places of self-discovery, but also a place for fun. They became an education, not only about what was, but also about what might be—an expanding of brain by exploring thoughts. Beautiful Michael, if there were no other transformations, that one alone is worth the struggle of our love.

Verge

11/24

Dear Verge,

I can just see and hear that scene at the tollbooth on thc Triborough Bridge. Having driven over it with you that very same day, I can well imagine what happened to those scurrying people when a snag developed. You must have been in fine shape when it was over, mm, mm, mmm.

My head is a spin. Missing you has never been this bad before. In addition to all the other I-miss-Verge-hurts that lay me low, I now get flashes of smells of you and feels of you that turn me around looking for you. I don't have the reality of this time's separation in my grasp yet. There is still a space in my head that is holding on to our being together. It is causing me to hide inside myself, so I walk among people and react appropriately, but I am really way down deep inside with my arms over my head hiding from the truth

Don't feel bad about crying on the phone when I called. A huge ball of pain had been welling up inside me, too, since we parted. You have every right to feel frustration and uneasiness. How you feel at home doesn't ease things, but Milo getting married and so far away is the thing that is jabbing pins in you now. There is nothing wrong with feeling discontent, or sad, or uneasy. They are just regular old human reactions. I know I don't have to tell you that the wrong part is if you let them destroy you, if you take no action to resolve them inside yourself. At this point I run the risk of offering advice where it is not wanted, but you know me, can't shut me up when it is about us. Mortgage, beg, borrow, steal, go into debt up to your pretty ear lobes, but go to Arizona for the wedding. Tell your boss you need a few days. Tell him you are going to be sick. Tell him anything, and then get on a plane and go, early even so you can be part of whatever is going on. I think you will love yourself for it. I know full well that what I am suggesting jeopardizes our seeing each other at Christmas. But I give that pain to you—my gift. I place your happiness and well-being before any pain I may endure. Maybe our personal imps will see fit to arrange Christmas, too.

I spent yesterday running around on a Twelve Step[7] call. It was the first time for me, as far as dealing with a stranger goes. I got a phone call the evening before, from the AA Central Office. They said a man was asking for help and gave me his name and phone number. I called. He was too stiff to talk. Wife desperate. Said I would see him in the morning when he was sober. Wife more desperate. I phoned my sponsor whose spouse is in Al-Anon and had her talk to the wife. The wife said she couldn't leave her husband to go to a meeting because he might hurt himself. Still desperate, she called the Central Office again through the night and they telephoned my sponsor who happened to have the night off. Sponsor and I went there in the morning when I got off work. Man sick, kneeling on bathroom floor in front of the toilet. Sick! Finally talk to man. Wife desperate. We told him he should get in hospital. "No way," says he. Wife wringing hands. We told her he must decide. Not to force him. We said that the other way would be to duke it out at home. No drink—just for today—for this hour, and tomorrow we would take him to an AA Meeting. "OK," he said, "I will go in hospital for three, four days maximum." We told him that ten days was the minimum stay. "No," he said.

Sponsor and I leave. Go to sponsor's house. Talk. Drink coffee. Phone rings. Wife: "He'll go for five days." We said, "Sorry." Then I go home. My daughter greets me at door, wife on phone. "Hello, he'll go, but not to Rosary Hall," (where we had a bed waiting). Man wants to go to Serenity

[7] Step 12: "Having had a spiritual awakening as a result of these steps, we tried to carry this message to alcoholics, and to practice these principles in all our affairs." Ibid.,106.

Hall, which is way out on the west side. I said I would have to see if they had a bed. (I don't know the procedure so I call sponsor. Not home. Call again fifteen minutes later. Home.) Hospital has bed. Get back in car. Get sponsor. Get man. Wife relieved. Drive, drive to hospital. Nurses leap into kindly action. We take care of business. Time to go. Weariness setting in. Lots of pressure. Heading for elevator. There's John who works with us at the Post Office. Chronic. Good to see him in there. Talk. Talk. Time to go. Weariness has really set in, now. Go to elevator. "Wait!" John's counselor wants to talk about John. Go back to her office. Talk. Talk. Time to go. Sponsor and I walk straight to elevator, looking neither right nor left, fast. Down. Get in car. Gone! Sponsor's understatement, "Twelve Step work takes a lot of time."

I guess I don't even have to tell you that I know how tough these days coming are for you. I am always with you.

Michael

Thanksgiving 82

Dearest Love, My Michael,

As I review my year I find many things I am grateful for, and most of them revolve around having you in my life. I am thankful for the self-discoveries we have made. I am thankful that Milo has found a love with whom to share life.

Our oven is on the fritz, so I fooled around most of the day at my friend Elle's house, across the lake, cooking a turkey that was given to Eric at work. He had brought it home mumbling that he would rather have lobster, anyway, but when I brought the leftovers to the house tonight I noticed he made a goodish dent in them. I had no more than walked in the door when Dad's wife called to ask what time I would arrive tomorrow, as they had decided to hold off their Thanksgiving dinner until I came. Oh my, I will be dieting until Christmas.

Sunday: I thought I would finish this letter and get it off to you, but I must have gotten right into the middle of my own dry drunk or something. I've been working on it for a couple of weeks, since you left. I let myself get into the middle of some heavy "poor me's" and depression. Sorry—guess you were getting a good bit of it in my letters. It all culminated Friday morning, before and during my drive upstate. On top of everything else, I didn't get your letter even though I begged the postmistress. She said everything had been put in the boxes. I know she lied. You were right—it was Milo's wedding bothering me—and I knew I was going upstate to my father's house to burn my final bridge (their offer to pay airfare). It was all tied up with wondering if I were doing this to myself because I eloped and didn't invite my parents to my wedding, and on and on and around and around. I am calm now, and decided, and sure I'm doing the best thing for me.

When I got back, I had received Milo's answer to my letter telling him of my decision. He said, "We would love to have you at the wedding, but you are right. I have finals until the sixteenth, and we wouldn't have much time to be people together. We are excited about you coming out in the spring and look forward to it."

Michael, I would like to be a human being to my daughter-in-law and not just a face. Also, when I get out there, I want to see what the country looks like, as I might only see it once. I couldn't afford to go again, right off soon, so I am now satisfied that my head made the right decision from the first. I just had to agonize over it until my heart fell in line. It was the shilly-shallying of not declaring my intentions that was driving me nuts.

Soooo, if you think you can that easily get rid of the chore of figuring out what to do with me for a week, you're crazy. No. Uh, uh. Sorry. That ploy won't work. My Christmas visit to your house is officially a tradition. Seriously, I know with what love that letter was written, what sacrifice and what heart wrenching. Don't let me get away with saying, "Oh, woe is me," anymore. Dad and his wife offered the airfare and are offering it for the spring. I had free choice and I have chosen. Thank you for saying you care more for my happiness and well-being than for your own pain. But that doesn't work. Our happiness and well-being are one and the same

Your first Twelve Step call sounded like a baptism by fire. Heavy stuff. You're a brave man! It's easier in Al-Anon, 'cuz its not quite so messy, although, come to think of it, I guess that is relative. I went to a meeting at a safe home for women needing a temporary refuge. The home is trying to offer a beginner's Al-Anon Meeting and has asked women from established groups to attend for support and guidance. *Las cucarachas* were scrabbling, the babies were either screaming or strangely wide-eyed and silent, and the ladies were not exactly. I used to move in and out of that sort of tough side of life, following Eric around on his "sociological studies" in bars we should never have been in, during the early years. It has been a while, and this experience was a little hard on the nervous system. Despite that, the common bond was instant and strong. Probably few of the women I was with had ever experienced that sort of dirt-poor, basic living, but the bond was strong enough to jump them across the aversion to the scene to something like compassion and equality.

Michael, this program works! (There were a few coats taken off and shaken outside by the cars, but nobody had any smart-ass things to say.) I was proud to be part of such a group. I guess my biggest surprise was that the indigent women accepted the Al-Anon people without the normal barriers of pride and suspicion. Somehow all the posturing, that would usually have had to be cut through, faded as soon as the talking began. No feeling of superiority or inferiority existed. I guess you will probably question the absolute veracity of the above, writing it off as the mad ravings of a proselyte, envisioning the sweet ladies of your Al-Anon Group in the same situation, but I swear it worked.

Verge

12/2/82

Dear Verge,

Dawg gone it! I thought my ploy would work. I am just going to have to sharpen up my ploying skills—employ them so to speak. Now I will have to put up with the likes of a tradition. What does one do with a tradition? Breathe it in so it becomes a part of one's own essence? Hold its hand and walk in new and exciting places? Does a tradition's merest touch fit all the puzzle pieces together? Seriously, I am very happy that you were able to resolve your head and your heart over your son's wedding.

Would you believe it, the Twelve Step man's wife called today to ask me to look for his teeth in my car? No teeth in my car. I think he lost them in the hospital while he was dry heaving into a wastebasket. This woman needs a good dose of Al-Anon. Couldn't you stop by for a while and help her out? If nothing else, Twelve Step work is good for teaching patience.

I went downtown today to do a little pre-shopping Christmas shopping. The milling and hustling crowds and the Holiday decorations made me call for you. We would have had a fine time together. What am I saying? We were together. We did have a fine time.

I am full of the joy of us.

Michael

Sunday Night, 12/5/82

Dear Michael,

Thank you for taking my phone call even though you should have been asleep. Sorry to dump on you again, but I needed to hear your voice saying...anything, really. You make sense when none seems to exist. You give me the gift of sanity. Thank you for being in my life, for being there when I need you, in just the way I need.

I still don't believe Eric got to me in that way. He has the unerring sense of where the vulnerable spot is and the most vulnerable time to strike it. Like weasels and ferrets! God, the insidiousness of this disease! I hate it. Daily I hate it! The deal was that I was going to buy gas and things he had been kicking in for, since he had gotten a job, so that we could send Milo a respectable gift for his wedding. If Eric had even left me the opening for a question that perhaps I had misunderstood—that it never had been intended as a collective gift, it would not have hurt so much. (Originally I agreed to the plan, with alacrity, because it seemed to give him a goal, and seemed a good place to let him take some responsibility.)

The point is not the money so much as the breach of the little bit of trust I trusted, on what I thought was neutral ground. The *coup de grace* was the intentional zing of him saying, "I suppose I could send him a note saying this was to him from us, love Mother and Dad, but the love seems to have gone away somehow, so I'm just going to send it from me. If he just thinks a little bit he will know I could only send it because you supported me." He can really run some emotional Mack Trucks over me. Just when I thought I had all of my storm windows closed tight and tidy and thought there wasn't one more possible thing he could do to hurt me! I wonder how long it took him to figure out this one, or if it just came winging in as an alcoholic inspiration. Sometimes I am hard pressed not to believe he was just plain born mean, above and beyond his illness. Yes, I know, it doesn't do one whit of good to pursue this kind of thinking, but being smacked in the face again with my tiny edge of trust in just a tiny bit of normalcy, hurts, damn it!

I'm going to hang in there one hour at a time. I'll make it. I feel your support like hands.

Verge

12/15/82

Sweet Verge,

I couldn't write last night because the post office decided to train a group of us highly skilled technical folks on the proper way to operate tow motors and fork lifts for the purpose of licensing. Not only do I already know how to do that, but also I rarely have the occasion to use either vehicle. It made me kind of cranky. Now the boss has told me that from now until I go to Oklahoma for training, I will be working with another guy to become familiar with the machine I will be trained to repair. That will seriously cut into my free time to write.

I agree with you about making decisions, then turning them over to H. P. [*Higher Power*] I also agree that one must act in the direction of that decision with the confidence that it will go as it is supposed to, whether it is as planned in your head or not. Even when it doesn't go as planned, somehow the outcome seems better, in an imaginative way you never suspected. It seems faith in self and faith in old H. P. is the key to it all. That sort of attitude surely makes many of life's paths easier to travel. I still have a hard time with the idea of a Higher Power who could possibly have time to look out for individual needs, but as you said, the more we work along the lines of the Third Step[8], the more we see evidence of something. Maybe there are Green Imps assigned to various people to kind of guide things along. All we have to do is believe in ourselves, and Imp, or H. P., or something. I don't understand, but I'll take it. (As I look back at myself of two years ago, I see what I just wrote as a far departure from what I would have said then. Healthier, I think. Do you find that true, or have I lost sight of the self of two years ago?)

Michael

12/16/82

Michael, My Sweet Lovin' Man,

Sometimes I want to pick you up and give you a big hug. Never mind the logistics of that. The idea of loving unconditionally has been much on my mind since being away from you this last time. To know there is

---

8 Refers to the Third Step of the Alcoholics Anonymous Twelve Steps: "Made a decision to turn our will and our lives over to the care of God as we understood him." Ibid., 34.

no but, or any wish for even tiny alterations, is unique. We each gave the other every chance to inspect things that we felt were unfavorable about ourselves. When the other looked without flinching or distaste, even those things changed perspective and no longer seemed so terrible, after all the years spent worrying about them or hiding from them. Just the way we were with each other was therapeutic. I don't mean that was our conscious intent, but that is one of the rewards of our relationship.

To know that I am known, in the deepest, most personal way, and to know that I am deeply loved, not because of who I am, or despite who I am, but just as I am—a real person with imperfections—that is a beautiful thing.

Verge

12/19/82

Dear Verge,

My thoughts have been with Milo and his bride the whole day long, and with you. If my thoughts can carry the power I felt for them this day, they will know all will be well. I smiled to myself as I thought of how many times I have heard it said of young people about to marry, that they are so young, or too immature. I was hard pressed to think of any young folks that weren't or aren't. If Milo and his bride have just a little piece of what we have, they will carry each other through.

Just in case you haven't noticed, a strange phenomenon is taking place—a departure from natural law, so to speak; time is moving backwards. If the condition persists I will soon be back in childhood. I'm not sure I could take that. The adolescent part was a breaking free time and picking it up again in recovery it is a growing, discovering, loving Verge time. But the childhood bit I choose to leave where it is. Could you prescribe anything to stop that backward flight of time? Please hurry!

I am mailing this on Sunday morning. That means it won't leave here until Monday. I guess I have to think of this as the last letter you will receive before you leave. I can't wait. My heart and spirit are so full of you I can't speak of it. The feelings won't change into words, except I love you.

Michael

1/2/83

My Love, My Michael,

Having spoken to you twice today, I am twice fortified, but I still have the feeling that I must not move too fast, speak too loudly, or exert myself in any way, because there is something in me too fragile—a hairsbreadth from breaking into a billion shards. The feeling that my lungs are breathing breath only because they remember breathing, that my heart is beating only because it remembers beating, that my blood is wandering its course only because it remembers wandering. I am like a star that shines to Earth but may have disappeared eons ago. My shell is here, but my vital forces are stuffed in the niches between your vital forces.

My only comfort is, that experience tells me I will not die of this thing that feels like dying. I know when this initial unbearable feeling is past, I will have new memories and discoveries to assimilate and to nourish my soul and brain and spirit. Should the time come when this separation and distance is no longer a necessary part of our relationship, I have had enough to last a lifetime so I will never, ever be careless of any time we are allotted.

I told you on the phone, there was a letter from Milo's wife with wedding photos. I forgot to tell you she mentioned he has a new job. I am presuming that means he will be able to go to school this semester. As you said, I have to turn it over and stop being a wart. (Sensible advice from one old worrier to another, what?)

Tomorrow I will get busy and forget all of this nonsense and pain.

Verge

1/6/83

My Sweet Verge,

You mean you get that feeling too? The just let me hurt for a while because I know she is hurting too feeling? This time, though, I was into that, and it started to get real hurty. I could feel it welling up so the shadow of too much pain was right over my shoulder. My only defense was to get real cold with myself. I remembered what you told me about my getting cold with the world, and I didn't want to hurt anybody, so I just turned self off from feelings. I pretended that whatever routine thing

I was doing was the most important thing to do and shut out all feelings. Self isn't easily deceived, but it helped to keep the pain from crushing. Now that a few days have passed, I can lean back and think about us together, and sort out all the beauty we shared, and smile, and feel it and enjoy. Missing you is still there, but it mixes with your presence and it isn't so bad. Besides, now I can start to count days and fantasize about seeing you in a few weeks and that makes the world shine more.

I am having countless interruptions tonight, and it is hard to maintain a thought, except I love you.

Michael

Monday Night

Dear Michael,

Exhausting day, but reassuring. When I spoke to you Sunday, I felt nervous about casting the high school play. You advised turning it over to H. P. and promised me a talented youngster or two—so I did. It seems when you practice The Program it comes up and hits you over the head with its presence when things get tough, even if you don't consciously call upon it. As a baby example, as many times as I tried to pick up the script and fuss over it, my head absolutely refused to. At school today I wanted to fuss again, but my brain kept me occupied with necessary work. When I got to the high school, everything went smoothly. I did indeed have some students who were good. One lad shone out especially; he has no background (said he played a rabbit in a first grade play), but he is a natural. I have two more nights of auditions and do need the central character, but feel confident I will find her.

By the time we finished, and I had gone to get a few groceries, and stopped off to pay the rent, it was a long day. I showed my landlady Milo's wedding pictures. She saw her doctor today and he told her that although she had been to death's door, she seems to be improving. He was encouraging about her recovery. I have grown fond of her over the years, so I'm glad for that good news, although she still looks mighty frail to me. I selfishly hope she recuperates, because I depend on the lake as a constant source of serenity, and I don't know of any other house there for rent.

I wanted to share my good day with you, because you were in so many ways responsible for the positive feelings.

Verge

1/12/83

My Darling Verge,

It doesn't matter what I write down here, it is all going to say I love you. This is a down and hard missing you time. Maybe because I am in flat, flat country all by myself, but more likely because I'm twelve hundred miles further away. As I told you on the phone, I wasn't off the plane and inside Will Roger's World Airport ten seconds before I started figuring ways to start building our nest, my mind racing with thoughts of you coming here.

I just got back from an AA Meeting. I needed it, too many ghosts around here! They keep beckoning from bygone days. AA is pretty active in this town, but the trouble is, without a car, it is hard to get to meetings. One meeting on Monday night is within walking distance, but the rest are a long Oklahoma walk. Old H. P. took care of business, though. There is another guy from Cleveland down here who asked me to go to dinner with him. He drove his car down for the training. As we were driving around the town he pointed out a clean, reasonably priced motel where he stayed the last time, when his wife came to visit. After dinner he wanted to go shopping and I threw caution to the wind, asking him if he would mind dropping me off at an AA Meeting. He was good with that. As I thought, I readily arranged a ride home with someone at the meeting. In fact, that person gave me his phone number and said he would be glad to drive me to a meeting any time or arrange for someone else to do so if he couldn't. Uncanny, what?

I'm glad you wrote about not being able to capture my face in your memory. This is not a me-too-ism, but the very truth; I have the same problem with your face. I have studied every mark and line and feature, storing away for when I won't be with you. Each time I failed, and each time I determined to study harder. Details are locked in my memory, but the complete living picture is never there. I asked for a photograph. The ones you sent help me to smile and dream, but they don't do what I had hoped. I have been keeping this in a secret place in my head, thinking it must be some flaw or quirk in my makeup. After all, here is the one human being in the world who makes it shine, whom I love more than anything, and I can't even summon up her living face in my memory. After your letter I felt better. You said it just right. It makes sense to me now. I'm glad we share that, too.

Michael

1/13/83

My Sweet Man,

Tonight I had my first blocking rehearsal for the play. Only two of the kids claim to have any real theatre experience, but I lucked out with finding willing, quick learners. I forgot how much I liked doing this. Of course I realize that directing is a perfect example of being the "controller" that Al-Anon and AA warn about. It does appeal to that defect in my character. I hope I am putting it to constructive use and it is not a regression in this instance. It is amusing to twit myself about controlling as I do my directive duties, but as long as I don't take myself too seriously and do see the parallels, I think the situation is healthy.

One fun thing about us keeping the same time schedule while you are at school is waking at night with the comforting sense of you beside me waking. That sweet, safe, heart-bounding feeling of you waking beside me, is a feeling I'm still trying to describe to myself. I have only now discovered that it is actually a feeling I didn't know I was waiting all my life to feel. I guess it's called bonding, that rush of heart spilling, mind lulling, peacefully held and holding, interdependent giving and taking, soothing balance of want and release, braced and relaxed, suspension of bodies in time. Now, at night, waking with you, I can feel you there that way, and all is right with my world. How very much more I love you.

Verge

1/16/83

My Anointing Woman,

Do you know what Oklahoma means? It is derived from two old Choctaw words. Okla means people and Humma means red, so, red people. Bet you didn't know that. Bet you didn't know that currently thirty-five tribes of Indians live in Oklahoma. Yup. That's true. I have been studying up so I can impress you with my Choctaw when you come.

Presently, I am trying to find just the right feather for my bonnet so I can wiggle it at you.

Is Green Imp helping you get all your grades together for the necessary deadlines? I am excited right along with you about your play. I know well that feeling of getting back to something you know and enjoy after a long time away. Yes, one of the things I liked about directing was the feeling of control, almost a sense of power. I don't believe that is unhealthy if you are using it as a form of expression, and if you realize the dangers involved. I know you are making progress on the control problem. It shows. Progress is all that asked of any mortal.

I have been fantasizing like mad about you being here. The beauty part is I know our time together will far outshine any fantasy I can cook up.

Michael

1/19/83

Dear Michael, My Love,

Nine days, tra la! I procrastinated and procrastinated about officially proclaiming my going away. I wasn't ready for the trick bag of questions. I did a number on my head trying to pre-guess every question Eric might have, until I got all worn out and put it off for another day. Just plain courtesy demands a little notice, yet I let it slide down to the bottom line of notice time.

I'm at the point where I would like to say, "I'm going away for X number of days, and I don't care to tell you where, so don't ask, and I won't lie to you." But that, I feel, is against human nature. I'm still afraid of Eric manipulating any truth he might know about me, so I don't suppose I can ever make the jump to total truth with him about anything that is not directly related to him and me. Every piece of personal truth he ever knew about me he turned against me, or betrayed. I learned to lie to him, either directly or by silence, for survival reasons and ultimately betrayed myself by becoming a non-person in my own home. I can neither blame him for what I did to myself, nor can I blame him for treating me like I didn't exist, because I treated me like I didn't exist. This is not a "poor me." It just recently became clear to me that I have to do as both of The Programs teach, to "place the blame squarely where it belongs—on my own shoulders."

I can't believe when you get this there will only be three days between us. I think I can; I think I can; I think I can make it!

Love,
Verge

2/6/83

My Love, My Michael,

I promise this will be the last official Valentine Card this year (unless one attacks me as I walk by). As it is the last one this year, I must tell you some newly observed reasons why I love you. I love you because your ears fly up your head when you smile at me. I love you because you are able to remain dispassionate and neutral through my emotional tirades, no matter how much you might be tempted to give an opinion, thereby giving me the perfect climate to see problems in a clearer light, without them being clouded or swayed by you. I have a fair idea of the personal expense that costs you.

I love you for the new trust you show by opening your own hurts and fears and self-revelations to our mutual view. For a personal man, such as you, to try to let another see that level of self is most courageous. As you have rushed to assure me on numerous occasions, it is not in a voyeuristic way my heart is gladdened, but only to know everything that has made you into the present perfect-for-me human you are. A new level of personal talking to each other seems to be evolving. It is like taking the lid off one's brain and showing it to another person all uncensored without the need to put thoughts into pretty words—just laying them out and letting the other decide for himself whether he wants to look at them or not. For myself, it seemed that some of the thoughts forced their way out without allowing me to fancy them up if I had wanted to. Almost like they were saying, "Look, this is who and how I bottom-level, really am. Can you still love me?" The overwhelming response from you was, "Yes. Yes. Yes." Most people can only hope God loves them that way.

Michael, I love you in ways now I could never have conceived of a week ago. Surely we will soon need a new language to tell each other of it all.

Verge

2/9/83

My Love, My Verge,

Among the extraordinary things about you and me in Oklahoma, was the way we talked wide open and were not afraid of it. I understand what you were saying about coming to some turn off point with other people. It is not planned or deliberate, it just happens. It isn't even a matter of clay feet, because many times I readily accepted that, but all of a sudden something pops and things are not the same; my interest wavers for no reason apparent to me at the time. As I think about those turn-offs, I called myself being turned off by the other person when indeed I could have been turning myself off. After just so long in a relationship, I catch myself worrying about whether I am boring the other person and feel unsure. To defend myself, I blame the other person. I never feel that way about us. Every unexpected corner brings a new turn-on.

Everything appears normal with the new baby. She is a pretty baby. I don't remember any of my babies being so unwrinkled and alert right after birth. Maybe it is because this new one was lifted from the womb rather than fighting its way out. Daughter and granddaughter are doing fine.

Love,<br>Michael

2/9/83

Michael, My Love,

I am heartsick tonight, for I have struggled all day with selfish thoughts and projections. I don't know whether the thoughts themselves are making me feel so lost and lonely, or the fact of being ashamed of feeling so selfish is causing the bad time. Probably both. I am unbearably sorry that I made you feel bad when you called to tell me of your granddaughter's birth. There is a creature inside me that I don't even want to recognize that comes jumping up at the most inopportune moments. It has no manners, it is unbelievably willful and childish in nature, and it does things that embarrass me at its weakest show and frightens me at its blatant heights. I do not love that creature in me, Michael. One of its most destructive qualities is jealousy. I thought I had conquered that, but it seems to be part of the present problem. I'm not sure I can even sort out all that I feel, but if I do make a halting attempt maybe I can deal with it, and it won't leave you hanging out there wondering what on earth has gotten into me this time. I don't condone any of the ways I am feeling, so bear with me while I work them out. Please God, someday let me grow into a mature human being!

A new life! A small, helpless, growing, needing entity to claim your affections and your attention. If I were there with you, to watch you give joy and take joy with that child, I would probably be the happiest woman alive. I have watched you being a father to your own children and it is a beautiful side of you. But, I am not there, so I fear one of my least palatable feelings is envy that it is not my baby, and I will never know that with you. I wanted to have another baby in my lifetime, and now that time is past. This innocent baby has hardly been born and I have projected you through the next seventeen years of its life.

My head tells me that she is a beautiful gift in your life and that she will be the source of much joy. How could I possibly be so meager of heart to resent anything that gives you happiness? On the phone you said such events are springboards in life. Maybe I fear that. Maybe I fear you will spring right out of my life. The worst thing about this is that my attitude is just the one that could cause you to run. Not the event itself, but the way I am reacting toward it scares the hell out of me. Please don't give up on me. I'm starting right now to work on that attitude.

I was shocked when you said that your daughter and Doreen detected some hostility on my part toward the pregnancy. I guess, in light of the above, they were seeing things I did not know I was feeling at the time. My resentments are not about the child, but about you and the child. As I ponder this, I guess I'm also kind of angry that your daughter never attained some measure of independence or came to recognize her potential before this responsibility became hers. She is still very much a dependent child herself and the whole climate of the house is geared to keep her one. There is someone ready to jump in and take care of her slightest problem, so she has never had a chance to test her capabilities and probably doesn't even realize her inner resources. (It's the old controller's lament: people just won't act in ways you want them to. They can't see what's best for them. What is the matter with them anyhow?) As you say, "What's a mother to do?" I am not even going to say that it is none of my business, because I love that girl.

None of this is that innocent baby's fault. She's just a wandering spirit who has found a home and never asked to be born. Now we all in our separate ways will deal with her being. I shall probably be the biggest fool of all over her, because I have had the least chance to be around a tiny baby in a very long time, having avoided my family over the years of birthing and growing little ones. To me watching a baby learn to see and hear and do is a miracle and makes everything fresh and new and wondrous. A birth is a celebration.

Done. I hope I got it all out. If there is anything more, I am not aware of it now. My brain has just been struck like a hammer blow with the thought that I feel like I did when you told me you were going to stop drinking—fearful of how it might change our relationship—and look how that turned out.

Love,
Verge

2/12/83

My Fine Honey Woman,

As I write the date up there, my mind goes into automatic and snaps back one year, then two years. No way can I allow this February to slip by unnoticed or unclaimed as a sobriety anniversary. What an unlikely month to hold so many treasures for us. I am tempted to say something usual, like, "Where did the time go?" or, "Who would believe a whole two years have passed?" As I inspect the incidents of our life, though, they seem timeless. We have grown together as we lived through those experiences and continue to grow as more come along.

I'm going to tell that baby the next time I see her, that my honey woman is beating herself over the head about her. What do you suppose the creature will say about that? Will she get all wide-eyed and say, "Me? I ain't done nuttin'," or will she say, "Give that woman a hug and tell her we are all in this together," or maybe she will say, "That honey woman needs a spank," or maybe just, "Goo." But, I'll explain to her that my honey woman is a human with feelings; sometimes they creep up on us humans, and sometimes we don't stand a chance against them unless we wait them out. If we do, and don't get nervous, we can watch them fade away like early morning vapor when the sun comes out. We mustn't be afraid of feelings, but must not let them beat us up, either. They are part of being alive. Don't forget the good feelings far outweigh the bad ones, the ones we wait out. The good ones grow and get stronger when they are fed with love, like my honey woman and I do. Usually they get so big and strong that after awhile the bad ones don't even bother to come around anymore. I'll tell the baby, now she is here too, "The best and safest road to follow is one that seeks out love." Being human, she will probably look at me and say, "Goo."

To you, my honey woman, I say I admire your courage. I understand how you feel, and I feel proud that you can talk to me about it. Even over the phone, I could sense you were having the same feelings you had that February, two years ago, when I stood on your sun porch telling you I was going to stop drinking. You sat on the couch full of fear of the unknown changes such a drastic reversal of lifestyle would bring. There was nothing either of us could do; just wait and see. I felt helpless, because no matter how I might declare my unchanging love for you and promise never to forget, neither of us really knew what was in the future. But we had faith in each other and we grew together because we trusted and looked life in the eye and allowed ourselves to learn. I love you, as you are, feelings and all. In fact I adore you.

Michael

2/14/83

Dear Michael, My Mirror Man,

No meeting tonight. I went out an hour and a half after coming home from rehearsal and found, not only was it snowing, but all-out dumping. Wind whipped daggers of snow. I got the car up to the top of the driveway, assessed things, parked and came right back down to cuddle under my Michael blanket, giving dawg and dinosaur little pats. Such a comfort those goofy presents have been!

I was not only touched by your baby-chiding letter, but as I read it I was doubly delighted by the way you took the sting and preach out of it by writing as if you were talking to the baby. My experience of loving you has changed the whole idea of love, as I understood it, to something so vast and in other ways so minute, that it would have been out of my past range of recognition. Like the sound of a dog whistle, there is visible proof of its existence, but it is out of the usual range of hearing. Loving you has keened up my ears. Man, do I ever hear those dog whistles!

I finally got a letter from Milo. I never learn how to keep from being attacked by foreboding imagination and worry about him. Every time my brain gets a worrisome scenario cooked up, I hold off until I can't stand it one more second, but when I finally call his aunt to see if she can provide information on whatever the pressing worry is, the very next day I receive a letter from him. It has not once failed, no matter how long or how short I am about giving in to the phone call. I am always left with a personal blush to myself. It is as if good ol' H. P. is giving me a little nudge saying, "See? You didn't have enough faith." Or maybe it is a green imp game. Anyway, it happened again. I have been fretting about visiting him and his wife at Easter, as I had said I would when they got married. He had not mentioned it, and I had not heard from him recently. On Sunday I called his aunt to see what she thought about my coming out to visit. She said she thought it was already decided, and his wife was looking forward to meeting me. Today, his letter came full of chat about new job, new college courses, new life. He said if I come out they would like to show me the Grand Canyon. His aunt also invited me to stay with them for a couple of days, so the trip is set.

My clock tells me that about thirty-five of the forty topics I had thought to write about will have to wait. I need to have my head together tomorrow for there are only two rehearsals before the four-day weekend. I am going upstate to see Dad and his wife over the weekend to take them up on the loan for airfare they offered when Milo got married. Love and hugs.

Verge

2/16/83

Dear Verge,

I am glad we humans are endowed with memory. Sometimes, as we live through moments, they go by so fast that we can't catch all of their meaning right then. It is nice to savor them later. In my "sophisticated" days, when I knew which way the world was going, how it was going to get there, and why, I sincerely believed that reminiscing was a pastime reserved for folks with shallow imaginations and weak minds. (I am not sure how I justified my own occasional engagement in that occupation, as you can be sure I didn't place myself in either of those two categories.) I even presumed to wonder why man bothered with such musty, useless things as history and tradition.

Self-sufficiency was the key, whether as a race or as an individual. There was no time to spend worrying about the past, or how those before us did things, or proscribed manners of doing things. When I heard, "roots are important," or "we learn from the past," I would say, "Piffle!" I thought, "That is for sissies. The only way is to forge ahead, stand on our own worth, and shake the dusty past from our shoes. We have the capability to go in any direction or as far as we want; all it takes is guts, ingenuity, and a dream." I wonder how I thought we got where we were at that point in time? I suppose I figured that each age was struck by a bolt of inspiration that had all of previous learning programmed right into it. "Okay, this generation is going to harness atomic energy. Let's get cracking!" I was pretty sure my thinking was flawless.

Now I have to wonder at what I thought was a clear head. Our love has taught me that life is full of continuity. By building on what we learned together, and drawing on the past, one from the other, we grow. How precious those past moments are, and what joy to examine and learn from them. You make my life a joy.

I think it is great that you are going to spend a week with Milo. I see you becoming more and more your own person, and it is beautiful. Have you told Eric that you are going? Are you going to?

I am here in the brand new library for the first time. It is kind of friendly and cozy. As I have almost no down time at work anymore, I have had to find a new writing environment. This arrangement seems like it will work. But time surely does fly by when I write to you. I am going to dash home to eat and to bed, perhaps to dream. I love you.

Michael

Sunday, February 20, 1983

Sweet Michael Man,

It is nearly your second year, sober anniversary. Two years ago on this very day I went to Poughkeepsie to pick you up. Stupid truck was stuck under an overpass, holding up traffic, and I, who was going to meet the train and you with open arms, got there late. You were casually leaning against the train station smiling a humorously mocking smile of, "I gotcha."

Four days were never more blessed. We lived those days like living a lifetime, refusing the panic of the changes to come and holding each minute like a precious jewel. I think we firmly learned just how compatible we could be, during those few days. We had always been honest with each other, but knowing we were on the brink of major change, and not knowing where it would lead, we were honest on a new deeper plane. We had known and appreciated each other's silence in the past, but we found a soul communicating silence in those rainy, foggy afternoons and gloaming evenings. Then came May in February! We were plotting how to remove a large tree limb that had fallen onto the ice by the dock. When we returned an hour later after taking Eric to work, the limb and the ice had magically sailed away, the lake was free, and the temperature had risen into the 80s. We seemed to be the only people in the world that afternoon. I'm convinced that everyone else had a usual February day, for I mentioned the phenomenon to numerous people and none even knew what I was talking about. The next day you went away and we began a sober life, which became the direct route from there to here with never a waver between us. It has not been without its pain, but between us, things just grew until it has grown so huge now I don't think I will ever finish exploring its nooks and crannies—and still it grows.

The trip upstate went well. I had an eye-opening conversation with my father's wife. She is making inroads with the whole clan—here and there I see breakthroughs—and she certainly does take good care of my dad. She told me that her previous husband was drug addicted, originally through illness, and later through fear of illness and a few doctors that were less than scrupulous. He had to be institutionalized off and on, and, in between, she got the full benefit of behavior similar to what I have experienced with Eric. I had begun to get some glimmer of this before, through observing her behavior, and was able to draw her out in an Al-Anon fashion. (Could she ever use that program!) Actually, circumstances forced her into practicing a lot of its principles when she married my father. Before they married she told him she was going to continue her church involvement and volunteer work, and he would have to change his mind and set ways on a lot of issues. When my mother was alive, she never spoke up for herself about any personal wishes. As little self-confidence as my stepmother has, she does let her wants be known. As she said, "I had a lifetime of miserables. I don't take time away from your father, but when he is at work I want to be able do some things I enjoy doing with other people." He has even stopped pouting about that. A lot of things she has talked him into doing, like attending a grandson's Jewish wedding and dancing, two things he had a narrow minded prejudice against, he ended up enjoying, learning from, and thanking her for forcing the issue.

During the conversation with Dad's wife, it was easy to tell her about Eric so she could understand some of my seeming standoffishness, such as not inviting them to my house. It made a bond of mutual understanding and may help her to smooth the way with my father, if the time comes when I have to leave Eric. The family has never had a divorce. I trust that she will keep my problem secret, as I have requested, because there is no reason to worry my father at this time.

You asked if I was going to tell Eric about going out to see Milo. Green Imp took care of that so I wouldn't have to agonize over it. Eric overheard a phone conversation mentioning that I was hoping to go out at Easter, and that Dad and his wife had offered to pay for the trip. He asked me if I was going, right after the phone call, so it was out of my hands. Although he was non-committal, and only showed interest when it was first discussed, I think the hurt may be setting in, now, when I obviously went to get the money from my dad. Probably that was the justification for a goodly weekend slip, while I was away, that he has not even tried to cover up. Tonight, he is cocky as all get out and has tried to get a rise out of me ever since I returned. I'm just hanging in here keeping out of his way. What really sets my teeth on edge is that it is just like a little kid that's done bad, trying to make up by being cute. (He wasn't going to drink until his birthday, again, remember?) Now he has the music up full volume on a song he knows I hate, trying to get my goat. "Easy does it. God grant me the serenity," etc. I work at understanding, but I guess I haven't grown that much. I feel myself stumbling, crumbling back to Step I. I'll never conquer this fear. It is like all the little devils in his brain cannot resist shifting straws about, balancing just one more and one more, almost willing the collapse of everything. I've heard numerous people in Al-Anon say that it doesn't bother their essential self when their spouse drinks, that they have been able to keep their serenity through slips and all. Well, it bothers the hell out of me! Every time there is a relapse it feels like emotional blackmail. One step forward with Dad's wife, and one step back with Eric! Does that mean I am stationary, or just teetering? Well, problem for tonight solved. Thank you, H. P., for his 11 PM to 7 AM shift.

I have offered numerous times to help Eric make the trip out to see his sister and his son, but he has refused. Now that he has a regular job, he can save up his own money and go out if he wishes. I can't let his hurt keep me from going. I refuse all guilt.

You haven't told me what life with baby is like. I admire your ability to adjust in gentle ways to what you need to do. I got a laugh out of your youthful impatience with the past and remembrances thereof. For me, you were always a good balance for Eric's pessimism of the future and constant looking back. You gave me courage to believe there was good up ahead for my child. Some better with the bitter. Yes, thank God for memory, for the learning it offers, and for the hope of a future to apply it in. Good night.

Verge

2/24/83

My Sweet Verge,

I hugged the brief recount you gave me of our two-years-ago February time together and drifted off in a reverie. I can easily remember the new feeling of love that started to grow then, a growth spurt in a new direction involving complete trust. That May-in-February day was two years ago this very day. As we sat on the dock, insulated in our own capsule of sun and water and clouds, I didn't think it was possible to feel any more happiness and joy. Little did we know the riches our future held.

I left that night. The next morning I arrived in Cleveland and it was my last drink day. I can still see the orange liquid running from the glass into my mouth, and saying to myself, "Well, self, this is it. No more." Not, "Good luck, self," or "Maybe, self," or, "I hope, self." Just a feeling of determination. If I had known how dog sick I would be for the next three days, I might not have had such confidence.

I know what you mean about Eric and the slips and all. It seems the hardest part is understanding and accepting that behavior as a disease. I hate to count how many trips I have taken back to Step I. As someone said at a meeting yesterday, "The falls don't count, just the getting up's."

The baby in my life...she hasn't pushed into it too hard yet. Everything seems to be sliding into place all by itself. She is a pretty baby, quiet. She is there when I come home, either sleeping or eating. Daughter changes her, coos around with her for a while, then she goes back to sleep. She seems to be very bright, but who can really tell at this age. I have held her several times, and I am glad to report that skill has not diminished with time. I welcome her as a new life. I still find that to be a miracle, the insinuation of life where there was no life.

Now, I have a question to ask you. What goes through your pretty mind as far as meeting your daughter-in-law? Is it a frightening thought? Do you feel confident? You know, all those things that swim in and around a head when new adventures looms.

Michael

3/4/83

My Sweet, Sweet Love,

It is so hard to get everything answered and to tell you all those fantastic things I think through the day. I just spend my life slaving over a hot pen. Sometimes, when we are together, a half hour's silence is more eloquent than tomes. You and I didn't used to talk a blue streak to each other. In the past I have told you that I valued the fact that, "You always know enough to not talk things to death." Since we have taken up talking, I would never use that phrase again, rather, "We know enough to talk things to life." Have two people ever enjoyed each other's company as much as we do? Part of the joy is that we taught each other to talk. This letter writing was one of the main tools that we used. It taught us to organize our thoughts enough to specifically state what we meant. It would be silly to send a blank piece of paper back and forth if we were to communicate, so we had to say something more than the state of the weather and that we missed each other. With experimentation, we found words could create feelings and change moods. Then we found it was fun to build a thought together. Everything didn't have to be presented in a final form. I could say, and you could respond; then I could revise, and you could give your opinion; and eventually we could arrive at some understanding collectively. I believe that was when our talking took off.

Before that, I always cast myself in the listener role. I was drawn to talkers (or *vice versa*), and not one of them had the patience to get me to talk. I never developed conversational skills and became more backward as time went on, 'til I wasn't sure I had anything worthy to say, anyway. I knew I wasn't stupid, but I wasn't sure I was very original, either. Because of my painful hesitancy, people rushed to fill the embarrassing gaps I left in a conversation, so I felt it was easier to remain silent, especially if I had a friendly drink at hand. Between us, there never were any painful or embarrassing gaps of silence, because we both hid there and neither minded the quiet. Through letter writing, we found that we owned undeveloped skills. We liked each other's letters and what we had to say, so we tried harder. Thank Goodness, for letters became a lifeline through some very painful times.

You asked what I feel about meeting my daughter-in-law. I don't feel nervous. I would like to have the same kind of relationship with her that I had with my mother-in-law, until the sickness got the best of me. I loved her, and felt accepted and comfortable with her. I don't know why relationships with mothers-in-law are depicted as difficult. I just know

I want to be a person with her and not some bad joke. I am very glad to have contact with your daughters to remind me what it is like to be twenty. I need reminding that being twenty is many unformed things that will soon be formed, but aren't quite yet. Just as a two-year-old does perfectly right things for two, that are not charming at three, twenty looks grown up and formed, but there are often miles to go before being fully adult.

Sometimes I read over my letters to Milo and get a panicky feeling that they sound like every clutching, guilt-laying stereotype of a mother's letter ever written. I become suspicious of the subconscious intent of every word, and I don't know whether to send it or to tear it up. I have the occasional giddy wondering if I will feel the same way about every word that comes out of my mouth to his wife. But I don't allow myself to speculate upon that too often. I will try my best to convey my "me" to her and try to find her "self", and see where we go from there. It feels like an adventure.

I try not to look at a calendar. It tells me things like it is still almost a month before I will see Milo and his wife, or you. I am desperately trying to do "one day at a time." I take my child in hand, if I can catch her, and tell her, "Now stop that! You must not expect things to happen when you want them to, not that very second. You must learn to wait, and wait, until the stars cross the meridian, and the sun and the moon line up, and then, if you have been very good, maybe you will get to see the boy who has been waiting for the same sun, and moon, and stars to move, and you can go play, while we grown up, mature people, Michael and I, have tea and discuss the weather and politics. Now, sit there, and don't get your dress all mussed up!!

My little girl says, "I think Michael would love me anyway, even if I did have dirt on my face and my sox were falling down." I ignore that last pouty remark and busy myself about the kitchen so my little girl will not see the half smile tugging at the corners of my mouth.

Verge

3/9/83

My Woman,

I have been having uncomfortable gnawings at the back of my mind for the past few weeks, (I call them plateau gnawings) and I have been hitting meetings even when I haven't intended to. I have also been skirting away from doing any AA leads, ducking them the best I can. In fact, last Wednesday a man asked me to lead the following Wednesday (today), and I even lied and said I wouldn't be able to be at the meeting. I didn't intend to go today...but, after gym, I headed right there anyway. Last Friday H. P. got even with me. A man asked me to give my story at a Sunday afternoon meeting in April. I was feeling bad enough about what I did a few days previously, and it was on a Sunday afternoon with no night work excuse, so I said OK. I guess I will never get immune to the strange way things work in The Program, but it surely beats where I would have been without it.

~

*Are you the little girl who has been waiting and waiting? Me, too! I hate waiting. But now I don't mind. You have a little smudge here on your cheek. Is that from jumping up and down? And your socks? Let me wipe it off? Your cheek is so soft and pretty. It looks like a tear rolled down through the smudge. If I kiss it, you will forget about it. I'm glad you waited. I kinda like you. You're nice...the way you smile. You have pretty hands—soft on my cheek.*

*I never talked to any old girl like this before. I'm gonna get my catcher's mitt. Come on, let go my hand! OK, OK, I'll fix your socks. Then I'm going. You have cute feet. I like the crazy way you hold them on the floor. Do you wear your socks all the way up, or folded down? Up? Your legs are pretty, too. Smooth. Strong. I like that. How fast can you run from home to first base? No? I bet you could be fast. ...I gotta go.*

*Hey, will you wait for me? Yes, I'll hurry back. Please wait.*

Love,
Michael

3/10/83

Sweet Love, My Michael Man,

Oooowee, Babe, tonight I'm tired and miss you unbearably. Do you believe that last night I had a guilt dream about drinking? I don't consciously think about drinking at all anymore. In fact, the only times I have thought of it has been in social situations where I felt awkward and unsociable by not drinking with borderline acquaintances and strangers. That passed when I realized that a bartender is just as happy serving Perrier with a twist, or a Coke, or pretends to be. In the dream I am speaking semi-formally to a group who had presented me with a gift box of cordials. As I am talking, I am absent-mindedly sipping the liqueur as one might absent-mindedly pop chocolates or hors d'oeuvres. Suddenly, I am aghast at what I am doing. I feel as sharply embarrassed as if I had committed some social indiscretion like wetting my pants. I am in a panic because afterward I'm supposed to meet you for dinner. I am trying to think whether I am acting like I have been drinking, and trying to think how I can disguise the smell on my breath. I feel so miserable and ashamed of what I have done without even being aware of it, until it was done. I know there is no way to undo it.

I woke in a cold sweat, crying. My God, Michael, the far-reaching effects of this disease are just mind-boggling!

Love,
Verge

3/12/83

My Sweet Verge,

I don't know what got into my system this night, but suddenly I was inspired to clean out the storage part of my tool cart. (Running out of room to put accumulated letters is the real reason.) Nine years of collected manuals, electrical prints, drawings, notes, check lists, all mostly outdated. And letters! Even I had to be a little taken aback by the volume. If I had saved them from the beginning, I would have to be issued my very own room for storage. Did you think you were such a prolific writer? I never dreamed I could be. I have never done so with another soul in this life.

~

*Do you always spend your summers sitting around poking at the ground with a stick? Hi! Yeah I know it is hot. That's all I feel like doing, too. Sometimes I sit for hours just watching the clouds drift by.*

*Sorry. Well, I couldn't. That night when I got home my Dad told me I was going to spend the month at my aunt's in Michigan. The next morning I was on the train—gone! Boy, that's something, how parents don't care how they just move kids around. Like kids don't have things they gotta do.*

*What did you do? Are you kidding? A chicken? I never knew anyone who had a chicken for a pet. What does it do, roll over and play dead with its feet up in the air? I'll bet it follows you around faithfully with its tongue all hanging out, panting and panting. Here, Henny Penny, fetch! Hey! OK, OK, I'm sorry. Just kidding. I'm sure a chicken is a very nice pet, all those pretty feathers and everything. They probably have their own special cluck—each different—so their mother can tell them apart.*

*You have a pretty smile. Yeah, you light all up. It's fun to make you smile. Can I see her? Your chicken. Sure I'd like to. ...Does it bite? Don't be mad. I won't tease you again. You're smiling. I know you are not mad.*

*It's kinda fun to be with you. I don't know, I just kinda feel good. Easy like. Like I've known you for a long time. You do? Funny, huh? Where's that chicken? ...Hey, she's cute! Well, I don't mean cute—nice, I guess. That's really something how she sticks to you. Never saw anything like that. She must like you a lot. Pretty nice.*

*Did you ever fish? Oh, yeah? No kidding? Yeah, I go now and again, but I never catch anything. I'd rather play baseball, or football, or something. What's there to learn about fishing? All you have to do is stick some bait on a hook and throw it in the water and then just sit there, and sit there. Really? I didn't know that. Wow! There is more to it than I thought. Maybe you could teach me. I could teach you how to hit a ball, sometime. Wanna go tomorrow morning? Oh. Way up there? Canada is a long way off. How do you get there? Does your dad like to drive? I guess he does then. Sure is a long way to go fishing. For two weeks? You must catch lots of fish. Fun, huh?*

*Well, guess I won't see you for a while, then. Are you taking your chicken? Want me to feed her and stuff? Sure, I wouldn't mind. I'll come over every day. Just tell me what to do, and I'll do it. Yeah, it's OK, I can do that, easy. I'll take good care of her. Well, I hope you have a good time. Gotta go. S'long. ...I'll... miss you.*

~

Wouldn't you know, I've written myself into a corner. Time goes by when I write to you almost as fast as when I am with you.

Michael

Tuesday night, 3/15/83

Dear Little Boy, My Michael,

Ooooooh, "Here Henny Penny, fetch!" That was a funny, funny letter.

~

*Can I come home to supper with you? Can I, huh? Maybe you would show me what your room looks like. Do you have pictures of cowboy stars on your wall? Y'know, the kind you get from the movies with their names written in the corners? You are not like my brothers at all. I like you. When you tease it makes me feel like you like me and stuff. My brothers tease me all the time, but they make me feel bad. Sometimes I just get so mad at them I stand and scream as loud as I can so I can't hear what they're saying anymore. When they play cowboys and Indians they always make me be the sheriff and I have to guard the jail. They go off on their horses and almost never capture any outlaws for hours and hours—not until they get mad at someone—and then I have someone to talk to for a while. If you wanna sometime, you can come and be the sheriff and I'll be deputy sheriff and we could play house in the jail until we get some outlaws. You won't like my brothers, though; they're mean. I didn't know boys could be nice like you. I bet even if you were mad at me you wouldn't twist my arm around and around. I bet you would let me catch you at tag, sometimes.*

*Maybe I could stay overnight with you. Would your mommy let me? Why can't girls stay over with boys, if I'm your friend? We could pull the covers over our heads and see which one needs to breathe first. I'd scratch your back for a long time, and then you could scratch mine. You never had someone scratch your back before? Don't you have a best friend? Maybe you like to have your feet tickled. I tickle feet real good....I bet you just don't want me to stay.*

*I have an idea. I have a tent. Sometimes I stay in the tent—well, for part of the night. It's just, sometimes there are funny noises that wake me up, or sometimes the moon is so bright I can't sleep. We could walk in the moonlight and I could show you how the moon sparkles on the wet grass. Did you know you make shadows in moonlight, too? You do. Grey ones. You could come and stay in the tent with me like we wuz camping. I don't think my mommy would care, 'cuz I used to sleep with my brother when my little brother was born, until I got my own room when my grandma died.*

~

Last night we put up the set, and tonight we had our first rehearsal in it. I've done well until now, but I'm suddenly suffering definite serenity slips, and boy, do I hate that feeling. I remember it well, and I do not want to be like that again. At every turn there is too much for one person to do. I think I should not have loaded my camel's back with this advisorship. Mind, I have enjoyed the kids, but the hidden work involved, just because no one is knowledgeable, sucks my energy. Thank God I have a person to do lights, because that is the only thing I know nothing about, and I am forced to accept whatever the light person does. I despair of ever getting this show polished. I'll be really lucky if a couple of people learn their lines.

Lord, where does the time go? I have to catch a couple of extra winks tonight, or I will be in trouble tomorrow. I was a holy terror all day today, and that is just plain not fair to the kids. I love you, Michael, from my very height, and breadth, and depth. Sounds like a mechanical drawing problem. But, you know how very seriously I mean it.

Verge

3/19/83

My Sweet Verge,

Aren't those drinking dreams weird? I have never experienced more realistic dreams. They come on so heavily, and just stick. I am sure there are scientific explanations for them. I told you about the one I had a year or more ago, when it was not until I had made coffee and was sitting down drinking it that I realized it was all a dream. What a relief! What deep remorse connected to them! It is enough to keep a body from going back out. Thankfully, I haven't had one in quite a while now.

I suppose by the time you read this you will be at sixes and nines over the prospect of an all too soon opening night. Not a second to yourself, one last minute crisis after another, too many things yet to be done. That is just the way opening nights are, even if you have a year to rehearse with a star-studded cast. If you feel a hand on your shoulder it is not your imagination, it's me giving a pat and being proud.

~

I *think I know your brothers. They seem like pretty nice big guys. They don't pay me any attention, but the other big guys at school like them.*

*Sometimes I wish I could be like them. I wonder why they treat you mean. I think you are very nice. I don't have any sisters, so I don't know about them, but I think you would be a nice sister.*

*You know, my brothers treat me kinda mean, too. My older ones. Sometimes I get so mad, like you, I scream at them, and cry at the same time. The other day, one got me so mad I swore at him. It just popped out of my mouth. I never said those words before. That made me feel bad. It just made him madder, and he chased me. I knew if he caught me that would be the end of me. I ran into my mother and father's room and locked the door. I knew he wouldn't dare break their door. I stayed there feeling really bad, until I heard him and his friends leave. His buddies were nice, though. They kept trying to talk him into leaving me alone. While I was waiting, I though, people are only mean to people in their own family. Funny, huh?*

*Can I pet that ol' chicken? What's her name again? Can I pet her? She doesn't bark or scratch her back leg, or anything. She's nice though.*

*Can I bring my dog when we're camping? He knows some real good tricks. He'll guard us too. OK, I'll hoot like an owl, so you won't get scared.*

*...Hooot. Hooot. Hoooo....Shhh, what do you mean shhh? That was a good owl. What do they say, but hoot, hoot? OK, let's hear yours. Oh, yeah. That sounds good. How'd you do that? Is there room enough for me in there?*

~

I mentioned on the phone about going to the islands when you visit. When I hung up I laughed to myself, "I'll just bet Verge thought I meant the Bahamas, or something. I'll bet she thinks you're a big time traveler. I'll bet she is impressed. Anyhow, I don't know what time of year thing start happening on the Lake Erie Islands, but I am going to check it out.

Michael

Tuesday, 3/22/83

Dear Michael,

Tonight, before rehearsal, I went home for a cup of coffee, and a fast change of makeup—just long enough to receive the unpleasant news that our landlady has died. I don't know where that leaves me. I hope her relatives will let us stay for at least a couple of months so I can find another place. Neither this day nor any day until I'm safe in your arms is the day I wanted to hear that information. I'm just too busy this week to think. Come hell or eviction, I'm going to leave Sunday for Arizona and I refuse to carry this problem along with me. You know it entails other things with Eric, too, and I don't have the strength until I get back to face that either.

Limping time, Babe. I will be with you soon, yea!

Verge

# PART II

# End Of The Pact

4/12/83

My Sweet Verge,

I like the real stuff better. Writing letters is okay, but I'll take touching you, seeing you and being with you as my first choice. Alas, at this time in our history, we are relegated to writing. With you, I am more myself than at any other time in my life, past or present. What you do to me is a true miracle. Take my most ill timed sickness. I could feel myself slipping under its heel that night you held me, and chased it away. It could have been a disaster, but it stepped back and held back until it was time to part again. If there must be sick times, okay, but not when we are spending our few precious minutes together. The beauty part is that I felt comfortable enough to honestly tell you that I felt sick and trusted you would accept it without pity or impatience. We celebrated the joy of being together despite the inconvenience. But, I feel I left something unresolved. I let you slip away when I know your head was loaded with stuff you wanted to share. I worry that I let you down. Now, I am like dawg, straining at the leash for the minutes to hurry so I can hear your voice and soothe this terrible ache.

...I have just talked to you, and I feel new again. The sound of your voice and your laugh—oh, your laugh, what sweet magic it does—have literally healed me, just as you did on that fever night. Talking has lifted a weight, as always when one or the other of us is hurting. I am left new again. Don't forget that you owe me a story about our kids in the tent.

Michael

Wednesday, 4/13/83

Sweet Man, My Michael,

It was a sunny day, so Elle and I took the canoe out for the first time this year. She has had an unhappy year at work since returning from a sabbatical, and I think she finds the same soothing effect in the lake that I find. She doesn't bother my space, and sometimes her presence keeps me off my own self-pity.

When we rounded the point, going toward the swamp, we were shocked by an elegant pair of swans regally swimming, with two geese in front of them and another pair behind. I have never seen swans on the lake. We both involuntarily sucked in our breath. After watching them out of sight, we paddled back into the swamp and found cowslips, just before flowering, ready for eating. Like dandelions they get bitter after they flower. We collected enough for dinner, and I showed Elle how to cook them. Just what I needed, a spring tonic!

~

*Hi! I thought you decided not to come. That was the dumbest hoot I ever heard. Maybe I'll call you Hoot. Just like that cowboy in the movies. Betcha ride a horse. ...Aww, come on, I didn't really mean it. I was just mad 'cuz I thought you weren't coming.*

*Please, please, pretty please come in? I'll let you read my comics. Just got a bunch of good ones from my friend. I have to hide them 'cuz my dad gets mad and burns them up. He says they overwork my imagination and that's why I wake up in the middle of the night crying. I cry because I'm scared. No! I never get scared in the tent. It's just in the house. I'm the only one sleeps downstairs, 'cept my Uncle Bill, and he sleeps real hard, and snores, and everything, and the house makes noises—cracks, and snaps, and the stairs sound like someone is walking on them, and stuff. Out here it is just the crickets and owls and things I know what are.*

*Did you bring your dog? No, I put my chicken to bed in her barn. You can't teach them not to squirt whenever they want to, so they are kinda messy. Your dog can come in, too. He is a nice dog. I like him 'cuz he likes you so much. I like his thumpin, thumpin tail.*

*Wanna eat? I brought banana and mayonnaise sandwiches and oatmeal cookies. Oh, they're great! They really are! Kids always try to trade their sandwiches for mine when I bring them to school. Just try a bite. Here. See. See? I told you so. I don't know, my mom just always made them. We have strawberry Kool-Aid to drink. Didn't you ever have any? It's some new stuff. Comes in different flavors. I like lime best, but we had that last week. We only get one kind a week. It uses a lot of sugar, and Mom gets all kind of crazy when we use much sugar. It is really yuck made with honey.*

*It's starting to get a little chilly. Let's get in the sleeping bag and then we can read comics. Darn! My shoelace has a knot in it. Can you untie it? Gee, you can do everything. I like the way you do stuff. It doesn't seem to matter to you that I'm a girl. You make me feel like it is fun to be a girl, and, you know, somehow different from you, but, as good as you. Do you know what I mean? My brothers make me feel like I can't do things as good as they can because I am a girl. They're bigger than I am, and maybe they can do things better because they are bigger, but not just because they are boys.*

*I'm chilly. Move off the sleeping bag so I can get in. Of course I only have one sleeping bag. There's enough room. It'll be all warm and snuggly. Your dog sure minds you good, lying there on our feet like that with his tongue hanging out and his eyes all looking up at you. Good dog! Let's turn out the flashlight.*

*Whew! (pant, pant) It's hot in here! 'N your dog needs some Listerine! Lets eat the rest of the sandwiches and drink up the Kool-Aid, and then I'll show you what the grass feels like when you run barefoot in the dew.*

*Come on, Hoot. Betcha can't catch me. Betcha! Owww. Owww. Don't tickle me. No. I promise. I PROMISE. I'll never call you Hoot again.*

~

I may call you Hoot, sometimes,
Verge

Friday, 4/22/83

My sweet Verge,

I think you are funny! Calling me Hoot, indeed! What's the matter with my hoot? That's the way I heard people do it in the movies. I meant to tell you, along with disparaging comic books, my mother also didn't like using all that sugar in Kool-Aid. I think sugar was rationed during the war. She didn't believe in soda pop either. She said it wasn't good for children, and I got the impression she thought it was immoral, too. My father used to buy us a coke when we were alone with him—sort of like a special treat. "But, don't...don't tell mother." I can't even imagine Kool-Aid made with honey. Running in the dewy grass in the moonlight sounds great. I love those kids.

Thanks for the offer of a loan, but Green Imp came through. It has become a game with Imp and me. When the money situation becomes a problem and my back is to the wall, because of one bill deadline or another, I tell Green Imp, "It's up to you. I haven't got the money, but I ain't gonna worry about it. Can't do anything about it anyway. " It's uncanny! It always works so the necessities are okay, but no frills. That Imp is a joker. Makes me smile at myself a lot. The same seems to go for how things work for us. Sometimes mischievously, but when it is serious the solution works out in a serious manner. The jokes seem to be set aside, and Imp gets down to business.

This all sounds childlike, but when I am at a point where there is no answer anywhere in me, and I can't do anything about it, what choice do I have but to turn it over—especially since I have found that it works? I used to try to run the world and force my will on the conditions, but all I ever did was to mess everything up. I do enjoy the chuckles we get from the "mysterious workings" and the way life goes on in a more gentle fashion. All of me loves all of you.

Michael

4/24/83

My Rainmaking Man,

The rains still do come down. Yesterday morning I went out to the lake and watched the pair of swans. I can't get too close, but they tolerate me at a distance. The sun shone for a brief bit, but it soon clouded over and again the rains. It begins to wear a body down. This day, besides the rain, began on the wrong foot. Eric worked last night and I had to pick him up this morning at seven. Missing that extra hour to myself, and having to get up at 6:15 on Sunday was not my favorite. I had thought he would go to bed after a long night, and I could ease into the morning. Another wrong foot, he decided to play chess with himself. Just when I had worked myself up to my grouchiest best, he decided to make some "suggestion" about my leaving information when I go off on my jaunts, " ...Because people call from school, kids call, your father calls, and I'm embarrassed because I don't know what to tell them."

That was one wrong foot too many, considering his history of unannounced and unexplained comings and goings all the years of our marriage. I cut him short with, "Tell them whatever I've told you, and that I will return their call when I get back."

He said, "You never hear me out." I replied that there was not much he had to say other than about his schedule that I wanted to hear. As far as I was concerned ours was a financial arrangement, period. What I did with my life was my business.

Michael, I still cannot talk to that man in a sane, gentle fashion. The only way I can ever tell him what I mean is when he pushes me too far and it comes as an outburst. When I try to speak necessary truths to him, he pulls all of the strings to make me feel pity or guilt so I soft-peddle, and they never get said. I have spoken nothing personal to him in over a year. Conversation consists solely of the running of the house or car arrangements. I avoid being in the same room with him. I go no place with him. What I said has been said in a million non-verbal ways in the last two years. Like a hurt child he said to me, "Even the poetry?"

Most of all I have avoided being entertained by him. I have walked away repeatedly from that thing he has used with everybody on earth to control them—entertaining. I fail to believe he can be that blind. I had hoped to not have to say it in words. I had hoped to allow him to save his own pride by not making me say it.

He went off to pout and came back later saying he didn't know what Al-Anon was teaching me, but that I had become, "just plain mean." Lord, he is a hard man to break away from. Just when I am sure he has finally gotten the message, I find he's flung another stinging, hot ray around my ankle to trip me up. Michael, what an awful, long, struggling, bad death this is becoming. I know, at every turn, everything I do hurts him, but I know I do not want to be with him. I don't feel malice. I don't wish to "get even." I know the man is sick. I simply don't feel anything! It must be a terrible blow to his ego, without any intent on my part. I keep "turning it over"... "The opportunity will present itself."... "Things will evolve." It is a wearying process.

I owe him the telling of how I feel. It keeps coming around to that. I must tell him. I have to put it into words. That prospect scares me. He still intimidates me when I talk to him—that's why I don't. He so quickly knows how to make me sound like a fool. But it is like being pregnant, nothing is going to stop this process, the when just hasn't happened yet. Michael, it is sinful to have a relationship with someone for twenty-six years and not be able to talk to him.

You and I, have had an unvoiced agreement, but let's put it into words. Michael, don't ever shut me up and don't ever let me stop you from saying anything, not ever. No matter what it is, how much you might not want to hear it, or say it, if you feel like saying it, do. I can see me sitting with you on the lawn swing down by the lake. The children were little, so it was long before we had started to write to each other. I said to you, "Michael, please don't ever shut me up." Even then I knew that to survive I had to communicate.

I'm sorry for a gray letter. Because I trust and respect your judgment, I talk about such things. I know it pains you more than you would ever tell me, but you also know why I have to talk about this with you.

Verge

4/25/83

Michael, my Loving Man,

You made a laugh catch deep in my throat when you said you love our imaginary kid selves and that you get all caught up in them. Strange, isn't it? When I write about them, they feel so real; they seem to say and do things that I just record. Apparently they exist for some very special reason—something about taking our hands and walking us through what I found to be a bad, awkward, shy, mentally painful time, comparable to yours, from what you have told me. It is like walking through it with you—a new, delightfully shared time. I love how gentle you are with me, and funny. That is what I missed in the living of it. I was so thin-skinned, sensitive, and serious during those painful years. I love our laughter with our kids. They are an entity in themselves; it seems all right to analyze them, because nothing can fade their aliveness. They create a feeling of growth for me, as if I were being allowed to rearrange my past in a more bearable way, being able to live both ends of the spectrum of my life simultaneously. I am starting to get into muddy thinking here, because my brain is still riling up its waters trying to make sense of it. Can you add anything? Do you feel any of this, or is it just my natural madness coming to the fore?

I have to tell you what I observed this afternoon. The two swans were on our side of the lake. Late afternoon had let a little sun through and a little warmth, but a stiff breeze was whitecapping the lake, blowing up quite a swell. The swans had started to swim across the lake. The larger one, presumably male, was ahead by quite a bit, paddling into the wind and the smaller one seemed to make hardly any headway. Transferring my feeling when paddling the canoe under similar circumstances, it seemed that only an occasional stroke was pushing her forward, mostly she was just staying in place, or worse with a weaker stroke, falling back. The other swan kept looking at her anxiously, and each time he turned to look, the wind would push him back perceptively, as well. After watching this for several minutes, I saw what looked to be a few moments of totally giving up on the smaller ones part, and she was rapidly blown back toward shore. Then, with what seemed like a capricious decision, she made a forty-five degree turn, opened her wings like putting out full sail and with a lurch went running down the wind full tilt toward the north end of the lake. The other swan gave her such a look, and sedately, regally turned and paddled up the lake following her, but on his own steam—none of this turning yourself loose to the wind stuff for him.

She kept flipping up her wings, looking for all the world as if she were thoroughly enjoying her free ride after that mighty effort. When she got all the way into the cove at the end of the lake, she began to feed. After the male arrived, he kept swimming back out toward the point and open water, trying to get her to follow, but she was having none of it. He would come back and then start out again, coaxing her. She totally ignored him. "God grant me the serenity to accept the things I cannot change, courage to change the things I can, and the wisdom to know the difference."[9] It works for man or beast.

I love you heaps more,
Verge

4/30/83

My darling Verge,

Thanks for telling me the swan story. I could just see you watching and calling me to look. I like how we both see the drama in nature, how we tune in on the same things when we go hiking or canoeing. Female swan discovered something of herself, and decided to keep that piece of independence she found. Male swan probably said, "I ain't trying any of those dumb female tricks," and then went around the point and practiced it himself.

I have to relate everything to us; my mind only works in us gear. We help each other over obstacles and are ready to accept and incorporate what the other offers, if it fits. No stubborn, prideful games between us. As you said once, neither of us has ever had to stop and wait for the other to catch up. We seem to grow along at a pace together.

Our kid's stories are no exception. I have felt since we started writing about them that I was recording what I saw—or remembered? I have been puzzled by the same question as you: how does that sort of sharing relate to the health of our relationship? I wondered if there was some perversity in examining their sexuality, but I ruled that out, because it carries the innocence of childhood, part of their growing up. It is like we are exploring, getting a chance to walk through that tough time together, and picking up what should have been if time were not out of joint. It

9 The Serenity Prayer used by Alcoholics Anonymous and Al-Anon. Ibid.,125.

helps me see and understand my childhood self better, and helps to put things in place.

~

*Ginny!...Gin! (I hope her father isn't up. I'll just try throwing this small stone. What if her brothers answer? I'll hide in this bush.) Oh, hi! Hi. You are up already. I hope you don't mind this early. I couldn't sleep. I don't know, just couldn't. I brought this old fishing pole and some worms. Get yours and we'll go, OK? Will your mother and father be mad?*

*I brought some bananas and this half'a jar of peanut butter. Yeah, they're good together. C'mon. I like this early part of the morning, don't you? All quiet and cool. I like to watch the animals getting up and looking for breakfast.*

*You can sit on the stump 'n I'll sit on this clump of moss right next to it. Hey, you're good at those worms. I like you. I don't know, just the way you do things and kinda look after yourself when you are given half a chance. I do that too. Look after myself. It is better than those dumb old brothers and my mother telling me what to do all the time. I could do all that 'ol stuff myself if they wouldn't be tellin' me all the time. I know. We just kinda do things together and don't be tellin' each other what to do. It also feels good when sometimes you ask me to help you do stuff.*

*Do you promise not to tell anybody that I said I like you? My dumb brothers would ride me, and tell my friends, and they would call me a sissy—for liking a girl. Oh, Gee, I'm sorry. I didn't mean it like that. I like liking you. You don't make fun of things all the time. You like to do what I like to do, and I don't have to do stuff because everyone else is or you'd make fun. Want a banana? Peanut butter? I brought some bread, too. Sun feels good. Look at that coon washing his breakfast. I wonder why they do that. Do you know?*

*I don't know, I just don't feel like jokin' today. Maybe I'm half asleep. ...I've been sorta thinkin' about last week... in the tent. That seemed kinda serious. Did it to you? I mean more than just playing, then going away and forgetting it. It stays on my mind.*

~

You are serious on my mind,
Michael

April 30, 1983

My Sweet Honey Man,

I love you. All day that has thumped in my chest more violently than usual. Various school pressures are beginning to build as usual when the year's end approaches. This week, with two seasonably warm days, the kids have just remembered it is spring. All those antlers sprouting at once are a handful. Tomorrow I am being observed in my mechanical drawing class. I am at a struggle point now where I am doing the plates just ahead of the class. The problems are simple enough when I understand the process, but mind-boggling until the light strikes. I enjoy teaching that class, though, and look forward to it every day. Today I had to call a teacher, at the high school, who has been a saint of patience with me from the beginning (as soon as I could get over my pride and asked for help.) He did a whole problem with me—akin to instructing an outback doctor through an operation over the phone. I got it, though, and the plates came out as promised. He keeps telling me the first year is the hardest. I enjoy it because I am learning a skill with the kids, and essentially I like learning things. It makes me happy and excited inside to battle with my brain. I have found with increasing self-confidence, learning things is easier because I don't feel hampered by a foreboding that I will fail. The awareness that I might fail is there, but if I do, so what? I can try again or choose not to try again, but worlds don't end and skies don't fall. Sometimes I feel so giddy with the freedom offered by The Program and your encouragement that I feel I must float. I can hardly believe the variety of things we learn from each other and with each other. I was going to say for each other, but I won't. We learn for ourselves and that in turn is for each other.

~

*Hey, Hoot, look! Your pole's jiggling. You've got a bite. My dad says not to jerk it real fast. Let the fish run with it until he decides to swallow the worm. I'm sorry it sounds yuck; that's just the way it is. Wow! Did you see the size of him when he jumped out of the water? You jerked just right. Ya got a good hold. What test is your line? Test. You know, how much weight can it hold. That's right. That is too, what it's called. Tests aren't just at school. C'mon, Hoot, stop teasing me!*

*...It's all right. You just try to make me laugh. I thought you really didn't know what test was. It's awful when you don't know and somebody*

*else teases you because you don't know and they won't tell you—just act like they are so smart and all. It makes you feel so dumb. But you have to find out before you know. And there's an awful lot of stuff to find out. Know what I mean?*

*Course I know you are trying to bring in that old fish. I don't know why I talk so much when I am with you. Guess it's 'cuz you look as if you wanted to hear what I might say. 'Cept when you're catching fish.*

*There, see! You've got him almost in. Don't let the line loose. Wow, Hoot, that's a real fish! Come on; let's go show my dad. ...He won't laugh. My dad gets real serious about fish.*

*You just want to share it with me? Oh, Hoot, I like you so much I feel like giving you a hug. You wouldn't? You wouldn't push me away?*

*I know, let's cook 'im. You scale him and I'll go get our camp fry pan. It's down cellar and no one will know. Sure, I know how to cook. I cook for my family every Friday when my mother goes to Grandma's. Dad helps, but sometimes I do it all alone.*

*What's that? A scaler? Hey, that's pretty neat. I always just use my jackknife. I'm allowed. See? Watch out, Uncle Bill just sharpened it! He says dull knives cut more people than sharp ones. Don't you have one? ...I'll be right back.*

*...Boo! Hey, Hoot, I made you jump! Uncle Bill taught me to walk real quiet in the woods, but I never learned to walk quiet enough to fool a crow. Good, ya got a fire going. I brought some cornmeal in this little bag I saved from the candy store by school. Here, hold the fish and I'll sprinkle the corn meal over it. My mom gets mad when I go there, and my dad gets fierce, but when I have some pennies I go with the other kids, anyway. I heard my aunt tell my mom something about the store man likes little girls, but I don't know why that makes them mad. I think more people should like girls. Now some salt and pepper from this twist of wax paper. Darn, how are we gonna turn 'im? We'll have to use sticks. Let's see if we can eat with sticks, too, like I saw in a picture.*

*...Think it's done? Sure smells good. We'll let it cool and eat it out of the pan.*

*...Hoot, this fish is really good!*

*...Oh, Oh, that's mom calling me. Gotta go. Will you put water on the coals? Bye—oh, I forgot, here. I've got two jackknives. I lost this one, and then I found it after I got a new one for my birthday. It was a little rusty, but it cleaned up pretty good. If you come over tomorrow, we'll get Uncle Bill to sharpen it. Gotta hurry or I'm gonna get killed. Bye.*

---

I agree with you that the sexual exploration between the kids is not perverse. It helps to purify what happened to me and to reclaim my innocence. We are ageless lovers.

Verge

5/6/83

My Sweet Verge,

I have always been fascinated by land's end places, also. I never considered Long Island, because I had the impression it was a teeming mass of humanity standing shoulder to shoulder. I always thought of the famous capes of the world, or the bottom of England, or Tierra del Fuego, or some such place, until I read John Steinbeck's *Travels With Charlie*. My mind's ear perked up when I read about his place near the end of Long Island. "Gotta see what that's like," I thought. As you said, our probings in that direction last fall were kindly and left me looking for more. From earliest memory I have been drawn to oceans, yet I have never been comfortable with them. To learn to sail knowledgably would be a realized secret dream I have, but in my present state of ignorance I would be full of trepidation. I think that would pass with time and experience, but I know I would always have a certain fear. A healthy fear and respect, I think. That time you and I, and Eric and Doreen went to Pemaquid Point in Maine was the clincher, the siphon that started the real flow. Prior to that I had been exposed to sandy shores. They were exciting enough in rough weather, but nothing like the rocks of New England. That ocean said, "Wanna try me? You are welcome, but I am not sentimental." I loved standing on those rocks with you, sharing what you were feeling, but feeling it alone, inside and private, too; a piece to share with each other and a piece to share with that force beating on the rocks. Wild!

I was glad you mentioned on the phone, about feeling out of sorts and discontent. Me too. I have been carrying it around by myself, thinking it was a passing thing. It nags me though. Persistent. Very disconcerting. The spring in my step, that felt like it had become an automatic part of my life, has to be remembered and worked at. The sights and smells and feel of the world are elusive, where 'til recently they jumped up and never let me get away without a notice. There are even times when I have to remind myself of the joy that is inside me. I chalked it up to missing you and our long separation, although hardly a month. When you spoke of your feelings, speculating they were forerunners of growth, it added a new dimension for me. It didn't change anything, but knowing that mysteriously we are going through the same thing together adds depth and purpose to it. I'll bet pretty soon, when we are together, we won't even remember what we are feeling now.

Love,
Michael

May 8, 1983

My Michael,

All day I have wished it was next week, and I was with you, laughing and being kind to each other, instead of being in the difficult day this has been. There is no nice, neat, unhurtful way to say to someone, "I don't want to live with you anymore." I don't care how many times your head has chanted that, over how many years, and no matter the provocation, it damn well hurts to say it.

The letter came Friday. Dear Mrs. Blake, the house will be put up for sale to settle the estate, but that will be several months. You will be notified when that occurs in plenty of time to relocate. That was roughly the import—not the exact wording.

Eric needling and needling, and me being silent until finally, just like last week, the words formed and jumped out, "Eric, I can't imagine sharing another house with you. I cannot live with you unless each room has an outside door. It is senseless for us to live together anymore."

As much as I was standing apart from myself saying that, it was like a knife cut and a white, hot cauterization. Such awful pain. I didn't say it nice. It hurt more because I couldn't even get it to come out with some humaneness. But nothing was going to keep those words in. I don't mean they were said with anger, just with an awful finality.

He just took it. Saying only, in a sort of dull, mild way, "You finally said what I've been thinking. We really are very bad for each other, now." Then he told me that he has been looking for a job, to be self-supporting and that he would like to know when—that he didn't want me to just spring it on him.

"When we have to move." was the closest when I could answer.

Now that is today. I hope to heaven he remembers it and believes it, because I can't go through that personal turmoil again. Even with the pain, there was the steadying, clear knowledge that it is the right thing for both of us. I'll never get myself together until I break with him and neither will he, if he ever will. Whoever said not to do this in haste before you start to get your head together and figure out the options, could not have said it truer. At any given point before this I know my cowardice would have overtaken me, and I would have wavered into half meaning. He would have seen that weakness and jumped in to twist my mind.

Was it just last weekend I was saying to you that I have to turn it over and wait for old H. P. to show me the way? I did relinquish it. It has been an increasing nag at the back of my head, because my landlady was so sick, and of course her death made it almost incessant. After I talked to you, I said, "Take it H. P. 'cuz I don't have the answer." I truly did not think of it all week, for the first time in months. It is breathtaking to look at it from that perspective. I don't want to spend our time together talking about this, but I suppose we shall. I had wanted to talk to you before telling Eric, when I got back and got my courage up. At least, you are spared that.

Yesterday I dug up the end of my garden. I haven't had much heart for one after letting it go to weed last year. Just for the mental health of it I decided to plant lettuce and radishes and maybe green beans, if I get carried away. It feels strange not to have any hunger to put seeds in soil. Usually it is an undeniable itch. I mourn my lack of earth-lust.

I'm certain there will be other gardens in my life. This is my fallow year—necessary for partings and changes. The lesson of the land is a fallow year gives earth time to gain back strength and to rid itself of disease. Being a good farm girl or at least aware of my roots (*pardonez*) I'll try to take that lesson to heart and build hope on it.

I'm not destroyed by this day. In certain lights it fills me with wonder. I do feel sad and drained, but also released from a heavy burden. I was grateful that Eric spoke the one thought that has weighed heaviest on my mind, "We are not good for each other now." I am as responsible as he is. My only request to H. P. is, "Please let him remember, tomorrow."

Verge

5/17/83

My Sweet walking with me Verge,

I have to check my watch to see what day it is. Everything is shadowy and transient, an out-of-focus photograph, except the four days past. I know the present will take its rightful place, but just for now I choose to study and savor our time together until I can weave it into the beautiful scape of us—an uscape.

What you said in the car as we were driving back to La Guardia has been running through my head. You wondered if we went back to seeing each other, with long intervals between, would the intensity of the feelings we have for each other diminish. I have tried to remember as honestly as I could what it was like then. Did I become *blasé* as time passed into months? Missing you got easier, but the thoughts of you, the looking for you, never went away, from the first time we met in Eric's kitchen, twenty-three years ago. I have told you how sad I felt when you left that time, and how happy I was to see you at his mother's house, later that summer, when we drove to New York to get his things. I told you how I would look for you in strangers, when I knew you were miles and miles away, I didn't even know where. I told you of the leap my heart took two years later, when Eric was in the Air Force and stopped on his way to announce he would be stationed at Stewart A.F.B. in the same town where you worked. I didn't even know where Newburgh was. I knew I had no right to the joy I felt, but nothing could erase it. I had no reason to believe you even remembered who I was. I did not see you again until you and Eric were married and you were pregnant, the summer you drove out to visit us. By that time I had not seen you in three years, and common sense tells me we should have been the next thing to strangers. There was no strangeness; we fell in with each other as if life long friends after a brief separation. Even then we were off walking and talking as if we grew up in a sleeping bag together

Other than periodic visits for the next few years, we had no communication between us other than a passing mention of you by Eric in his letters. Even at that, we never needed any period of reacquaintance. Each time I saw you I learned to love you more. That I loved Eric is no news to you, and it was always a thrill to see him, but hindsight and the little bit of self-honesty I have achieved, tells me seeing you grew in importance with each visit. Each chance I got to know you better convinced me of a unique bond between us. Out of loyalty to Eric, I tried to deny it, because I had no right to feel what was true. When the visits became a regular family affair, beginning in the summer of 1970, you had already become deeply entrenched in my life, and love just took off and flew. Our mutual concern about Eric's increasing "psychological problems" drew us ever closer, as over numerous drinks we tried to understand his changes. Never did it occur to us that alcoholism was the problem. Even then our communication between visits was an occasional family phone call or reading your newsy letters to Doreen. I cannot forget the jittery feelings I would get as the day for departure from Cleveland neared, and how they increased as I got closer to Newburgh. I still get those jitters and shakes each time seeing you is at hand. "Anticipation jitters," I call them. Pre-CLICK jitters. Then as now, they disappear the moment I see you.

Would we cool down if we went back to long separations? I can only believe, no. The growth might slow, but the more I look at our history, the more I am convinced that some seed was placed in our hearts at birth and we needed only to nurture it. Now it will continue to grow and flower despite what we do. You make all of my life a joy.

Michael

5/20/83

My sweetly sane Michael,

I don't find it necessary for my heart to bump against my breastbone every time I walk into a room and see you there. That I should feel like fainting when I turn to find your eyes brimming with that love seems excessive. Having attacks of wanting to burst into operatic arias at the mere thought of you is perhaps overdoing things. But it all seems to increase rather than diminish. I feel more excessive about you today than I ever have in my life, and I have always been head over heels about you. Where on earth or out can it lead?

Thank you for that nostalgic walk through our years. It's a marvel. Never a falter or a false turn, never a distrust, a misunderstanding, or a basic disagreement. Each step of the way increased our respect and regard for each other.

Yesterday, Eric announced that he would not be working at the place he has for almost a year. They are cutting back on guards. The offer of job replacement was either a day job in Peekskill (roughly a 90 mile round trip) or 40-hour weekends. He is supposed to find out tonight. Of course he cannot collect unemployment if he quits. That prompted me to offer to pay for a used car, and if it was reasonably priced, for the next year's insurance. I knew he would need it for transportation. Broaching the subject had seemed insurmountable, as he has always refused to have anything to do with our car except drive it, and I had projected all of the various objections he might have. He only said mildly that he knew nothing about owning a car. I simply replied, "You will learn." I believe that this separation will be as good for him as it will for me. Everything seems to be falling into logical place, and I am at peace that this is the right time.

I have just found out that that one of my worst fears has come true. Eric returned early. He is without work tonight and has to go tomorrow to get another assignment. I said fairly casually, "Well, you better get it straight with them, for soon it will be your livelihood and not just spending money." It was then that I found he refuses any remembrance of ever having had communication about our separation. He has been outwardly sober and acts fairly normal. I began to believe some strides were being made. You would think that an announcement that shakes your whole world would be remembered, from its shock value, if nothing else. Right? No. It wasn't easier, telling him a second time, but the words came out more succinctly. I also wrote it down on paper in black and white in a concise, straightforward and unemotional way.

After mulling that over for a bit, he came back to say that if I just give him the money I would spend for a car, he will leave as soon as he has it and go to Phoenix (the old geographical cure.) He says he will ask his sister's husband to help him find a job, that he knows how to live in a big city and survive. I could give him the money, but those other people just might have other plans. It never occurred to me that he would take that tack. Well, I can't live their lives for them either. Somehow I have the feeling that I'm going to end up being all around unpopular. He's got me going and coming. Somewhere is an insidious alcoholic thought that if he threatens to do that, I won't go through with the separation to protect Milo. But I will. I turn them all over. Old H. P. is going to be working overtime with that group. Good luck. Ain't life innerestin?

Love,
Verge

5/24/83

My Verge,

I am caught up in reverie tonight about us at the ends of the earth: sand dunes, clouds of Beach Plum blossoms covering hillock after hillock, the ocean spreading its jewels on the beach, and me teasing you about picking up each one. If only I could stretch my arms out beyond my ability to stretch and sweep them all to you. Your laughter, your delight envelops me. How joyous to blow multicolored bubbles off over the ocean from the very end of land. Only with you can I let the child peek out. Doesn't time melt into time when we are together?

~

*Hi Gin. I'll race you down to the pond. Oh, no. No head start. You are just as fast as me. No. Well, OK, just one giant step. But I shouldn't. I've seen you run. Come on. I said one giant step, not one kangaroo leap. OK? Go!*

*Whew! Told you. You are faster that me. I ain't givin' you any more head starts. ...You're kiddin' me. I didn't let you win. What does being a girl have to do with it? No. I don't believe that; some people can do some things and some people can do other things. Sometimes it is easy to let other people make you believe wrong things about stuff. Like your brothers telling you that you can't do this or that, or mine telling me I'm too little or too skinny or something.*

*I've been practicing my hoots. Wanna hear? Hoot. Hoot. ...Hoot. That does too sound like an owl. What kinda owl do think it is I'm doin'? There—no wonder you don't think it sounds like an owl. I'm doing a Barn-Swooping-Over Owl.*

*Well, just because you never heard of it doesn't mean there is no such thing. Go ahead; ask your uncle. He doesn't know everything. There is too!*

*(Long silence as kids look under rocks at the edge of the pond.) Gin! Look at this big crayfish. There he goes. Let's get him. He's under that rock over there. I'll roll my jeans up and wade in. You comin' in? Hey! Hey, stop splashing! I'll show you splashing! Now look. We're all wet, what's your mom going to say? SSShhh! Someone's coming. You go that way and I will go this way. I'll meet you on the path by the big tree.*

~

I will meet you in my dreams. I get to writing about the kids and time disappears.

Love,
Michael

Saturday 5/28/83

Dear Michael,

Old yo-yo time at the ranch. Eric was informed that he will work Sunday night through Thursday, the eleven-to-seven shift, same as before, at another place. Five guards were let go, so he is lucky to have a job. A few days ago Eric left a note in response to my written notice about separation, saying that, oh, yes, he did remember my telling him, after all. It was a classic alcoholic response, using a variety of ploys to gain sympathy/give guilt, but no further mention of Arizona. At least now I have a confirmation that he has received the information. Let me just hang on to my sanity and some measure of serenity until this is over. Not having to be constantly on guard will be the one thing I will be most thankful for.

On Friday, when I called the high school to decline the invitation to continue next year with the theatre group, I was informed that the annual High School Awards Assembly is coming up and I have five awards to present to students from my group. You know how public speaking terrifies me. Please give my hand a little squeeze that night. It will be my first time since being in Al-Anon. I wonder if it will be any easier? If I could get over that fear I would feel I had made a major accomplishment.

~

*Hey Hoot, how much money you got? Uncle Bill gave me fifty cents for weeding the beans. He really owes me for a bet I won, but my daddy wouldn't let him pay me 'cuz he says betting is like gambling, and he won't have any gambling in his house. Grandma taught me solitaire and when he saw the cards he threw them in the stove saying cards wuz gambling, too. I'm not sure what gambling means, but it must be awful bad 'cuz my dad gets all red and angry when he talks about it.*

*Anyway, let's go buy some pop and have a picnic. What kind do ya like? I like Birch Beer because in our house you can't even mention about beer.*

*My dad and Uncle Bill talk about drinking or people who drink like they were monsters. I saw my girlfriend's father drink a beer once and he didn't seem like anything but a nice man. I like him. So saying Birch Beer is like saying about drinking only nobody pays any attention.*

*Why is it some words get big people all mad and if you just put it with another word it is OK? Like in the barn, everybody talks about the cow's tits and nobody thinks anything of it, but my brother got into a lot of trouble with my dad 'cuz he said something about a girl and her tits.*

*Hoot, I'm not ever gonna understand about anything. I don't think I want to grow up. Grownups always know what is right and what is wrong. I'm never going to be sure what's which. They don't seem to have any question about it.*

*So, do you want to have a picnic? Will you ride me to the store on your bike?*

*OK, I've gotta go get my shoes on. You go get your money. Sure you'd rather do this than go to the movies on Saturday? Cross your heart and hope to die?*

*See ya in a minnit.*

~

Tomorrow I need to start getting some of my matted pictures in frames, for the art show next Sunday. It is outdoors, so please, no rain on Sunday next! I haven't worked much at getting things together because my hopes for a sunny day are small. Today I worked on a painting I have been at, off and on, all spring. I am still not satisfied with it. It's of a green heron on a post sticking out of the lake. I like the heron, but I am not satisfied with the water. It is in acrylic and I just haven't mastered getting that medium subtle, like oil paints. I miss using oils, but I've noticed that the turpentine makes me feel high, so I stay away from it. Elle is also exhibiting her photography, so I will have her to chat with, if we can get a spot of fence next to each other.

My calendar reminds me you soon have another AA lead coming up. I suppose you are an old hand at it now and probably don't need any hand to clutch, but just in case you need a sympathetic smile, my spirit will be with you.

Verge

6/3/83

My Sweet Verge,

Your letter is what I needed today. You always know how to treat me, and what to say to me, even if it is before the fact—you just know. For the past few weeks I have been feeling unme. I guess I have mentioned to you on the phone the negative thoughts that won't go away. I said I just chase them away, but they won't go for long. Crazy thoughts full of self-doubt, universal doubts, seeking, lost, wandering. Everything feels like square one again. I feel confused as to where all the good stuff went that I have accumulated over the past two years. At the present, I persist in chasing them away and ride on what faith I am able to muster. I know this must be some sort of growing thing, but it is very confusing. Sometimes when I can't convince myself that I really am a part of the universe and that I belong here for real, I think of how I know you feel about me, and a new pride and sense of worth grabs me and I feel new again. Thanks for you.

The AA lead is over. I feel drained, exhausted. I didn't run one mile, didn't swim one lap, and didn't lift one pound, yet I feel more used up than when I do those physical things. How do you explain that? I don't even try anymore. There are many schools of thought on the effectiveness of such therapy, but I quit trying to analyze them. They just confuse me. Besides, none that I know of put their finger on that thing that happens inside when you give a lead. I can't name it; it is something that defies explaining, but it is there and I don't want to fight with it.

The lead itself went well. There were numerous comments, many sincere thanks for the help, flattery and so forth—much to gobble up and feed to ego. Any actor could fly pretty well for a while on that. Strange, though, I didn't feel that way. Sure, I was pleased that I had gone through it in a fairly articulate fashion and that people could relate to my story, but no ego. Now at the library, in this quiet place I wonder what happened? What stirred? The only thing that comes to mind is a certainty that the gears have meshed and are starting to turn again... slowly. Do I feel suddenly new again? No. Is the head still messed up? Yes. But, I feel a little movement forward, rather than swirling.

You were there. I didn't see you sitting in the audience; you were standing right beside me, holding my hand, tightly. Thank you for your love.

Michael

6/6/83

My Michael,

This need, want, crave—this thing will not be denied. It will stand in the corner if it must, but proudly; it will be silent if it must, but the singing in its head and shouting will not be stilled; it will even turn away and whistle and kick stones to pretend non-interest, but the more it does so, the more intent it is on not being denied. Sometimes the want and feelings come all tumbling around to such an extent I have to just say, "Whoa, girl, stop and let me out for a few minutes. Just carry on and I'll be back as soon as I can make it." At times like that, there are words I can hear from numerous voices saying that when feelings begin to grow again it is very painful, sometimes confusing, and even conflicting. Perspective will come, they tell me; it just takes time. I sometimes have to hang on to that to keep some sanity to it all.

You told me this morning that you have been having a hard couple of weeks. I know you speak truth when you say you are glad when I feel comfortable enough to cry on your shoulder. When I do, I don't expect you to have answers or to get involved, only that you will allow me to form into human words for another human ear a statement of my grief or trouble. Forming it into words gets it into manageable dimension. The statement of facts as I see them often exposes my confused thinking and forces me to face THE THING—whatever it is. Voicing it often shows me the answer, or at least a range of choices to resolve the problem. At most, what I expect from you is perhaps a couple of choices I may have overlooked. I have thanked you thousands of time for just listening. You do it so eloquently. So why do you wait for two weeks to form your disquietude into words? You know everything I have just written is true. I hope you don't think you are protecting me from your hurts. If you do, you are denying me the privilege of returning to you what you so beautifully have given me. It is only good when you allow me to give some back. Strong, silent suffering is stalwart stupidity. It did a lot toward getting us as sick as we were. There is no side of you that is not beautiful to me.

I suppose I'm not allowed to complain about my sunburned nose and my red arms. Not after you so kindly allowed me a day of sun, with just a hint of late afternoon gray creeping in. The art show goers were so bedazzled by the brightness they forgot to buy anything. Perhaps they will all come pounding on my door next week? Exposure is good. Unless they see my name around, no one is sure my work is any good, so they won't buy it. The whole field is purely subjective, having more to do with whim and opinion than to do with art *per se*—especially on the level I am dealing with. I can't look at my own work objectively, either, but it suits my whim and fancy, so I will just go along having a love affair with my own art, and if the poor peons can't see its unquestionable value, it is their loss.

I finally wrote to Milo tonight. I have had a hard time telling him that I am leaving his father. I have no idea what his feelings on the subject will be—not that I can let that make a difference. I didn't justify or explain further than that I have to figure out what I am going to do with the rest of my life and that his father has to take charge of his own.

I have had no second thoughts on the matter. I waited until I was sure what I must do. Thank God for it, because I feel sure even the slightest waver on my part would be instantly pounced on and poked at, until I was a mass of quivering indecision again. The decision feels good, but the necessary waiting and the inaction are nerve- wracking. I have waited so long; I want to do it all, now! Old H. P. is forever trying to give me lessons in patience. The whole Program is based on "time takes time" and patience. Having frittered away so many years in time-wasting pursuits, I feel a little panicky about having enough time left to reap some of the benefits of new insight. I know that is projecting, but sometimes I can't help it.

Verge

6/9/83

My Sweet Verge,

I would feel terrible if I had consciously been pulling that strong, silent suffering routine of years past, especially with you. If I had been shutting you out of this pain period I just went through, I would be hating myself for sure, because that is definitely not where we are as an us. I feel no need to hold back from you. I was not churning inside like I used to, resenting people in my life because they were supposed to know something was wrong without my having to tell them. I have learned how selfish that is.

I don't blame you for thinking I was being a stalwart fellow and sparing you the grief, because that is the way I was behaving. I didn't mean to. I'm sorry. What happened is it snuck up on me—the bads. At first I just thought I was having a bad day or two. Then I was mired in; it was getting worse; I didn't even realize it. I may have mentioned on the phone that I was feeling bad, but it wasn't until the pain got heavy that my protective devices kicked in saying, "Hey, you! What cha doin'? This is starting to hurt." Now that is a thick head, that hurts and doesn't know it until it is banging on you. Anyhow, I did a stop-all-motors routine, did some thinking, did what I have been told by The Program, and the rest is history. I talked about it to some good AAers, wrote to you, prayed, and luckily there was the AA lead in there, too. Things started to get better, and now I am fine, or at least I feel fine.

Those folks didn't buy your whims and fancies because they were awestruck. The realization of what they saw is just now sinking in. When it has, they will be beating on your door. I wish I could have been there. I love to watch you doing things. The more you are expert at what you are doing the more I love to watch; you know, things like painting, cooking, dealing with a child, combing your hair, eating a lobster. You go about your business with your head high, your shoulders square, and your movements sure. I love it even more when you know I am watching, and you let me. Those times rank among the most intimate to me.

I saw a TV show featuring a woman, Betty Edwards, who believes that the right side of the brain is responsible for producing art. She has developed a method of teaching that stimulates that section of the brain, so anyone can learn to draw well in a relatively short time. Numerous non-drawers told her they would be the exception, and they were proven wrong. It amused me, because I am sure I would be her downfall. In fifth grade, it was coming on to Easter, and we had the unusual occurrence of a real art teacher doing a project with our class. Even in kindergarten I was unable to produce anything artistic enough to hang up in the classroom. Teamed up with someone considered "good at art", the results were still less than desirable. I always wanted to do well, but just couldn't. This time I was determined—fancy art teacher—Easter time. The teacher started with basics. I just knew if I started from the very beginning, I could get the idea. Everyone else seemed to know all that stuff, and I never figured out how they knew.

My motif chosen, it all began encouragingly. I was right on track! Then, somehow things started to go awry. I could feel myself losing control. The teacher would stop and point out a few things, and, again, I would feel back on track. As the days went on, the intervals between on track, and off, grew shorter, and I could feel the panic start to rise. Then, I noticed the teacher didn't even stop by anymore, and the other kids were back to knowing, as second nature, things that had me stumped. When I was sure the teacher was taking a circuitous route, I gave up.

Needless to say, the project was a disaster, even in memory's eye when I give it the benefit of being a preadolescent attempt. I give the teacher credit, though; she stuck to her word and put up all of the pictures.

There mine hung to haunt and embarrass me, for what seemed an eternity. I tried my best to learn to like it, hoping that familiarity would, in this case, breed love. It was futile. Every time I walked into the room, there it would be. I tried to sneak up on it with a sideways glance; I tried to face it head on; I tried to ignore it, but nothing worked. It shouldn't be too hard to imagine my relief when the time came to redecorate the room. Since then I have never made any attempt at seriously doing art.

That's way more than I intended to say, but it felt good telling you. Now that I look at the episode, I think I must have been carrying a resentment ever since. I have always had admiration and even envy for people who could paint or draw, or trace even. I am glad I can tell you these things without being afraid. I shake my head in disbelief that I have carried that little child thing with me all this time.

Michael

6/11/83

*Hi Hoot!*

*Why are you just sittin' here with dawg? Whatsa matter? Are you sick? ...Hey, I didn't mean nothin'. Do you want me to go away? Why did you squash that bug? I never saw you do anything mean before. Bugs are too, good! What would birds eat if we didn't have bugs?*

*What did your brother say?*

*You are <u>not</u> too skinny. Look at you. You are pretty all over, 'cept for that scab on your knee*

*Look! There's a dog in the sky. No, you have to lie back. Over there—see how that one cloud makes a floppy ear and there's his head and his tail. Didya ever notice when you lie on your back and look at the sky the world seems to be movin' so fast you could fall off? Makes me all dizzy!*

*Hoot? Why I wanted to find you was...do you like flowers? They're gonna mow hay in the big field over in back tomorrow and it is just full of daisies and black-eyed Susans. I thought maybe we could get us a whole arm full—the biggest bunch in the world. I need your help, 'cuz one of us has to hold um and the other pick. Do you wanna? OK, let's go.*

*Oh, there goes a killdeer. That bird running along with its wing down, like it is broken--see? It says, "Kill deeeeer, kill deeer!" It does too sound like that. You should laugh, with your old, hooot, hooot sounds, like a chicken with whooping cough Hoot? Kin I hold your hand? I dunno, just like to. Wow! Look how tall the grass is from all that rain. Something's made a path through. Lets follow it. I'll go first—in case it's dangerous. We better hurry because we have allll these flowers to pick before dark.*

~

You mused about what would have happened if I'd never said out loud that I love you. Just as botanists say trees communicate chemically, I think we've always known that we loved each other. I don't think it is possible that those words would have gone unspoken. The actual saying of them was not premeditated. As we drove down the hill to the lake house that summer day, bringing corn to the others for dinner, I could feel the words forming in my mouth without my volition and flying out. The occasion had an aura about it that left me watching and listening to myself, as if separate and at a distance. I wish this didn't sound mystical, for one tends to dismiss mystical as exaggeration or fantasy. It did feel mystical at the time. I have experienced that since, sometimes when avoided thoughts can no longer go unvoiced, and sometimes when someone new in The Program asks questions and I know I have no answer, yet a thoughtful one comes out of my mouth.

By the time we'd moved to the lake, I knew that things were never going to be right between Eric and me. I knew I should leave him. I knew I would have to give up myself to live with him. Two things I wanted, more than self, convinced me to stay. First, I knew I could leave anytime I wanted, but Eric would do violence before I could get away with our son. Second, I could not figure out how to keep you in my life without staying with him. His advantage was powerful. Although my marriage was a myth after that point, I was determined to make the best of it, and with good alcoholic denial on hand, I did. My joys were real and huge. They were watching a child grow and become a man, and being part of this other growing thing with a man so attuned to me that time and space did not seem to matter. They were made that much more precious by the pain of watching another man I loved, hell-bent on self-destruction.

That brings me to thoughts on the joy of starting a new life—the giddy thought that I can begin to let myself grow in a non-oppressive atmosphere. I made a choice back then to live the life I did, but I have come to believe that we not only have the right, but the obligation to develop our selves to the fullest degree. Only as we begin to develop self, do we begin to grasp whatever meaning there is to life, and I think we are meant to grasp some meaning to add to the body of common knowledge that evolves generations forward. You and I do something catalytic to each other; we stimulate each other's brain and vital forces to push beyond the complacency of, "Well, I'm all grown up. I put this many years into being here, and that is that, and now I just want to chew the cud of life." We delight in our growth and discovery.

The basis for that growth is honesty. You are the only person with whom I have ever been totally honest. I always shaded the truth with others if the full truth made me look bad, if it had a consequence, if it would upset someone, or if it didn't suit my belief about how things should be. I thought there were justifiable reasons for not being completely honest. Just as those confessional words came out, directed by some force other than my conscious self, I am forced to be honest with you, no matter how I tremble at what has to be said. You have always accepted my truths as gifts of trust, without judgment, and I have done the same with you.

One thing I look forward to most is coming to my own home to relax. The constant vigilance of looking at the smallest act to decide if it fosters Eric's dependence and the uneasiness of not knowing what the day might bring of disaster or destruction combine to make an atmosphere of distrust and inquietude. That makes home a place to avoid. I also look forward to being able to invite someone in without fear of the person walking into an embarrassing situation. The scary part about going it alone is that there will no longer be a convenient excuse for things that are wrong. If something's wrong, it must be something about me. I will have to look at that with a cold eye as it sinks in. Maybe everything will be Gin's fault.

Verge

6/22/83

Dear Verge,

You talked briefly on the phone about poling a raft around your farm pond when you were a kid. That reminded me of an era in my childhood when I was ten and eleven, when I used to spend much of my time down in the park where the zoo is now. The zoo was much smaller then and the park was much larger and wilder. At first, during summers I would spend time there with my brothers; as I got older it was with buddies. In the park was a swampy place called The Square Pond. My child's memory tells me it was tucked off in a very secluded, secret area. If I were to see it now, it probably would be in an obvious place, not too far away. That is one good thing about child land; places and things can be tucked away and secret even if they aren't. Most of the boys of my age knew of The Square Pond, if they spent any time at all in the park. When the older ones outgrew it, they passed it on to the younger ones coming up, as did my brother and his buddies. I used to think that he and his army were the coolest people to walk Earth. On the very rare occasions when they took me along, or were forced to, (my mother always worked) I was in ninth heaven. It was easy then to forget all the mean stuff they pulled on us younger kids. It was enough just to be with them.

The swamp was a real kid fun place. We poled along on rafts which I am sure were also handed down from one age group to the next. We would spend hours exploring. When we left, we hid the raft in a secret place in a special way. The next time, next day or next week, the raft was always there, although someone else had obviously used it in the meantime, but it was easy to ignore that fact then. At the end of the day's adventure, I always hated climbing the long hill from the park back to civilization. I was sad when they drained that swamp years later. I get a charge out of our childhood similarities in spite of their vast differences.

You told me, during that same phone call, that you believed you could teach me to draw. You said that you believed anyone could learn that skill acceptably enough to communicate with it. I trust you. I accept your very courageous offer gladly, but I must admit to a certain amount of anxiety. It is me I have to fight. It is exhilarating to think I could learn a new means of expression. You will surely start from the bottom, you might even say from the pit. I know, I know, I have to get rid of negative thoughts. I am honestly working on that, but know that your skills will be challenged. The gauntlet has been cast.

Michael

6/24/83

My Michael Man,

My head is just a mass of quivering jelly tonight. I'm only writing because I know how desperate I am for your letters just before seeing you. And, Babe, I am going to see you soon!

I don't want to get my hopes up too high, but Elle showed me a little house just down the street from her that I might talk the owner into renting. The woman has been in a nursing home for a year and a half and a nephew has to come to check out the place. It sorely needs someone to tend its little lawn and its insides. I am in the process of trying to get in touch with the nephew, to ask if he is not dying to have a handy little lady occupy his house. (Now, come on, you have to admit I'm handy. Maybe the rest is shaky, but I'm working on it.) Empty houses always collect mouses and ratses. My good cat will do her share to keep the place in shape. Maybe? It is not right on the lake, but just up one street with beach access and a place to keep my canoe.

~

*But Hoot, it pulls when I stuff my pigtails up inside this old baseball cap. Why have I gotta? This flannel shirt is HOT! Like (pant, pant) H. O. T.! Kin I at least roll up my jeans?*

*I don't know why you are trying to make me look like a boy. You said girls were just as good. You don't give me any head starts or nuthin'. Jeepers! So what if some of the guys saw me? You afraid they'll laugh cuz you're playing with me? What do you mean, the older boys might see me? What do you mean they might bother me or stuff?*

*Of course I trust you. Didn't I tell you my most secret secret about being scared when they made me kiss my grandmother, with her all funny in the coffin feeling like your cheek feels when you've had Novocain? Didn't I trust you enough to let you look at me all naked? What do you mean that's what you are trying to tell me about the older boys? Oh? They might? Don't they have anybody to look at?*

*Sure, I do wanna go see your secret place. But if it is a secret place, why should anyone else be there? Oh, you mean it is a loaned secret place. OK, Hoot, I'm sorry I made you tell me instead of just trusting you. I hate almost knowing something, but not really knowing, cuz your mind makes up some awful stuff sometimes to make you think you know the parts you don't know. When you finally, really, truly know, it usually isn't nearly so bad or scary as your head makes up. So people should just tell you right out, instead of hinting.*

*Hey! Listen to those bullfrogs. It's the middle of the day and they're grumphing. Gee! Darning needles all over the place—big ones, little ones, red, green, blue, PURPLE! I never saw a purple one before!! Cat tails! Wow! They sure are tall and thick. I like the way the bogs just shake back and forth underfoot and make the cattails bounce over your head.*

*Whattya mean, ssssshhh and wait? Crimminy, you think I can't be as quiet as you? What did you see? Nothing? What did you want to see? Nothing? Hoot, you're crazy!!!*

*You want me to go up there and look? I'm not afraid. I'll go look. Aren't cha comin' with me? Well, what is it? Hoot, tell me so I'll know if I see it. It's not SNAKES is it? Well, no, I'm not afraid of snakes, but I don't like being surprised by them. Yeah, I know that's usually the way you see snakes, but once I know they are there, they don't bother me.*

*OK, I'll go look. Maybe you better come just in case I don't know what I'm looking at. I'll know? OK, here I go. HOOT! HOOT! It's a raft!! Oh, Gee, Wow! Oh boyohboy. I always wanted to try a raft. Always, since my mom read me Huckleberry Finn! Is this your own? Did you make it? How did you get it here? Wow! Come on lets try it out. Have you got poles? A whole family of them? Hoot, what do you...Oh, Hoot! That's an awful joke. I mean, do you? Really?*

*Oh gosh, Hoot, when I'm with you I never can seem to shut up. I talk a blue streak. Don't you ever feel like saying, 'Hey Ginny, shut up?' Usually people are always asking me if the cat's got my tongue. Boy, that's really a dumb thing to say. You'd think people would think what a dumb thing it is and not say it. Either that or they talk about me when they think I am not listening and say things like, 'She's always daydreaming.' I like listening. People say interesting stuff, and dumb stuff, and funny stuff. Whatever they say, it is like walking around in their heads. I like walking in people's heads, but I don't like them to walk in mine. I like to keep my me all secret so nobody will laugh at me or think I don't know anything. Sometimes I feel nobody will like what I think anyway, so I'll keep it to me. I don't feel that way with you. It all comes busting out, anything and everything like I overstuffed my brain, and things in there that I even forgot I knew come falling out.*

*Come on, Hoot, lets go up this way. Thanks for showing me your best secret. Do you suppose I am the only girl who's ever been on this raft?*

*Hoot? You're my friend, right? ...And you are a boy and all. Hoot? Would you mind if I just thought in my head...and didn't tell anyone...Hoot N. is my boyfriend? ...Hoot, why aren't you talking to me? It's OK if you don't want me to. ...Hoot? That's an awful funny look. Why are you looking at me like that? Hoot! C'mon, say something.*

~

I'm glad I can tell you that I love you out loud without ever having to go through that moment of awful silence again. I am just hanging on minute by minute to the life raft of next week. There is no way I can make that brat of a girl behave. She gets dirty the minute I put a clean dress on her. I found her out drawing HOOT, HOOT in the mud yesterday, ankle deep in the muddiest puddle. She drives me crazy. Maybe you can do something with her. I'll see you tomorrow if you get this letter on Monday.

Verge

July 21, 83

Dear Michael,

As the plane took off, you were there in the airport window, waving. After arriving in New York City, the bus trip home was a nerve-wracking affair. The driver sped through a fierce storm with zero visibility and lightning strikes everywhere. By the time we got to Newburgh, the rain had subsided and there was faithful Elle waiting for me. I treated us to dinner, and then we went to look at the house.

Although the electricity was off, and the light was waning, I could tell from my first look inside that it is perfect for me. All but a few personal effects have been removed. There is a gas stove and a nearly new refrigerator in the kitchen, and baseboard heat throughout. The grounds need a lot of work, poison ivy needs to be sprayed, but there is potential.

...Today I called the nephew to say that I am interested. Tomorrow I'm to meet with him. He is anxious to make arrangements, because he wants to rent by August first. I want to paint inside, fix up the yard, and move boxes, but I don't want to pay two rents at once, and I do feel obligated to provide a place for Eric until October first.

Events are moving me along with their own momentum. A piece of my head complains, because it is all happening so rapidly, but there is the lesson of the Band-Aid being yanked off. Right? If negotiations get settled tomorrow, I will start work on the house and be so busy there'll be no time for question or complaint.

Last night I told Eric about the house. He was docile. He told me that his sister has reservations about him coming out to Arizona, so he is not planning on going there. Other than making a crack that perhaps a drunken husband could live in the garage, he accepted the news. Today he asked when I am moving, if I get the house. I told him, September first, but hopefully he would get this house free for the month of September, due to the original deposit. He asked if he could use my address for his mail, asking if I know how hard it was for a middle-aged man who was single to get a job? I told him that having his mail sent to my address would not indicate his marital status. Tomorrow I will suggest a P.O. box. As far as I know, one is married until he is divorced—legality will be my next week's adventure. I'm not sure whether that was a ploy to have daily communication, a sly attempt to sabotage my legal standing, a "poor me" attempt for my sympathy, or just not thinking too clearly. Anyway, he can't use my mailing address.

I received a friendly letter from Milo. He told me of his grades for the semester and light chitchat. His only comment about the separation was to ask when I was moving.

Thanks for sending Hoot with me for company. He is a dear lad, but he is very shy. I half ignore him and watch him out of the corner of my eye until he gets more comfortable with me. Hopefully Ginny hasn't wandered off looking for Hoot. Try to keep her tidy until I get back.

Love,
Verge

7/23/83

My Sweet Verge Woman,

I watched my life walk down the plane ramp, turn the corner and be whisked away. I zombied through the rest of that day until bedtime. Since then I have kept busy to avoid facing the loneliness. Tonight I did a mental hoedown when I found a letter in my mailbox, smiling at me.

The house sounds like a perfect Verge house. Boy, you and I could roll up our sleeves and do a job on that yard. I wish I could be there to help you. I know we could make great fun out of all that work.

I give you a lot of credit for not wavering in the face of Eric's various attempts to hold on. Everything you are doing takes a lot of courage. I stand cheering you on. I also have to admit to fear and worry about the changes the new life will bring to you. When I think of the growing you will do, I get scared. What if she finds her new life leads her down a divergent path? I said all those things just before you left because they sounded brave, but I didn't feel very brave. I meant the part about our trust and love, though. We will walk along hand in hand and leave no room for fears.

You sure know just how to handle that Hoot! I can tell from what you say you are doing to help him with his shyness, that you are very sensitive to him. Since we are on that subject, I have to tell you about Ginny, not to be a fink, but to keep you abreast, so to speak.

You weren't gone very long, maybe you were still in the air, when the heavens gave a great display of color and movement and electricity, and then opened up. Heavy rain. We were standing on the front porch watching, before the rain started. I was telling her some stories about the clouds and storms—some fact and some fiction—hoping to set her at ease by understanding it all. You know—explode the myths. She was listening, I could tell, but was very restless, jumping up and down, first on one foot then the other. I told her there was no one in the bathroom, but she said she didn't have to go. I told her she could take her shoes off if they hurt, and she did, saying they didn't hurt. Just then the rain fell all at once, and like a shot Gin (I call her that sometimes) was off the porch and splashing in the river-like puddle that was forming down the center of the alley. I could only chuckle to my self; she looked to be having that much fun. Suddenly a large lightning flash and simultaneous thunderclap sent poor little Gin straight up in the air. She let out a shriek, and I dashed out and swooped her up. She clung to me, hugging my neck, and didn't want to let go even inside the house. Slowly she stopped shaking and I put her down. I stepped back to inspect her. There she stood, all mud speckled and drenched. Her braids were dripping water, and you know the crazy things she does with her feet. I couldn't help it; I had to laugh out loud. She looked furious. She was ready to stamp her feet, when instead she began to laugh, too. There we stood laughing at each other. I guess I was a sight, also. Suddenly she ran to me and gave me a great big hug and just hung on—laughing. I could feel the love passing between us. It was quite a moment. The deluge had stopped by then, so I took her upstairs, drew a warm bath for her, and left her alone to undress and soak.

Later she sat at the kitchen table in fresh white shorts and blue T-shirt, and let me take her braids out so we could dry her hair. The rubber bands were pulling—you should have heard her shriek—so I snipped the bands with scissors. I couldn't blame her for yelling. Cutting the bands saved her a whole lot of pain. As I dried her hair, I explained in serious talk all about thunder and lightning. We had a good talk about it. Afterwards, she seemed to feel better. Her hair pulled at the comb, so I held the mirror and let her comb her own hair the way she wanted it. It wasn't beauty shop perfect, but she was happy with it. So was I.

By that time the sun was shining again. She went out to play with the girl next door. She looked so shining bright and happy. I just loved her. She ran off the porch, then ran back and poked her head in the door, smiled, and said, "I love you."

That took me by surprise, and filled me up. I said, "Pull up your socks." As she ran down the steps, I couldn't help calling, "Ginny, I love you, too." She turned and smiled again, then skipped away. I think we will get along just fine.

My very own Verge, I love you,
Michael

July 26, 1983

Dear Michael,

Let me see; are you on my list? The good Al-Anon people have told me to make lists to calm myself and to figure out priorities. Everything is moving around me so fast I feel like I'm in the eye of a hurricane, but I'll just keep doing one thing at a time. Presently the hardest task is to keep an even emotional keel. I go to the house and get elated planning my attack there. Then I come home and get into sorting and packing, trying to be ruthless about it, by shutting off my sentimental thoughts, yet I find waves of depression lapping about my feet.

Eric is staying mostly cheerfully detached, except for an occasional stickeroo. Latest was bemoaning having to throw out his books. Not outright asking, but getting across, would I store them for him? Lord, I have always been a sucker for books. I never could discard one, and always brought home the discards from various libraries I inhabited. I'll probably live to regret it, but I said I would store some for him. I still have the uncomfortable feeling that he thinks I'm going to eventually relent. I must do the lawyer bit immediately to firmly and legally establish my position.

~

*Hoooot! Hoot where are youuuu? ...There you are! I have been calling and calling for hours. I've been calling so much that my mother said that you were probably off playing with the boys somewhere, and why didn't I find something else to do?*

*Here, have a molasses cookie. Mom just took them out of the oven and they're still hot. She makes lots. She doesn't care how many I take. 'Sides she likes you. I just know. When you don't come around she asks where you are, and when I have nothin' to do but just hang around the house and pester her, she usually tells me to stop moping around and go help Uncle Bill or find Hoot to play with.*

*Anyway, it sure is a good thing you are here. Now you can go with me to get ice. ...To the icehouse. Come on; get on the truck. Dad's going.*

*Here he comes. Daddy, are we going to go now? Hoot is going to go with us. No, I didn't tell him he has to work.*

*The ice is for making ice cream. It's for my birthday. I know today isn't my birthday, but I went up to Aunt Lindy's cottage on the lake yesterday. I s'pose you were disappointed, 'cuz you didn't get to give me a birthday spank after threatening for a whole week. No, I didn't. Nobody asked me; they just stopped and picked me up. Course I wuzn't sorry. Would you be if you had a chance to go swimmin'?*

*Is that why you stayed away all day today? You did, too, know I was back. I waved to you last night when we went by your house. Hoot! What do you mean you guess you will have to give me my present next year? Well, of course it is not my birthday now, but I had one. You're so pigheaded Hoot, you make me mad.*

*...Don't oink at me! Well, gee, Hoot. ...Sometimes I laugh when I'm mad!*

*Oh, that's a great idea! Tomorrow? We'll have an unbirthday picnic, just you and me, and you can sing happy unbirthday to me and give me an unbirthday present. ...Oh, all right, you can give me an unbirthday spanking too. But I get to do anything I want to on my unbirthday. ...I always smile like this when I'm happy. I don't care whether you like my smile or not. Stop. I don't want to be mad at you anymore. I missed you too much. I'm glad you missed me too.*

*There's the place. Dad's got to get Mr. Blakeman. Look at those big tongs hanging on the side of the crib. Ice crib, Hoot! Isn't it wonderful, how it can be so hot and sticky and right in that sawdust is real, honest ice taken off the river last winter?*

*...Wow! Look at that big piece. Come on, Dad; let's get home before it melts. Ooooh, feel it, Hoot. It's sooo cold.*

~

This is getting unmanageable. I will have to finish it next letter.

Verge

7/30/83

My Sweet Verge Woman,

I can feel the excitement in your letters as you tell me about planning and plotting, concerning your new home. I can feel the quickening in your chest when you awake with the sun peeping at you, and you realize a brand new life is just beginning to unfold. I understand that feeling, of the push for growth, that cannot be denied. I know I am a part of it, but I can only stand aside, and watch, and cheer, and delight in the release it brings you. I long to be there with you, helping with the physical stuff and giving emotional support.

~

*Boy, Ginny, you do a lot more fun things than me. I never rode in the back of a truck before. You know how we get ice? This guy, Carl, rides up and down the streets in his ice truck and looks for his sign in the people's windows. The sign has his name on it and numbers, 25, 50, 75, 100. You put the number of pounds of ice you want in your window, and he delivers it to your ice chest.*

*This truck is fun. The bouncing makes my dupie numb. You look funny when we hit a row of bumps. It looks like you have three faces and your pigtails fly up and down. Ha ha ha ha ha. Me too? Ha ha ha ha.*

*I'm still not going to tell you what I got'cha. –You weren't here. Yeah, tomorrow. But I can't stay all day,'cuz I'm going to scout camp next week, and I have to get ready. Yeah, all week. Sunday at noon until the next Sunday morning. No, I don't have to go, but I wanna. Sure I like it. I wait all year for it. No, you can't visit. Because it is a long ways away. No. Not even if your daddy drives you. Because you can't. No! I'm not being mean. The scoutmaster said so. He's not being mean either*

*I know I will be gone. I just told you. Awwww, with all the fun you have, you won't even miss me. I gotta pack my stuff tomorrow and there's lots of stuff. I'll be here most of the day. Awwww, Ginny, don't cry. I ain't dyin'. 'Sides, I'll be here early tomorrow morning for your birthday picnic, and OK, ...I'll give you your present. I like your smile, everything lights up.*

~

It sure is easy to get carried away writing about Hoot and Ginny. Do you mind my picking up your story line? Do you know how wildly in love with you I am?

Michael

Saturday, July 30

Dear Michael,

You will be on vacation and all it entails when you get this. Sorry for sounding like a spoiled brat this morning on the phone. That Ginny! She pops out at the most inopportune times. As we both know, she is not quite civilized. Even if she has her sox pulled up and her ribbons straight, never depend on her being ladylike. Of course I wish you to have a relaxing and happy vacation.

Today I painted, and Elle helped by doing some hedge clipping. She had started mowing the lawn, but one of the neighbors, a gentleman about my father's age, came over with his riding mower and did it, telling her she shouldn't be doing that much work. He also tried to help me get the pump started—I think it is air bound—but we were not successful, so he said he would call his plumber. Another neighbor, a young woman with four young children, has been over to chat and even offered me a package of panty hose that came in the mail. She said she usually wears jeans or shorts and has no use for them.

The point is, I have had more neighbor contact in one week than I've had in the last 15 years. Everyone has, in his or her fashion, gone out of the way to be pleasant. It must be my time to learn the lesson of graciously accepting neighborly help, for it is being heaped on me from all directions. My old head still wants to say, "I don't need your help. I can do it by myself." My growing head tells me that people feel good when they help someone else. It takes them out of their life for a while.

Eric even offered to come over and mow the lawn. I refused—politely. He asked me if I was trying to hide my little house from him. I hedged an answer, but my head told me it wasn't a very mature thing to do, and yes, I was trying to hide. There are ways he can find the place if he wants to, and he's more apt to do something dumb, out of drunken spite, if he has to look for it. Logic tells me I might as well be open about it. Besides, by then, I will have the law on my side, if he wants to play stupid games.

Thanks for the Gin story. I fell in love with your relationship with Ginny. I haven't quite assimilated the grown up to the child relationship yet. I was almost a teensy bit jealous until I gave myself a smack and said, "You dope! That's the bratty child, you, he's loving like that." Funny, how that changes the light on the kids. It made me feel like you took the fear of thunder and lightning away from me and healed me up. Ginny sure looks up to Michael, and in a fresh, natural way, full tilt loves him with whatever love is left over from loving a Hoot. You know just how to take the hurt out of things for a little girl, and at the same time to encourage her to take hold of life with both hands and find her way of doing things for herself. I liked how you cut the rubber bands out of her hair and let her comb it herself. You know when to pick up and rescue, and when to let go. There were so many things about you that I love in that little sketch. You understand her as well as you understand me. I know she is the young of me, but that doesn't make your understanding automatic, just from knowing and loving the adult me. You have to do mental gymnastics to know her so well. It is a further development of Hoot and Ginny that has a new potential for communication between us.

I know I owe you the end of the ice cream story, but I am falling asleep. Next letter, I promise.

Verge

Monday, August 4

Dear Michael,

I'm so excited I can hardly stay still; Gin's just jumping up and down! Now, you can't say no—it isn't even allowed. I have found the perfect birthday gift for you. I found this ad for a sailing school out of Cleveland on Lake Erie. You just have to promise to teach me everything you learn. You can take Gin along to keep you company. When she wants to learn something she can be real quiet, and study up by watching. This is just the thing to keep her interest. Perfect gifts come only once in a great while—so—accept. Next time I come out, perhaps you can give me my first lesson.

My man gave me my first sailing lesson,<br>
He sailed me so fine and high.<br>
My man gave me my first sailing lesson,<br>
He taught me how to fly.

As far as helping me with my move is concerned, do not despair. You have helped me every step of the way with the house and all of the emotional turmoil of change. Haven't you listened to my complaints? "Damn it, Michael, I hate sanding plaster!" "Michael, why would anyone cover a hardwood floor with this rotten linoleum we are now taking up?" Haven't you been consulted at every turn? Didn't you comfort me today and throw every piece of Al-Anon at me when I found out the pump is not drawing water. Didn't you lead me by the hand to the phone and make me dial the landlord's number, despite his living on Long Island and indicating he really doesn't want to be bothered by the house. Haven't you said to me all day that no one else would rent the place or buy it, if it didn't have water? That there is no way, after spending all those man-hours in good faith fixing up, he could or would even want to renege on his responsibilities.

Aren't we still cogitating just how we want to cut the overgrown foliage by the house to maintain an attractive privacy? Haven't we planned where we want our garden next year? Haven't we arranged and rearranged the house with what furniture we have? Don't you come to the other house with me each night, dog tired, and look at the sunset on the lake and cry a little each time—knowing that is going to be a big hole in our life? Having access is not the same as owning a world of lake.

Aren't you going to help me bake Mr. Mowing Man an apple pie for his good help? So how can you feel left out? I could not even start to begin without your support and constant companionship.

Hey, how about those kids? I would never willingly send that Hoot back. He is the greatest kid ever invented. I'll tell you about him and me, but right now it is ice cream time.

~

*Come on, Hoot, I'll race you to the cellar. Dad will bring the ice.*

*Whew! Can I help it if I won just because I knew where the cellar door was? You shoulda just watched where I was running. Well, I can't help it if you don't have eyes in the back of your head.*

*You have to help me get the freezer. It's hanging up on a nail in the fruit cellar. Don't you like it in here? It's all cool and dirt smelling. We keep apples and carrots and stuff in here almost all winter. Can you reach? Here hold me up. Chout!!! Sorry I dropped it. Did it hit you?*

*Here's the stairs to the kitchen. Mom! Hoot and I got the freezer down. He's going to help me make the ice cream. Doesn't that custard smell good? Is it done yet? We'll be back to get it in just a few minutes. Come on, Hoot!*

*Now comes the work part. We have to break the ice up into little pieces to put in the freezer. Do it like this, inside the burlap sack so it doesn't fly all over. Break off a couple of big chunks with the sledgehammer and I will help you chop them up with this smaller sledge. That's good. We don't want too much at once. Put a layer of ice in the bottom of the freezer. Yup. Just like that. Come help me carry the canister with the custard in it 'cuz it's heavy and if I drop it I will get skinned alive after we saved all that cream off the milk.*

*All right, now set the canister inside the freezer. Put the wooden paddle inside the canister and screw the top on. You put eight hands-full of ice to one of rock salt out of that cloth bag. Mix the salt along through as you pack the ice around the canister. Screw the top on from each side like this, then we churn. Me first.*

*It takes a long time to make ice cream. I'm sorry you don't like vanilla that much—that's the only kind we make. Mom makes a real good chocolate sauce to pour over the top, though. You'll like that. If you eat outdoors you can even stir it all up and make chocolate ice cream soup. In the morning we kids fight over who gets to drink the left over ice cream. That's my favorite. It is all melted and foamy. Because it is my birthday ice cream, I get to have it and I don't even have to fight. If you come over real early I'll share with you. No! If you don't come by noon it will be gone. A dead duck! Oh, you're teasing me again!*

*At last! Can't turn the handle anymore. Uncle Bill always has to check the last part to be sure it is done. Uncle Billll! Is it done? Huh? Is it? See, he is going to pull the paddle out and pack the ice cream down good. We get to lick the paddle while we wait. You lick that side and I'll lick this. Stick out your tongue and touch mine with it. Isn't that cold? Isn't this the best coldest ice cream you ever tasted?*

*It's getting dark. Look at all those lightning bugs. Get yourself a jar off the shelf. I'm taking this one. Pound some holes in the cap with this nail. Come on, Hoot, I bet I can catch more lightning bugs than you can before the ice cream is ready.*

~

And so my head sees them wandering off into the summer night bumping into each other, giggling, and exclaiming at each bug caught or not caught. Ginny and Hoot, best friends ever.

Verge and Michael, best everything ever: friends, lovers, companions, sidekicks, confidants, and imaginers. I just love us.

Verge

8/10/83

My Verge,

I feel the temptation to inflict goodly numbers of spanks upon my person for not having written. Truth of the matter is that my head has been in a race for the past three or four days and I have been trying to run along with it. Can't keep up, especially since it has been going in several directions at once.

The excitement of seeing you in a couple of weeks has just started percolating in my nerve endings and has my head spinning. The number two spinner is, of course, the sailing. I am sorry if I led you to think I may not want to do it; I am eager to. It's just the timidity of doing a new thing. Really it is not a new thing. You and I have sailed that little two-man sailboat off into the blue on your lake with next to no knowledge of what we were about, experimenting along the way. The foreign force will be that large body of water. For that matter, what is the difference between being a mile from shore at Orange Lake or Lake Erie? I know the newness will soon turn to excitement as soon as I get into it.

Another head spinner, the home situation, is pushing at my head for a closer look, for an airing, for a real and open evaluation. I am still at a point I can maintain. It is not a hostility thing. Things haven't changed that much. It is not our relationship that is making it unmanageable, although it certainly has given me insight and the courage to begin to face where my life is leading. I think that is the key to what is happening—growth—and I am becoming restless within the confines of what I perceive as an environment that is inhibiting growth. Can't slow down to take "one step at a time." My H. P. and I play tug of war. I should say I am playing. "Here it is, H.P....No, give it back. ...No, here it is. ...No. ...Yes." Wanting action and solutions right now and not waiting for the natural course of events are part of my problem. I am not trusting H. P. enough to accept that things have to happen in his time frame, not trusting that He will be kindly, even though everything in the past has been kindly. In other words, wanting to make sure it is my way—not trusting enough that his way will be right for me and us. I guess they call that grinding.

There is no way I can discount the us that is in there, because it gives me the energy, freedom, and insight to see what growth is and how it feels. What I must be careful of is not to run, not to run from anything and not to run to anything. I feel the urge to look at the growth in its own light, where it is going, what can best enhance it, and what will get in its way. I think only after I understand it as well as I can, will I be able to walk in the direction it leads me. The nearest I can come to an understanding now is that we have given each other that growth. I know this sounds jumbled, just laying it out, but even that has helped me to sort through some of it.

I love you,
Michael

August 10, 1983

My Michael,

On Sunday, I took a break and canoed over to the swamp with Elle. It seemed like all its creatures were parading for us. We saw a green heron on a tree branch we floated under, and at the mouth of the stream going back into the swamp, the pair of swans was feeding. Elle took several pictures of them as they made their unhurried way past us. She had just put down her camera to push us off a submerged log, when the great blue heron flew up from that place you and I sat watching dragonflies the last time we were there together. I was so surprised, or awed, or unwilling to share, that I did not point it out to Elle. I figured it was my personal Michael gift of the swamp. I had been avoiding going back there, because leaving it makes me so sad. As I paddled, it dawned on me, that it still is going to be there when I want it. I gave myself a good talking to. "You're just going to have another side of the lake to explore. You could be moving to an apartment, or a place in the city. Check out the good stuff that has been laid on you and quit bellyaching!"

When we got back, Elle dropped me off at the new house, and I invited her to the first dinner I cooked there. After dinner I attacked the faucet problem. I persevered, and finally got the handles off, just as you told me I could. Monday, I got the parts I needed and *voila*, it works!

Elle's neighbor, Herb, loaned me his electric hedge trimmers, and I attacked the overgrown barberry hedge. There is an untrimmed spot right in the middle where I narrowly missed walking into a bee's nest—thank you H. P. I have several bees' nests in the yard that are etched in my brain map, until I can figure out what to do with them. The hedge is uneven, but looks a whole lot better. After my busy day at the house, last night I went with Elle and Herb to Middletown to see an outdoor performance of Shakespeare's *Merry Wives of Windsor*, done New Orleans style with a Ragtime Band. Audience and performers alike had a rollicking good time on the balmy summer night. I'm glad I went.

I'm gradually moving three or four boxes each day as I go over to the house. Today Eric went to look at a car, a used Volkswagen station wagon. He put a binder on it and one of the men he works with is going to look it over tomorrow. I had held my tongue about him looking for a car, and darn, didn't I have to say something this very morning (casually, of course), just when he was all ready to go on his own initiative. Old H. P. spanked my hand and told me to leave it all turned over and to stay out of it. Eric's comment today was, "I thought I better get a station wagon in case I need a place to sleep." I didn't rise to the bait. I just kept on packing.

This evening to relax I took Hoot out in the canoe. He is getting much better about doing new things. This was only the second time he has been out, and I told him to sit in the back ,and I would teach him how to steer. I told him he wasn't supposed to know how, 'cuz he never had a chance to do it before. I said that I would be awful glad if he would learn, because my elbow still bothers me and being in the steering position puts extra strain on it. If he learned, we could go more often, could go further, and could stay longer. Then I basically told him what I knew about maneuvering the canoe. He caught on right off and wasn't embarrassed or anything. In an afternoon's time, we were a real team. I took him back to the swamp, and he said right off what a good place to catch fish that would be. I didn't tell him about the angling that had already been done there. I could tell by his dancing eyes and that sudden smile that lights up his serious face that he really liked it. Then didn't the blue heron fly up, to our mutual startlement? Hoot didn't say anything, but his eyes got real big and he took it all in. Hoot is the most taking-inest youngster I've ever seen. The way he observes, you just know he is searching out the essence of things. If you talk to him, he is insightful and has a droll sense of humor, but you have to draw him out slowly. Occasionally, he has forgotten himself and talked along at a great clip, words almost tumbling out, and then all of a sudden, silence, and back into his shell. He becomes aware of the fact he is talking and gets shy again. I leave him alone then and carry on one-sided conversations, or just let the silence be comfortable by doing some distracting thing to take the attention off him. We have good silences together. Hoot is just trying new stuff.

Soooo—if Hoot can learn to try new stuff, my Michael, you mustn't be afraid of sailing. Let the joy be greater than the fear. I hope I didn't put you in a force position by those sailing lessons, though. That never occurred to me. You have the option of maybe buying a hood ornament for your car, or putting the money toward some new tool for work or something, if you would rather. Right now my rather is to lay my weary body down and have a sweet dream of Michael.

Verge

8/15/83

My Verge,

I am afraid there is nothing in my head tonight, but sugarplums, as in the age-old Christmas poem. Only, these sugarplums are named Verge. They are dancing all right, but they look like parts of your body, or things you have told me, or things you have done. Ooh, look there is Verge's navel. It is so pretty; I can look way down in there. Or, do you know what Verge told me? She said she thinks I am fine. That makes me walk tall. Now you know how my mind is wandering this night. If someone could open up my mind, you would pop out.

Hoot has been prodding me to tell you some more about him and Ginny. This seems like a good time to do so, to get him off my back. He reminded me, that the last time, he told Ginny he was going away to scout camp for a week, and that he had to prepare all the gear that night. He had promised to be back early the next morning with her birthday present. He later told me, and asked me to pass on to you, that he spotted Ginny peeking in the window that night he was helping his troop prepare for camp, after telling and telling her she couldn't come around.

~

*The following morning around 6:30, Hoot carefully bounces pebbles off Ginny's bedroom window. The sun has just cleared the horizon with a promise of a hot, hot, July day. The heavy dew feels good on Hoot's bare feet. He carries a wrapped box and his constant grin is a dead giveaway of his excitement.*

*"Ginny..Gin...Ginnnny! Boy she sure sleeps hard. Ginnnny! Hey! Oh, Hi. I was looking for you to poke your head out your window. You scared me. Did you sleep outside or something? You mean you were up and waiting in the kitchen already? Couldn't you sleep?*

*Yeah, it's hot already. I don't care though. This? Oh it is just an old package. Hey! Don't be so grabby. Yes. It is your present, but we have to have ice cream and cake when you open it. Do you think your mother will be mad if we have it now? Sure you can open it now; I was just kidding. I can't wait either. It is something I want you to have so you don't forget that we are friends. Here...and Gin...well...I like you...a lot."*

*Gin opens the present, and when she realizes what the gift is, she is stopped. She looks at Hoot, then down at the silver charm, then back at Hoot. Hoot is scared. Maybe she didn't like the little silver fish. Impulsively, Ginny jumps up and hugs the embarrassed Hoot's neck. She whispers in his ear, "I won't forget. Ever. I like you, too, a lot." After a brief moment they both grin and steal into the house for the melted ice cream.*

*Later, sitting on a log by the pond, having finished their ice cream, they hear a frog splash. They look at each other and together get up to begin a hunt, turning over stones and poking into the pond with sticks. "Ginny, I saw you peeking in the window last night." She straightens up, poised to run. "Oh, it's OK I thought I would be mad, but when I saw you I felt kinda good all over. I wanted to rush outside and bring you in to help me, but I knew the guys would never stand for that. I.... Oh, nothing. No, I wasn't going to say anything. Wow! Look at that big one over there. Let's get him."*

*Morning drifts into afternoon. Both are keenly aware that it must end soon—not just for that day—for a whole long week. Something has been stirring inside Hoot, pushing to be said. Why should he feel this way, afraid but glad, shy but eager to open up to this girl? They vaguely feel the pressure of time and dread to leave the woods, not solely because of the cool shelter.*

*"I guess we better go. Come on Gin. ...Wait a minute. Ginny, let' sit on the stump for a minute. I wanna tell you something. Well...I always was real excited to go away to camp before. When I was there I was glad to be off on my own. Sure, I had fun doing stuff, but mostly I was glad to be away and doing for myself. When it was time to go home, I always felt kinda sad. Other kids would be homesick and want to get back home; their families would come to see them, and they were glad. I always prayed that no one would come to see me, even though I knew they couldn't. When I did get home I didn't hug and kiss anyone. I hoped they wouldn't notice I*

*was home for a while, so I could get used to it again. But.... But, this time... well...I feel different. Ginny, I feel like I don't want to go, but I gotta. I think I am going to be lonesome, even though I never have been since I was four, up in Michigan. I never missed nobody, except my friends when we got back home from camp and they went to their own houses."*

*They continue sitting on the stump in silence, looking closely at each other. "Gin, promise to hug my neck when I get back next week?" She hugs his neck right then and there, and they run together out of the woods. No one could quite decipher the little smiles each one wears. "Ginny? ...See ya."*

~

It's amazing how good those kids make me feel. Almost like the good you make me feel. Next time I tell you that it will be with my lips right against your cheek. Please hurry.

Michael

8/16/83

My sweet Michael man,

I fear I will have to trade spank for spank. I feel guilty and mean because I haven't written since last Wednesday night, and it is making huge holes in our communication. It is something like your reason, a spinning head that I can't slow down enough to get a handle on what I have to say, other than I love you, I miss you, I wanna now!

Spinning, also, because of trying to decide what furniture is to go to the house and where it will be placed. Tomorrow, Dad and his wife are bringing some furniture down in the truck and staying to help me move. I need to take a trip to the dump to get rid of what I don't want to keep. I keep thinking I'm getting organized and throwing a lot of junk away, but still find myself transporting things I don't really need. It is such a short distance to the new house that it is a temptation to hang onto stuff I can live without.

I have been puzzled for more than a week because Eric got a post office box at the same branch as mine and tried to put it in both our names. The postmistress, who is in the program, thank Goodness, told him she couldn't do that without my permission, as I already have a box. I can't, for the life of me, figure out why, when we are separating, we would want to share a mailbox. When the postmistress told me about it, I told her Eric and I were separating, and I asked her to be sure I got my mail in my own box. I didn't mention it to Eric, and he didn't to me until last night when I was not waxing enthusiastic about his offer to help me move. He said, "Not knowing where the house is makes about as much sense as us having mailboxes three feet apart at the post office." That created an opening where I could say I didn't understand why he even tried to put it in both our names, which led to my telling him I am going to the lawyer this week to get separation papers filed.

Then it was like suddenly the whole thing was different to him. "Why are you going to a lawyer? Why would you pay good money for a piece of paper?" I could take his word for it that he wouldn't bother me. I was forced to ask him what he thought I intended when I said I didn't want to live with him anymore? He said he didn't know; he had been wondering that himself. I told him that the separation would lead to a no-fault divorce in a year. "Divorce? You want a divorce? Isn't that expensive? Why don't you get it now?" I told him that way I could cover him with my health insurance for the year with the hope that one of the jobs he has taken tests for would have an opening by then, and he would have his own insurance. Either he was toying with me, to find out if I was serious or not, or the probability of a divorce really hadn't crossed his brain. Anyway, it is all out in the open now. I wrote it all down and posted it on the refrigerator so he can't say he doesn't know what is what.

He is taking a big step tomorrow. Tonight he paid for his car and tomorrow he will go take care of paper work. Paper work! On his own. That is a major accomplishment. Tonight he asked if I had nuts and bolts for his license plate. I said that the plastic ones they sell are better because they don't jar loose so easily. With his usual perception, he said, "I've lived in this town for twenty years and I don't know where to buy anything unless it is sold at Lloyd's. I could kick myself every time he comes up with one of those gems. How true it is. How much I contributed to his dependence on me! Through the years, I responded to his imperial command to buy this or that for him. It is true: you can't play king unless someone plays subject.

Wanting to respond to your letter about running away causes major spinning, too, yet a great hesitation has come over me. I have to be careful to not be saying things through selfish self-interest. I've tried to analyze every word I might use and that dissipates the energy needed to address the problem. I think I will wait until I see you in person, and then present all sides of the issue as I see them flash by like a merry-go-round in my head. Thank you for trusting me enough to think out loud with me. I will see you very soon,

Verge

8/31/83

Dear Michael,

This is your natal day. I send special dupee pats and navel explorations and commemoration of this day of your beginning. I also send blessings to your mother and to the memory of your father, in gratitude for their commingling that conceived the most precious person in the world to me—my Michael. I sent you a special hug during your birthday sailing lesson today—hope it wasn't too distracting.

After Montauk I felt like I had lived with you. Perhaps it was a fanciful version of "life with Michael," but it had a general all over feel of how you and I would operate with each other in a life situation. Now after our Erie Island sojourn, the fanciful part is gone and in its place is a pervading feeling of real, despite our not having to go to work or engage in the time consuming minutia of life. I am glad for your cheerful acceptance of me on the edge of worrywart panic, neither getting sucked into it, nor callous when I really panic. We balance and complement each other to the most delicate degree.

On Monday I went to the lawyer to read over the papers. They are shudderingly legal, but I'm glad I chose this lawyer because he stays human. There is a clause that says all rights and responsibilities are removed, unless the spouse is in danger of becoming a "public charge." I questioned the lawyer about it, and he said even if you are divorced that responsibility is there, and can be legally brought on a one-time spouse. He said in a case like mine it wouldn't be done, but it could be. Did you know that? My Goodness, one could be haunted forever by an active alcoholic. As if we didn't know that already!

Yesterday I picked the papers up and delivered a copy to Eric. I have to mentally compliment him on acting in a gentlemanly way through this tough stuff. For once in his life he has risen to the occasion, and has been generally co-operative, even after he knew I was serious. He throws in a whammy every now and again, but is far more helpful than I believed he would be. Last night he asked if he had to read the papers. I suggested he ought to or I might run off with his fortune. His reply, "But you are. You were my fortune." Such clarity of vision, and such warped thinking! This morning he greeted me with, "There is nothing in there about my stipend." I told him he would just have to accept my word on it as both lawyers said they would not write that in. He stayed reasonable about it. I suppose, if I obviously do not trust his word, then turn about is fair. My lawyer thinks I am a little demented, because he doesn't know how to handle no tears, no recriminations, and no anger.

I am so glad I feel the way I do about this. I do not feel guilty. I do not feel angry. I do not feel unsure. I can see where this would be an awfully tacky, hurtful business if one party wanted to kick up a fuss, or if there was doubt in one's mind.

Yesterday I spent the afternoon cleaning the old house. I had dreaded that job, as it had no rewards except personal pride and perhaps a touch of homage. I could not just walk away leaving my dirt behind for someone else to inspect, as I have just finished doing with this new house. I made one last try to get allll the BBs out of the cracks in Milo's bedroom floor. One last swipe at spiders that have had residence in the house for years—old friends—progeny of ones you and I have watched on various nights when we dared not look at each other. Accumulated ghosts I keep trying to shepherd away across the lake, but mostly they prefer to keep their old haunting grounds. I hope the new people are prepared.

Elle came this morning to help me move my plants in her camper, and to notarize Eric's and my signature on the separation papers. Eric asked me to have her do it, if she would, because he didn't know where to find another notary. After that business was transacted and the plants were loaded, I followed Elle in my car. Halfway down the road, I heard, "Yeeeeeoooooooooooowwww!" Cat was stowed away amongst the boxes in the trunk of the car. She has been nervously watching each room being emptied and has checked out my putting things in the car every day, but this is the first time, in the ten years I have had her, that she has willingly gotten into the car. She does not like traveling, so with dread I had held off taking her to the new house until I intended to stay. It is as if she knew what was happening, and she determined not to be left behind. As she is over here now, I did not want to leave her alone on her first night, so I am staying, also. This is the first night of my new life. Come join us in our dreams.

Verge

## Virginia N. & Michael N.

9/5/83

My Love, Michael,

I'm sitting at my kitchen table in my new house listening to a blue jay proclaim his territory to the neighbor's cat. The crickets and locusts are making a low level sizzling sound, and the lonely call of a heron floats up from the lake. My mind and body are balking stubbornly from even considering what has to be done this day. The Gin creature wants it done now, and I have to keep telling her that it is going to be a while before we will feel settled in our new home. Each day it is rearranged and things fall into their resting place, but it takes mental gymnastics to think where some particular thing is at the moment.

Thank you for reassuring me during our phone conversation about that leaving night's conversation, turning it around to where I was doing you a favor by calming your last night's afraids. I have worried that I had said too much, had been too selfish, and had put needless pressure on you. I've been around and around the conversation countless times since, yet if you were to ask me tomorrow what my thoughts were on that subject, I would have to say it all the same way. Honesty has been the strength of our relationship and has been the quality that has kept it pure through adversity. Even when it hurts, we have brought honesty to each other as a sacrificial offering. As Al-Anon teaches, say what you feel and what you need to say, but don't expect that to change the other person. Say it; then let it go. As I look at it now, the most criminal thing I did with Eric was never being completely honest about anything, yet feeling resentful that he didn't know me better. Accumulated little acts of dishonesty done in the name of kindness, or keeping peace, or any of the hundred other justifying reasons I thought of, built daily into the huge dishonesty of denying my self. There was no way he could have known who I was or what I believed in.

Thank you for standing by, listening to my grumbling and poor me's, and staying a neutral strength. I'm sure you have had days when it was difficult to do. I just want to run up to you, wrap you all up in my arms and legs, and roll around with you—sort of like a Pig Pile, only less knees and elbows. (Do you remember Pig Pile where a bunch of kids all jumped on top of each other and scroogled around—or is that just a rural sport?) I love you more.

Verge

9/8/83

My Verge,

I'm in the park today. It's a bright blue, late-summer day, clear for 100 miles, puffy white clouds, and low humidity. There are boy and girl type couples all around, sitting close together, talking and laughing. I must confess feeling resentful.

The conversation of that last night together is a good example of how we worry needlessly over things between us, that upon examination prove to be less foreboding than our imagination tries to tell us they are. When we look at them together, they diminish in size and fright potential. The beauty part is that we never let them fester between us. When things are ready to come out, they do, and we are usually ready at about the same time. I don't think we could have parted without talking about the state of our relationship and its current effect on the peripheral people. What you said, about getting honest in there someplace with others. is something I have told myself over and over. It made me look at it, accept it, and chew on how I can implement it in my life. You have helped me to see more clearly that there is no ready wrapped solution for us. The road is not easy, but if we do the footwork for our own growth, the rest will be as it should be.

Another thing I had mulled around in my head—stewed over, even—was the status of our pact. I could tell by the way you talked about it, that you had stewed, too. My thoughts had been almost word for word what you said. Namely, that the pact was mostly for the children, and now that the children are grown, the reason for the pact has ceased to exist. As far as I am concerned, the rest of the path should be traveled as growth and development dictate. Since you said you wanted to be released from the pact, and so do I, I hereby cast my vote to absolve us from it. I guess that can be considered a second, since you firsted it. It is hereby concluded that said pact, and all its bindings, is dissolved and no longer holds either party of the aforementioned to its precepts.

You didn't scare me when you told me that you were prepared to do whatever is necessary to preserve our relationship. When you said that, I filled up the way I do when I look at you and think I am going to burst from all the love that is pushing to be told about. I felt proud and relieved, because I couldn't fight off the worry that you would weary of all that patience stuff. I was relieved, too, that you understand the difficulties in trying to give someone to him/herself, not to mention finding one's own self.

I'm glad we had that talk. Along the vein of finding one's self, I thank you for writing about what dishonesty can do to self. How it can build into the huge dishonesty of denying who you are, causing resentments and cutting yourself off from the realities of life. Telling me about that made things clearer for me.

I never played Pig Pile, but there was a game called Buck, Buck—that's with a B. It involved kids jumping on each other until they all fell down in a big scrambled up heap. Can you do that with just two people? (Less elbows and knees, you say.)

Michael

September 13, 1983

My Honey Man,

First day of the new school year, and I think I have whatever ailment you had yesterday when you called. I had to concentrate on each little thing I did to keep my mind off feeling really rotten. Queasy stomach and sniffles and just not right. But I wuz brave.

After school, I took Eric over to get his car, then came home and had a bowl of soup and took a nap. I still feel less than fit, but writing to you always makes me feel better. Today's letter from you filled me with such gratitude that wild horses couldn't keep me from writing. I feel the same as I felt when you finally spoke to me after I told you I loved you that first time. I was afraid you would feel too insecure without the safety of the pact between us. Thank you for releasing us from it. That is a big step in trust. We think we trust all there is, and then we find we have kept ourselves one little reserve. That pact was our reserve against our selves more than against each other. Until we fully trust our self, there is always going to be a little place of not totally trusting the other. I think this will be a major growing step between us.

You talk of my patience and the hurty parts you feel responsible for in my life. Michael, you know you are not responsible for my hurts. I am. I choose to love you in such a way that I allow you to be my happiness. The Program says, as does every grain of sense one can muster, "You cannot expect someone else to make you happy." I do expect you to make me happy because history has shown that to be a truism. You being alive and kicking around this planet with me make me ecstatic. It is not some specific act you do. You have chosen the same dangerous route of letting me be your happiness. You hurt, too. What has that got to do with patience? Sure, sometimes I want it all NOW! If I can't have it now, then what? Can you think of any replacement you would care to put in your life? Me neither. Can you think of anyone you could possibly fill the hole with, that you wouldn't constantly be biting your tongue on, "Verge, look!"? Me neither. Elle has gotten used to me saying, "Michael, look!" and she is just a comfortable friend. Then, there is all that history, all those laughs, and shared tears. How could one even begin to get a tiny piece of what we have together? Impossible.

What is ultimately becoming clearer is that the time of martyrdom is coming to a close. A time of responsibility to self is dawning. The prospects, when I see glimmers of them here and there, Montauk, Erie Isles, are dizzying and nothing would keep me from hanging around to see how it all works out.

Verge

Friday, 9/16/83

My Sweet Verge,

You say that you like to watch me savoring things of life. I have spent so much of my life trying to hide the real me that it is a huge relief to be able to let out all the stops and really be me with no fear, just a good easy feeling of being loved and not judged. You make me so happy I could jump up and down and spit and stomp and everything!

Once you asked me if I ever felt connected to my parents or brothers. An incident came to my mind of a time when I was nine or ten. My favorite aunt, who was visiting from Michigan, had promised to take me to a movie I really wanted to see. I guess I had done some bad deed through the day, because my mother said the movie was off. I was crushed, but I don't remember feeling it was an unjust punishment. My aunt was a jolly type, full of life, who liked to do things that kids like—go to movies, play cards, drive a car. I loved her and respected her judgment. She whispered to me that if I would just go up to my mother, and hug her and tell her I was sorry, I would probably be able to go after all. I refused. Not because I was mad, but because the idea of hugging my mother was such a novel one, and truthfully, one which inspired revulsion. I was assured that if I did that one simple act my mother would relent, yet I couldn't, and didn't do it. I remember the feeling of trying to force myself, but not being able to.

If I keep scaring up all these weirds from my past, eventually I will have you scratching your head wondering what kind of nut I am. I thank you for accepting them in your own, just right, way. Whenever I tell you these never before told things, I always feel better and they lose their bothersome quality almost at the telling.

I do feel the trust between us has taken a giant growth step. Ding, dong, the pact is dead! I believe we had outgrown it and had been proceeding along without it before we even realized it. Now its shadow is gone. I can take whatever comes, as long as you are in there somewhere.

Michael

September 19, 1983

My Michael,

Even at a young age, I never believed a compliment anyone gave me. People telling about me made me squirm with embarrassment. It never gave me a glow, only a miserable feeling that no one knew the real me. A paradox there—an early hiding of self, yet a craving to be known. It didn't start with Eric. It was an old habit by then, because it seemed to me that no one liked the real me when I let it out. I have to say back to you, "You do it just right." I believe you when you compliment me. If I can't see it, I can let my mind say that, as you see it, I am such and such, and accept it as your true feelings.

Since I have been away from you this time, I have been studying myself in the mirror to see me as you physically see me. Even when I see a softness here, or a line there, and I wish perfection, I let myself look with your eyes, and I can enjoy some of what I see. This is not an act of self-adulation, but a voyage in curiosity. I haven't looked at myself more than superficially in years. I'm forcing myself to look, without cringing away or finding fault—just accepting. I am starting to be able to do it frankly, without the guilty feeling that there is something unnatural about staring at myself.

Michael, promise to stop saying things like, "If I keep scaring up all these weirds from my past, eventually I will have you ...wondering what kind of nut I am." You offer me the compliment of trusting my ability to understand a piece of hidden you, and then you keep yourself a hiding place to run back into, in case I react in a way you don't like. Don't apologize for trusting me; it weakens the trust. How do you suppose it makes me feel about some of the heavies I have laid on you? What repeatedly comes out of these revelations is that you and I put some awful, self-inflicted pain on our beings since childhood. It is eerie to realize how parallel our lives were even though we were separated by time, space and culture.

I've worried about the state of your health, all day today. What did the doctor say? I'm about ready to be sick and tired of my malady and hie myself off to the doctor, too. I've told myself it is everything, from change in drinking water, to some perverted guilt hypochondria, or just plain old pout over missing you. Perhaps all combined.

I admire your attempts to stop smoking, especially in your weakened state. I could tell you forty things I did to stop, but allowing myself to smoke a pipe whenever I had the urge helped me, at first, to cut down. It was messy, time consuming, and never satisfying. The real answer was to do it for myself. I had tried to do it for Milo, for the kids at work, and for you and your concern about my perpetual bronchitis. I always ended up feeling deprived. When I finally did it for myself, I was positive about it. I was getting rid of that troublesome pipe, and I was going to free my lungs from that onslaught to see what real breathing and tasting was about. The process was gradual, but I no longer had those wracking coughing spells, and I could take a deep breath without it hurting. I didn't recognize the taste difference until I lit a cigarette for you and woke the next day with that taste still on my tongue and realized it had always been there to find other tastes through. I'm in your corner for anything that increases your chances for a prolonged life. It is your lonely fight, though; don't do it for anyone but yourself. Good luck.

I can't resist saying that cold turkey is the best way, just as with the booze. Having just one or two sucked me back in every time. It didn't allow me to ever get the taste or the habit out of my system. I read that it takes three weeks to change a habit, each day being positive about the thing you wish to change. I finally ended up hanging onto the "one day at a time" slogan for dear life. They keep telling me in The Program, awareness is the beginning of change. Gotta sleep. I love you.

Verge

9/22/83

Michael,

I'm awfully sad tonight. I got a letter from Milo, as you will know from tomorrow morning's phone call. I feel so sorry for those kids.

Milo's wife went home to Papa, and I guess from the letter divorce is imminent. Thank God for Al-Anon telling me I cannot live someone else's life for him/her or keep pain from anyone. It also tells me from pain comes growth. I simply have to trust that some H. P. will watch over those kids in as kindly a fashion as I have come to believe myself watched over. They were two troubled youngsters seeking solace from the world, without either having the experience or maturity to know how to "give" enough. I don't know what precipitated the leaving, only that they looked so much in love, it seems a shame not to work on it for a while. I know how Milo keeps everything to himself, and I had hoped he would learn how to trust enough to communicate his feelings better. It is upsetting to see the worst of your own self replayed by your children. Makes one wonder if it all gets replayed ad infinitum. I've just finished writing a careful "don't pry, just be supportive" letter to him. Having spent overlong at it, I am cheating time on this one.

When you get this, it will only be a week before I will see you. I am still worried about the state of your health. On Monday I have a doctor's appointment to find out about my own health. The doctor did call in a prescription for me, but it has only made me feel worse—weird and really tired. I don't suppose I did much for the state of your health in April, but you said it made the illness seem less. I would consider it a privilege to nurse you. Please let the time hurry for we are overdue, Babe.

Verge

9/24/83

My Woman, My Verge,

You must not stop prodding me; I need it. I need to hear all the advice you can give, all the encouragement you can think of, and all the commiseration you can muster. If you aren't writing them or telling them to me on the phone, then be thinking them to me. I need them all. I will not think they are nags; I won't get exasperated; I will know they are your love. I feel like a child wandering in a wood. If this sounds dramatic, you are right. I have successfully cut back to one pack a day, but I can't seem to get below that. I feel lousy because that one pack doesn't do it for me. I feel like I am in withdrawal even though I am taking in that much nicotine. So, self says, "Might as well go the whole way if you are going to feel bad anyhow." With a cringe and a duck of the head, expecting the worst, I am at this very moment smoking my last cigarette in my last pack. See how casually I crumple it up and toss it into the basket? Kinda scary! You said that awareness is the foothold in the battle. I've gained some of that since starting to cut back last Sunday, aware of some pitfalls and habits, but aware doesn't mean licked. Do it for myself. I think my head is attuned to that concept. At first I was going to surprise you, but that fell through rapidly. There is much more involved than I thought. I need your hand. With the booze, at least there was AA and all those meetings and people to tell you and lead you. This will all be a surprise. You said that "a day at a time" is good. I am at the millisecond stage right now. This is me turning it all over.

You are indeed correct about giving trust with one hand and saving a hiding place with the other. My ego is so busy scurrying about, trying to protect itself, that it doesn't consider who it may be trampling. Thank you for the insight. I have no reason to do that to us. Thanks for another leg up in the growing department.

I'll be thinking of you on Monday while you are at the doc's. Don't show him your feet. My doctor asked, "Where did you catch those funny feet?" I couldn't answer him.

I, too, feel like a sad poppa for Milo.

Michael

Wednesday night, September 28

Dear Michael,

Now look Hoot, I ain't gonna talk to you, or write, or nuthin' until you apologize. You are a lie!!! No doctor ever, ever asked you where you caught your crazy feet!!! Besides everything else, you are older than I am, and YOU HAD THEM FIRST. If they were catching, I had to catch them from you, cuz you know we are the only two people on earth who have second toes shorter than the third ones. It is like the Potter put a special stamp on us so we would recognize that we belonged together. We were so busy recognizing other things that it took Eric to point out our "brand", our "watermark", after we had been intimate with each other's feet for years. I'll always marvel at never noticing until then. I guess I accepted them as normal, because yours were like my own and nothing particular to remark upon—everyone else's were peculiar.

Yea! Good for you and your non-smoking endeavors. You sounded so determined in your letter about THE LAST ONE. Every time you get a craving, think a positive thought. You won't have to endure nasty looks from non-smokers. You won't have to get resentful in restaurants that carelessly leave no ashtrays on tables. Ceilings stay wondrously clean. In one month, you are saving airfare to NY. You will be minus one habit that has chilled me for years—smoking half asleep in bed. I always had to entrust you to whatever divine providence watches over fate tempters.

I did detect just a smidge of poor me's when we talked on the phone this morning. I found that to be a sidelight of not smoking. I felt so deprived. Everything that I could usually swing with depressed the hell out of me. It was a shock to realize what a mood-altering drug nicotine is. Cigarettes seemed to have no particular effect on me when I was smoking. When I stopped, I found the addiction very apparent. Hang in there; it gets better once you detox, but that takes a while. The idea, that, for the first time, I will taste the real you unadulterated by tobacco, is exciting. Perhaps I will need an introduction.

I finally did what I promised myself not to do since Eric has made no evident attempt to find a place to stay. I told him there was an ad in last night's paper for a two-room apartment, reasonable, including utilities, in a nice location—a rare deal. He got me! He said that he did not want a permanent place where he would have to sign a lease, that landlords would never give back a deposit on short notice, and unlike me he doesn't want to make a nest. He wants a motel room. I could shake myself for expending sympathy on him. (I didn't take him a newspaper, saved my dignity that far.) I keep telling myself it is the disease, but I could shake him for sitting around looking pathetic when he has avenues to help himself.

Verge

10/3/83

My Lovin' Woman,

Now just settle down, Ginny. Simmer down. There is no need to get so all fired up, so foot stompin' (oops, sorry) mad. I know how it feels to have funny feet. I read what you said about me being older, and you having to catch them from me, but that ain't necessarily so. I read in this big ol' thick book called *The Foot Knowing About Book* that lots of times people catch funny feet from people who ain't born yet. That's right. It says that the being who handles the feet division for people who are getting ready to walk Earth rarely sets things up in time sequence. It says if there is a pair of destined humans with a special order attached for a benchmark to show them or the world that they are a pair that belongs together, he doesn't necessarily make them in order. He just gets them ready and on the designated day off one goes, because usually such pairs don't get launched on the same day, or even in the same year. He could have made yours first, and when the order came for me to be a match with you, he inspected your mark very carefully and made my feet just like yours, so I caught my feet from you.

Okay, Okay, I agree. You could have caught your feet from me. That is just as possible. I just wanted you to know what it said in that book. Or, maybe my feet changed like yours after I met you, because I never noticed anything funny about them before. The marvelous part is that we have got um to let the world know we are an us.

Thank you for those encouragements in regards to not smoking. I know you have encouraged me on the phone, but the written ones I can study and implement and they work. I am sorry about the lapse in letter writing, but this damn sickness has robbed all of my initiative, and the lack of nicotine has left me irritable. I get so angry! I have so much to tell you, but every time I get a thought my brain slips out of gear. It does seem odd that you and I have been sick about the same length of time, namely since we left the islands. Maybe we left our shadows there. Should we go back and get them?

Don't I know how hard it is to want someone to do something my way, yet not to say anything, and to watch him make the "mistake" of not doing whatever it is in the way I know will solve everything? I promise myself to "let go", stay out, and bite lip and tongue. Then, to break down and tell the person how it should be done, only to have it snap right back in my face makes me want to crawl into a closet corner. I know. Nobody ever said this growing up stuff was going to be easy. I'm just glad we are doing it together, hand in hand.

I have a feeling we are going to be very busy doing a haunting job at your house. I look forward to being in the autumn with you.

Michael

10/12/83

My Michael,

When I first moved, I felt disconnected and very lonely for you. I kept busy as a madwoman, trying to make this place into a home, racing to keep away the lonelies that seemed to snuffle and snirk under the doors and in the mirrors. Now, I feel your presence, your slippers cozily tucked under the bed, dishes you've touched anew in our privacy, your image caught in every mirror, a scent that lingers. Cat keeps going into rooms looking expectantly for you.

It seems strange that a habit you have had since I first met you—smoking—passed away nearly unnoticed. I had to think what it was like when you did smoke. I suppose it would have been more rewarding to you, if I had felt more impressed or aware of your great achievement, but it just seemed the way it was supposed to be. I did like your new taste and smell, but I always liked your taste and smell.

You were made more precious while you were here, by allowing me to see you uncomfortable and hurting, and yet able to talk about it, so I could understand your hurt and discomfort without confusing it with what I feared caused it. As sensitive as we are to what makes the other tick, it has been demonstrated time and again that we must tell each other what is causing complicated feelings, for half-told things breed fear in our rampant imaginings. It is best to discuss them as frankly as we are able to at that point in time, for we are not mind readers. It is not lack of interest or lack of trying that sometimes crosses our wires. We come as close as two people can to intuitive knowledge of each other, but to dispense with the margin of error, we give each other a gift by not presuming the other will "just know." With all this growing, sometimes we don't even "just know" about ourselves, because this is unmapped territory we have never traveled through before. Although it might be hard to explain what is going on to another human, that person may give a fresh perspective or offer more choices than one head can conjure up by itself.

We know ultimately we have to answer our own questions, or wait for the answers to come. However, getting around to answers does not have to be the deadly, lonely process it used to be. We can share a joke, or a kiss, or a sad heart, and somehow the weight of all those questions and answers is bearable, rather than overwhelming.

You talked about being irritable with comparatively blameless occurrences. It reminded me of last winter trying to tell you about anger. It came surging up out of nowhere for reasons beyond comprehension.

It shook me to my innards, because I didn't know how to deal with a feeling I seldom allowed myself, due to fear of repercussions. I had convinced myself that I was a cheerful person with no anger, believing if I could keep the home environment free of turmoil the beasties would be placated. That unrealistic view of myself exploded at the time in The Program when I discovered I had myriad feelings. People kept telling me that learning to feel again was a normal part of the healing process, and there is nothing wrong with anger; it is what you do with it that counts. Anger forced me to break my barrier of fear with Eric enough to tell him some of the unacceptables I would no longer accept. Some of that anger was so white hot that I didn't care what the repercussions were, as long as what was pushing to get out, did. I lived through claiming my right to be a human being. A lot of it was ugly, much of it was frightening, but it purged a festering hurt, and gradually I learned to express my anger in more appropriate ways. A simple statement of why we are angry directed to the cause of that anger may not change the situation, but it does air the issue so our feelings are known and innocent bystanders or blameless sources do not become the recipients of unfair rage. The last was the hardest to learn, but the most necessary.

Today, I was angry because one kid ruined a sculpture another student had worked on for two weeks. I discovered it at the end of class, just as the next class was walking in. I was frothing. I explained to that class what had happened and that I was very angry. I told them if I seemed perturbed it was not at them; I was trying to gain my self-control, but it might take a few minutes. Miraculously the class went about its business, held off on the dumb stuff until I got myself together, and seemed to respect my honesty. In the past I might have been a bitch all day, compounding my misery by making a lot of kids angry and rebellious by unfairly taking my anger out on them.

It is strange how so many parts of the growth process feel like regressions until they are dealt with, and the revelations they hold, dawn. Don't be hard on yourself. I have heard it discussed at enough meetings, and have seen it happen to enough people to say with assurance that it is part of the process of getting better. If you usually handle your feelings as well as you did when you were here, you are maturing much less painfully than I did, as far as the people around you are concerned. Keep on talking about it and admit what you feel, or it will take a far longer time to get through this phase.

Last night at the meeting someone said something very simple that seemed to make profound sense to me, "The Steps are not punishments.

They are tools for getting well." Sometimes a simple statement strikes at just the receptive moment and seems like a revelation. I have come to the place where I refuse to try to analyze The Program anymore. It works. I have seen it; I have felt it; I cannot explain it. I just plain give in to it. Thank you for the beautiful haunts.

Verge

10/15/83

My Sweet Verge,

Can it be just a week ago, my first time at your house, when we both were so ill we were falling asleep over dinner? We folded our sick and exhausted selves into your bed and instantly fell asleep. It feels like a forever ago, and it has only been a few days. Thanks for the good places you take me. Both the Storm King Art Center and Opus 40 stay with me as fresh quiet places where we could be as free of care as children. At Storm King, I loved playing with you among the sculptures on the hill overlooking the valley, experiencing the tactile joy of running our hands over their surfaces, and making up silly stories about them. And at Opus 40, who could believe that stonework could be so beautiful? Just knowing you are walking this earth with me keeps me going.

I like to think of your house from the outside as well as inside. It's so trim and gleaming and expectant, sitting up there on the hill. I like the little stir you have created in the neighborhood. I love your mock orange bush and your crumbling outside grill and your cute parsley plants on the kitchen window sill and your funny outlets, and, and just all of it.

Love,
Michael

10/20/83

Michael, my love man…Oops, Gin is stealing my paper…

*Dear Hoot,*

*"OK, Hoot! You told me after the last silly card I sent you that it left the field open for any retaliation. But, do I…have I ever once since I have known you…did I even nearly drop allusions to…HAVE I EVER SAID*

*ANYTHING ABOUT YOUR FUNNY OUTLETS?!! That was a dead unfair, below the belt, rotten assed thing to remark on!!! Oh you think you are sooo cool. You think sometimes you laugh at me to yourself and no one is any the wiser, including me. You think you will ooze something in and I'll never even notice, and there you are half choking on your ice cream cone thinking it is your own private, to yourself, insult. Well, I'm not so dumb as you think, even if I am not as old as you. I hear things. I'll get you back for that, Hoot, if it takes me a month. I hope the bottom of your cone breaks and half the ice cream melts and drips in your sneaker. Nooo! Don't try. Don't even try to sweet talk me out of it this time. I declare gonna git you back WAR.    -Gin*

~

Michael, I don't know what Gin is on about, but she is doing a lot of stamping and banging around after your last letter. Now it is too late to write.

V.

10/23/83

My Verge,

Just the other day, perhaps at the time you were writing your letter about communication, I had a serious think to myself about that very subject. I recalled that Saturday afternoon when we were walking in your neighborhood and I got upset. I had to tell you I was upset, but I also had to fight the urge to spare you the upset feeling. It was a battle with the old and new self—one growing and knowing to be open, and the other wanting to play the strong assumer of burdens, the martyr. As a result, only half of what I wanted to say came out, and that sounded way different from the real reason for the upset. Seeing only half of the scene, the distorted half, the only logical reaction you could have was to be upset, too. I saw you being upset, and hating for you to be upset, I clammed up. That solved nothing, because you thought what you suspected was right, and I thought you were upset for the same reason I was, which shouldn't have affected you that way. Rather, you should have understood and sympathized, instead of being upset with me for being upset, only you really didn't know why I was upset. Whew! It was a big ball of confusion and confused feelings all because half was said and half was assumed.

It is truly as you wrote. We should never leave things half said, or unsaid, or assumed between us. We strive to be as visible as possible to each other, but we are individual entities and no matter how hard we try to be open, we have a unique way of seeing, feeling, and interpreting life. The paradox is that although we value our sameness, our separateness is the agent that draws us closer.

I am glad we had the chance to clear up the misconceptions on the way to the airport. It was easy to talk about it then, and it felt so much better afterwards, even if we may have felt a little foolish for having assumed wrong, or for waiting so long to straighten it out. Lessons from our past should have proven that, but growing is not always in a straight line. I'm sure glad we are doing it together, though.

It is amazing, as you said in your letter, how learning to feel is such a surprise, and such a new thing, almost to the point of being silly or alien. I thought I was supposed to know this stuff long ago, or thought that I was immune to feelings, like who needs them? I'm glad you said the growth process feels like regression until it is dealt with. Such clear things are not always so clear until they are pointed out. I wonder why? I share your thoughts about not analyzing The Program. That always gets me off track and I start suffering again.

Hoot wants to get his two cents worth in to Ginny. No matter how I shoo him away he keeps coming back. He has a very intense look about him and says he will only take a minute.

*Gin,*

*I'd say you sure are quick to jump on a guy for nuthin'. All I said was you've got funny outlets. What is so bad about that? You didn't make 'um. They were in your house when you moved in. It's not like funny feet; if you're born with them, there is nothing you can do about it. But if you are so touchy about those dumb old outlets why don't you have someone change 'um? That's no big deal. Anyone who knows anything about electricity can do it.*

*Besides, I was trying to be nice about your outlets. I was tryin' to let you know that sometimes it is nice, or fun, to have funny or different things. Like your crazy feet. I like them. They are yours, and I like you. I wouldn't want you to change them. I want to keep liking you, so will you think again about that all out WAR? But if it must be, it will.*

*–Hoot*

*P.S. I thought that hope about my ice cream cone bottom and dripping in my sneaker was a very, very mean crack.*

~

Geesh, give that kid an inch! Now my time has run out. I just plain, real hard love you.

Michael

October 30, 1983

My Love,

It was such a happy thing, hearing your voice on an afternoon phone call. You sounded downright boyish. I wanted to jump over there, and did mentally, hooking my finger through your belt loop and following you around as you shopped. I made a big nuisance of myself, tripping you up, rolling the oranges down, and covering your eyes so you couldn't see the kind of cereal you were looking for right in front of you. I dragged you into the slowest check out line, although it did look shortest. I thought you needed a little tease.

But why I am writing is not for us. Gin has been in an absolute dissolve of tears and blue funk since her letter from Hoot. Usually she tells me right off what is wrong, but this time she would just burst into tears and walk away when I tried to find out what was bothering her. Finally, I just grabbed her and set her down on my lap and held her. She struggled some, but I just held on and she started to sob. Through the tears she finally said, "I didn't know that's what he meant."

"Who you talking about, Honey Girl?"

"Hoot!" and then more sobs and hysterical carrying on.

"What do you mean, Ginny?"

"When he said I had funny outlets."

"How do you mean?"

"Hoot said I had funny outlets and I thought"...(more heartbroken sobs) "I thought he meant my nose, and my ears, and my mouth, and...

all those other places! All he meant was the things you put plugs in. You know, you call them wall sockets."

I was certainly taken aback by the degree of her passion. She said she was so mad at him especially seeing as how she had let him look at... (Now don't get upset. As I understand it this was pure childish curiosity and an act of innocence between them. Don't you even get into it with Hoot. I know them well enough to know that Ginny would have been the instigator.)...look at all her natural openings. She said that she had told him it was all out war and everything, and now she doesn't know what to do because she says he is going to think she is really dumb not to know what an outlet is and that she started the whole thing just because she was mistaken. She says that if she could just sit on a log beside him, that just the way he is would make it easy for her to explain it, and she wouldn't feel dumb at all. It is just the writing of it part, when she can't see his eyes, or she can't just come up behind him and push him off the log so he will chase her and she can let him win and sit on top of her so she can tell him. Besides, someone might find the letter, then everyone will think she is dumb.

I told her that I am going out to see you, pretty soon, and that she could come and tell Hoot herself, but he sounded pretty worried, so how about if I told Michael and let Michael tell him that there was a misunderstanding. Ginny doesn't want any war. She will explain when she comes out with me. I hope you are following this complicated mess, for I've had quite enough emotion for one week. If I know Hoot, and he is as worried as he sounded, he must have been putting you through the same thing only in his silent way which is even worse 'cuz you don't even know to what depth he is hurting.

Anyway, Ginny agreed. She said that Michael was almost like Hoot when it came to knowing how to say stuff and do stuff that makes you feel good, even when you do dumb things. So it is in your hands. One of these days I'm going to just leave that girl with you for permanent. You do something magic to her. Give Hoot a hug for me, and tell him he is a saint for putting up with Gin.

As for myself, I love you, miss you, want you, and feel like a great big Gin "Now!" is coming on.

Verge

11/3/83

My Verge,

I just have enough time for a brief line to reassure Ginny that she is more than welcome to come along with you and to stay as long as she likes. We have always gotten along just fine. Tell her I said it would be a pleasure and an honor. Her room is all ready from last time.

Your letter explained a lot. Hoot has been doing some strange things lately, like staying in his room more. He brought out all his toy soldiers and tanks and things and lined them up on the table. He would puzzle over them a while, then change them all around, on and on. I thought it was odd.

As soon as I read your letter and discovered just what was going on, I got that boy by the scruff of his neck and gave him a good shake, and settled his dupee down good. In case Ginny is still worried about Hoot and his silly "war", I have set that straight. I chewed him out good for acting his high and mighty technical self. I told him that not everyone refers to those plates in the wall as outlets; some people call them sockets. It's just natural for those folks to assume that outlets are places from which things are let out. I told him to work on being more considerate of others and sent him to his room. (I did wonder what his smirk meant, though.)

The nicotine specter continues to loom larger as time passes. I continue to fight. The circumstances of the past few weeks have not been much aid, though, I'll tell you. I keep remembering what you said about substituting positive thoughts. It helps.

Lately, I have had a run of thinking various ego inflating situations were aimed at me, and I felt all puffed up only to find they were directed toward the guy next to me, or behind. For instance, at the Saturday morning discussion group a young woman at the table was quiet and seemed distressed. After a while, she spoke. I tried to keep the discussion going in her direction to help draw her out. It lasted for a few minutes then died away. After the meeting I stayed at the table in case she needed to talk. She did start to talk, and I just said what came to my head, hoping to help her distress. She kept smiling politely. Finally she ignored me, and struck up a full-blown conversation with the guy next to me, as she had been waiting to do, for they knew each other. She wasn't in the least distressed. I just slunk away. My stock was down again. That was just one of about four similar episodes in the last two weeks.

Michael

11/5/83

My Michael,

I don't understand you and Hoot! You have to be gentle with that boy. He is so dog gone sensitive, if you are harsh with him he'll never come out of his shell. I wasn't going to tell you, but he even cried in front of me once when he was here. He was mowing the lawn and got into a bee's nest. Four of them nailed him before he could get away. Without thinking, he yelled in pain, and when I got to him the tears were just welling up. He tried his manful best to stop them until I explained that the ability to cry is a special blessing God gave us to get rid of built up pain, whether from something physical like then or a hurt in your mind. I told him we are the only animals so blessed as far as I knew, but gorillas seem to grieve enough to cry and maybe you can't see the tears for the fur. Because it is given us for a reason, we should use it when we need to, without embarrassment. It is a lot of hogwash that men shouldn't cry. He looked at me like maybe I was a little crazy, but he stopped being embarrassed. We put ice on the sting and he was quiet and thoughtful for the rest of the afternoon. He went off to read when I told him we'd leave the rest of the lawn until the bees settled down because I was afraid of getting stung.

A few days later he said to me, "You know Gin cries when she gets mad, or else she gets mad if you catch her crying. Did you ever tell her it was all right to just cry?" I had to tell him it was pretty hard for me to tell Gin anything. Her brothers used to tease her and call her crybaby when she cried and other grown-ups told her to stop crying, or they would give her something to cry about, so she wouldn't really believe me that it was a right thing to do. Hoot said, "I don't think anyone ever told Michael that it was all right to cry. Someone should. You can always tell him stuff; maybe you should." I told Hoot that probably you already knew.

Anyway, go easy on that boy. His feelings run deep. I already explained to you that THAT GIRL is without doubt the instigator of all nonsense. She is the one who declared war on Hoot, all over a misunderstanding. I feel ridiculously like starting a parental war with you for treating Hoot in such a shabby manner. Those two kids are going to walk off hand in hand—best friends again—and I'm going to arrive all full of fluff and feathers at you. You better think of something to distract me.

See you soon,
Verge

11/26/83

My Verge,

I wish I could be a mouse, just for Sunday, instead of a ghostie, so I could scurry around and see all the preparing dinner things you do and watch the intense, satisfied look on your face as you skillfully evolve a complicated meal. I am always amazed at how you do it with such apparent ease. Ghosties tend to get themselves involved and interfere with bumps and generally getting in the way. How does it feel to be cooking a festive meal in your own kitchen in your own house? Will you tell me all the interesting stuff about your enigmatic neighbors? I want to hear how it all went from beginning preparations to last good-bye.

Something deep in my core wants to explore the mysteries of our sleep together, as if thought alone will produce the same peace and refreshment the actual act does. I have always resented having to sleep when the people I wish to be with are quick and about. I know you resented sleep when it took precious time away from our personal time and I would feel remorse for succumbing. Sleep was an interloper. It could have become a monster between us if we had not discovered that out bodies communicated on a different level as we slept. When I visited you this fall we both were so ill we were falling asleep over our dinner. Powerless over sleep, we left the dishes on the table and succumbed. We awoke revitalized and discovered we had had nearly identical dreams. It was as though our subconscious had continued to play freely and that we had tapped into some other plane of communication.

Why does it feel so good to watch us travel along that path? Isn't it enough to be like human life always was, and the way all other forms of life seem to be content, to eat, talk, sleep, wake and see, to be on Earth among trees and rocks and animals? Enough to live along as if that is the only element in which living things belong? It is, after all, the only life we experience and can substantiate. Aren't we satisfied with it? Why this special feeling when it looks like something more is happening? Why be driven toward it in such a way that we feel more complete as we approach it? Does it mean that it is so? Does feeling it make it real? These are some of the questions that buzz around me.

I seem plagued by questions. Why does the human animal need to be connected to history and tradition? Why can't he just pass through creatively, without hanging on to the hooks of the past? Why does a human have to share his problems with another? Why can't he just take care of his own stuff? What mechanism is at work that causes sharing to act as a relief valve? What causes something as nebulous as guilt to boil inside and fester if it's not talked about—or anger, or resentment? I'm not trying to dissect our love, but as our sleep experience progresses, I can't help wondering what is going on. Does that ever bother you? Do you have thoughts about it?

Michael

November 24, 1983

My Michael,

On this day of traditional Thanksgiving, I give thanks for you. That is not a small-visioned thanks, for it is a thank you, God, for life, and the will to grow. Thank you for another human being with whom I can discover the beauty and fullness of life.

Today I had turkey dinner with my father, his wife, and her sister. After dinner I went up to my favorite cousin's house. Her mother and father and sister were there dining with her family. We talked, and I sampled little bits of this and that. Later that evening two of my brothers and their wives came over to Dad's for cake and ice cream, a birthday celebration for one of the wives. In other words, I saw all of the family with whom I keep contact, in one day. I have to say I felt more comfortable with them than I have felt in years—relaxed, non-judgmental, uncritical, and unruffled. "Take what you like and leave the rest," "live and let live," and a whole heap more Al-Anon phrases made it all seem peaceable. I could also allow myself to feel their love and respect for me in return for mine. It was an all-time first, as far as I can remember. I still prefer to keep my basic distance, but it felt good for those few hours, to let my barriers down and accept and give. Because I live at a distance, have no part in interfamily strife, and pose no reason for one-upmanship, they can afford to love me for a day, and I can return it without feeling dishonest.

Big jump to Sunday night, 11/27

I felt good all weekend. I had an amicable time up-state with my family. I came home to Milo's letter telling me the marriage was definitely off, but I had already done my heart leaps on that issue and resigned myself to not being able to do anything about it. The Sunday dinner plans went a little awry, as one of the elderly ladies I had invited came down sick and the other one would not leave her. Even that did not shake my good feeling. Elle and I made a fine feast. We had festive flowers. It was a good day.

That is, until I went out of my way to spoil it for myself. The meal was tasty and I had so much extra, my Good Samaritan side just nudged me into trying to share it. I had the mistaken urge to "brighten" Eric's day. I took a meal over to him. He had to work horrendous hours over the Thanksgiving weekend, 16 hours on, eight off, and I felt sorry for the way his employer treats the men like animals. I took it over once, and he was not there, so later, I reheated the whole dinner and took it over again—a true case of not heeding the signposts along the way. That time he was there and he was stiff. He seemed deeply disturbed by something. I left the food and beat a hasty retreat. When I got home I called a mutual friend to see if he knew what was wrong with Eric, if he had lost his job, or what? Friend said he had not seen Eric for a couple of weeks. I no sooner hung up the phone than Eric called. He asked if he could come over for 20 minutes and a cup of coffee. I couldn't find it in me to refuse, so I agreed and then called Elle and the friend, telling them of the situation and asking them to call so I would have outside contact if I needed it.

Eric came. Apparently he had gotten a work assignment confused and traipsed to two separate jobs, finding that it was a wild goose chase and he didn't have to work today, after all. I asked him when he did have to work and he said Sunday from four to twelve. I said that it was Sunday, but he countered that was when he thought he had to work. He then pulled out a sheet of conflicting instructions he had written down that was so confusing I hope he figures it out before the event. He told me about a terrible blackout he had that frightened him. I told him it was caused by alcohol and he said he had hardly had anything to drink. I told him it didn't take much as the disease progressed. He said he was going crazy, and I said that I felt that way until I stopped drinking. Then I told him that he makes me feel very uncomfortable when he is drinking, and I will refuse to see him, ever again, when he is not sober. He said he had vowed never to call me if he had even one drink, but he was so distraught he needed to talk to a human being tonight. I told him I understood, but I would have to refuse hereafter. I asked him to leave then.

He did. He drove around the block and came back to tell me his gas tank was empty and would I give him money for gas. I did. He went to start the car, and it wouldn't start. He fooled around with it for several minutes, until finally I went out and said, "Let's go get some gas." He was sure that wasn't the problem, but I prayed a mighty prayer (for real and honest), that it was. We did; it was; and for one last time I insisted he come in to wash the gas off his hands. I was not emotionally equipped to handle a holocaust on top of everything else. He wanted another coffee, saying he was sober, but I said I wanted him to leave, as I had to get ready for school tomorrow, and I really couldn't handle any more tonight. He accepted and left.

I had called both Elle and friend after he first left, so I had blown my backup, and I had to do a lot of trusting of H. P. when Eric returned. It is futile to pursue the thought, but both had called while he was there, so it was almost as if the alcoholic in him drove him to return after my connection was blown, as if he knew.

Think that was the end? No. After he got home he called me to thank me for seeing him in his desperation, despite his condition. Enough? No. Half an hour later he called and asked me not to do that any more. "What?" says I. Not to bring him food anymore because it hurts too much. I am glad to say, I agreed.

Yikes! I don't learn easily. I have struggled through every step I have taken in this program, fought it every inch of the way. But slowly, slowly, almost despite myself I learn. I know; I deserve a shake. First, I had no business going over there. Second, I just have to realize that his desperate reaching out is the disease reaching out. I have to harden my heart to it. If he is going to kill himself or whatever, there is nothing I can do to stop him. I am powerless. I must leave God's business to God and stop trying to save that man. Without a doubt, this incident will be eradicated from his brain from beginning to end by tomorrow, and I only hurt myself by playing head doctor.

Poor Love, I bet you thought you were through with this kind of letter. Me, too! Please hold my hand one more time, and tell me one more time, that I will learn. Michael, tonight I crave the peace that only you know how to give me. Your quiet acceptance of this human who makes foolish mistakes, and your love without reproach is what I would ask for at this moment.

Verge

12/1/83

My Verge,

I liked your Thanksgiving thanks giving. I feel touched to be included in your life like that. It sounds like you did a lot of pigging out over the weekend. Once your elderly neighbors find out what they missed, they will never get over having so carelessly gotten sick. I wish I could have gone to all the places with you; tasting the foods and watching you interact with family and friends.

I know how those slips in behavior feel. The more you learn; the more you are sure you know; the harder it hurts—a deep thud hurt that makes you wish it had never happened and you could just disappear. I'm holding your hand tight. Nobody said we would ever be perfect; all we have to do is work on it.

It has been about a month now since I answered Eric's letter asking me to come and get him, and drive him back to Julie's place in Cleveland. I've had no response. Of course, as sporadic as our writing has been, that doesn't mean anything. When I wrote, that his company threatens my sobriety as long as he is drinking, but he would be in my prayers and I would do what I could to help him if he wants to quit; I could just see him balling up the paper and hurling it into the wastebasket, as only Eric can (after he got Julie's address, of course). If that is true, it is just as well. I figured by saying what I did, he would either answer, leaving room for information flow, or give up on me all together. I didn't think he would ignore it and talk around it, but who knows? "One day at a time," they tell me.

Hey, Verge, can you straighten me out? Does Ginny still believe in Santa Claus, or is she putting me on? I had an experience with her today that left me wondering if I had done the right thing, I wouldn't want to mess the kid up or anything. I had to go to the mall on an errand for my mother and Ginny was tagging along. I didn't mind because she is good company, even when I am in a hurry. She just kinda trots alongside making fun comments about stuff. She makes me grin a lot. Anyhow, I cut through from one section to another and, behold, Santa's domain!

Gin began pulling on my sleeve coaxing to see Santa. I was hurrying along and she kept tugging, "Please, can we see Santa?"

I was all set to say, "Come on Gin, you don't believe in that stuff, do you?" Although I had the feeling she was making fun, I bit my tongue for I couldn't be sure. After we stood and watched for a few minutes, I told her that we had to hurry today, but we would come back another day. Now, is she serious or not?

The mall is decorated for the holidays. I am usually not impressed by the commercial splash the establishments make in an attempt to put one in a spending mood, but this year everything looks lavish, and festive, and fun. Poinsettias abound and I couldn't be blasé. Gin and I walked slowly away. We must have looked special, because strangers nodded and said hello

Michael

12/2/83

My Michael,

As a continuation of the Eric chronicle, that same night, the phone rang at midnight, waking me. I ran to the phone with joy, thinking you must have worked, after all, that night, but it was Eric. I told him in no uncertain terms that I did not appreciate being awakened by a phone call at that hour of the night. As his question was about Milo, I also told him he would have to keep his own communication with his son and hung up.

The next morning as I was rushing around the house getting ready to go to work, comes tap, tap on door. It was a contrite, sober (I use that term loosely) Eric with a ten-pound letter of apology. Sigh! Lord, deliver me from that tortured existence.

When we were last together, you talked about how, early on, your love and my love was so mixed up with our love for Eric, that we could not really separate ourselves from it. I believe that is true. I thought of myself as loving you both equally, as if you were one person. To me, you balanced each other. Like the moon—you were the light side and Eric was the dark side. I'm not sure when that balance changed, but I believe it was long before I was aware of it. The last time I tried to make it so was that hot, hot night after you rode back to New York from Cleveland with me, and the three of us were celebrating being together, out on the dock under the stars. I said, "Oh, I love you both so much!" I knew I had lied the minute it was out of my mouth, and I hated the lie.

I remember the last time I was sure I loved you both equally. It was the night of the aurora borealis. We three were lying on the same dock, drinking, watching the unusual eerie lights streaking in the sky and mirrored in the lake. Doreen was too tired to wake up, but later Milo came home and joined us. I was content that if it were the end of the world, I was with the only people I would want to be with. Somewhere between those two times the balance was toppled permanently, and I became aware that you had been the most important light in my life for a long time.

I loved Eric like a god—an obsession. He was all-powerful, and without him I would blow away like a dust kitten. It was as if he animated me. I always felt that I could never think of anything intelligent enough to interest him. Yet all along I was talking with you, and you never seemed to want me to stop and always treated me as if I was smart.

We discussed loneliness at last night's meeting. Thinking about it, I realized that the worst loneliness I've ever experienced was when I really did not know what was wrong with Eric. I would sit for hours listening to him talking and talking, and I couldn't make any perceivable sense out of what he was saying; yet he obviously thought he was being very erudite and witty. Friends who still came around for drinks appeared to hang on his every word, as they always had when he was holding court. By sheer force of his convictions I would wonder if he were making sense and my mind was scrambling it up. That was lonely. Now I am seldom lonely. I walk, talk, joke, and live with your presence in my life. That's not lonely.

You ask me questions about Gin as if you thought I understood her better than you do. Often I speculate, but I seldom understand her for sure. You say she wanted to see Santa. Sometimes she gets very stubborn about growing up, as if it is all too much for her and she would rather hang on to childish notions. She has all sorts of magic formulas for getting through a day; counting her age a certain number of times makes expected events happen more quickly, kicking something three times will make it work, saying the alphabet backwards on D the toast will pop up, walking backwards to the barn will keep the old rooster from attacking, and nothing bad will happen if she keeps repeating, "Dear God in Heaven" when she is doing something that scares her. There are so many of them, even she can't keep track. She is forever daydreaming, and sometimes seems all caught up in her fantasy world.

When she plays alone she is forever talking to some one or another of her mental creations. She talks right out loud, and if you ask to whom she is speaking, she will seem surprised, or even annoyed, that a "real" person is intruding. So, if she asked to speak to Santa she may be trying to be little again, or it may have suited her fantasy, or she may just have been joking.

Apparently you handled the situation to her satisfaction, for if you had responded wrong for her frame of mind, she would have let you know instantly how you hurt her feelings. No one gets more crushed than that sensitive little brat. She is a confusing mix of brassy boldness and sensitive vulnerability. The contrasts are so sharp that if you are seeing the one quality and the other shows up, you feel like one child has been whisked away and a changeling has appeared. I told you I was tired of trying to handle her, so I left her with you. She adores you, so it is a nice vacation for both of us. She does make her whimsical little visits every once in a while, just to keep me in line, and then goes skipping off to you. She tells me, "Michael gets lonely so I have to keep him company. Hoot's busy growing up and sometimes Michael needs someone to make him laugh." I think she cares about you, in her way, as much as I do.

God knows, I wish I could go skipping off to you and trot along holding your hand and even say something silly like, "Let's go see Santa." Not that I feel a need for Santa in my life. Real is the best thing invented.

Verge

12/12/83

My Darling Verge,

Thanks for the insight you gave me about Ginny, but it was sparse indeed for someone so close. I think you treat her too harshly. I spoke with her about some of the things you said. We had a very nice talk. She got me to try the backwards alphabet on the toast and sure enough, it did pop up on D once and another time on B. It was a surprising feat. She hasn't kicked one thing since she has been here, and she says the people she talks to are real. She even introduced me to them, at least the ones for that day. They seemed pleasant enough even though I couldn't see them. They didn't mind being intruded upon, in the least, as long as I didn't startle them. She explained very nicely that sometimes she is cross or changeable because her braids are too tight or she knows her hair is snarled and the next time someone tries to comb it, there will be pulling and yanking, making her yell. I know how she hates that. We didn't touch on walking backwards so the rooster wouldn't attack. Something told me to leave it alone. She was getting fire in her eyes and I had the feeling she would take off on that subject and show me peck marks and all. I just wasn't in the mood for that.

She said she likes to visit Santa one time during the season. Once is enough. She said she doesn't ask him for anything, just asks about how he is and chats in general. She says she isn't sure about him and doesn't want to take any chances. This way he knows she is still around and being straight, and well, you know... "'n everything."

Ginny and Hoot are getting along famously. That halfway misunderstanding they had is long forgotten. It seems with those two, once they get together nothing else matters. The last I saw of them today, they were going off down the street toward the zoo, each pulling a sled. Hoot said he was going to show her a neat coasting hill. As they went off I heard them bantering back and forth about who had enough guts to go all the way down from the top. Ginny hadn't even seen the hill yet, but she was right in Hoot's face telling him how ain't no hill ever got her to back off. Hoot had that funny grin on which indicated he was gonna get all he could from that tease.

So off they went. I couldn't help watching them for a while as they moved on down the street, alternately nudging each other, and running from each other, laughing. Those kids perk up my spirits at the times when I seem to need it most. They are pretty heavy with excitement, as Christmas gets closer. I have to admit it is infectious. I guess I will go make some cocoa.

Michael

12/13/83

My Michael,

I have been trying for days to get a pat answer to your letter of questions written at Thanksgiving time. First of all, let me jump to say that I am content to walk along holding your hand, feeling the sun and breezes, and tasting good tastes with you. At this point we could exist on that plane of life very happily because we have built a background of specific trust and communication. If those elements were removed, perhaps we still could, although we know from the experiencing of it that each thing we add of our minds, expanded by introspection, books, and learning from others, makes a simple smile or a held hand all the more beautiful. The more body of comparisons we have, the more we can be certain that a particular taste is really special, or a particular person is the right one for us. The greater the body of knowledge shared, the greater variety of choice we have to make simple pleasures new and fresh. If we lived strictly on the plane of the immediate senses, it would neither matter what we ate as long as the food was nourishing, where we lived as long as we were sheltered, nor who our partners were.

As far as saying the only thing we can substantiate is the element in which we live, we can't even substantiate that. Our senses blatantly lie to us. Seeing, for instance. We never question the fact that a tree seen on a distant hill looks perhaps a quarter of an inch tall, yet when we drive by, it may be 70 feet tall. If our heads can allow that to be taken for granted, where else in our daily living, on how many levels, do we adjust our heads to our fraudulent senses? At every turn science and technology tell us that all is not as it seems. The teacher who ridiculed me in front of my second-grade class for saying that animals talk, would have been livid if I had said that plants communicate, too. What if I had said that by the time I was grown up there would be a real man on the moon?

Without allowing one's mind to accept more than what exists in its world of the moment, dreams, fantasy, free flowing thoughts, man would not progress further than any of the other primates. He would plod (perhaps more happily) out his cycle, and neither conceive of, nor have a use for, philosophy, or progress, or future.

I do not find our special levels of communication spooky or magical. I believe there are existing things that our senses are not honed acutely enough to perceive. Just as we know there are tones of sound too low or too high for man to hear, I believe there are other dimensions of all the stimuli of our senses. We have discovered to our satisfaction that we can communicate in extraordinary ways. The Russians are training people to develop their ESP for use in warfare (what else?). Scientists have proven trees communicate chemically to other trees about the presence of hoards of insects. I choose to believe we communicate on an extraordinary level that is not generally recognized, due to the intensity of a relationship needed to achieve it. Now aren't you glad you made such a chance remark? Do you have any other life-long questions I can answer for you?

Perhaps you missed the kids today. I borrowed them and took them shopping with me. Hoot was acting grown up and subdued—his idea of sophistication—wanting to escort both of us. Gin was trying her damnedest to bring him back to her level. She was bouncing around in the back seat, punching his arm, and making up goofy presents she was going to buy him. He kept saying, "Gin, stop it! Gin, sit down and stop jumping around. How can Verge drive with you carrying on?"

When I got to the mall, if the kids hadn't been with me I would have fled, for the crush of humanity was almost more than my nerves could handle. However, after we got inside and Gin started singing off key to the Christmas carols—albeit earnestly and with gusto—and even Hoot dropped his cool and forgot that he already had planned most of what he wanted, they got me in the mood and I started to enjoy myself.

Gin got her eye on something and dragged me along by my hand saying, "You want to do it NOW!" Before I quite knew what was happening, she had bought me a pair of onyx posts and a free ear piercing that went with it (she said it was her present). I hesitated, mentally feeling my intact ears for the last time. Did I really want holes where I had none thus far in my life? The nurse lady laughed at me when I asked if the holes would go away if I decided afterwards I didn't like them. She said they would grow together if I did not keep posts in them. The nurse also told me that she had pierced an 80-year-old lady's ears that very morning because the lady complained that she couldn't find any pretty clip-on earrings anymore that didn't pinch her ears. I could hear Gin giggling to Hoot, saying something about, "At 80, she should be so lucky." I chose to ignore them as they poked fun at my wincing when the posts were stapled through my ears, making faces behind the nurse's back. There was a pinch and a sting. The posts have to be left in place for four to six weeks until my ears are healed. Still feeling a little unsure, I asked the kids, "What if Michael doesn't like them?"

Hoot jumped right in with, "Oh, Michael will like them. He likes anything you do. He'd like you even if you didn't have anything on." He realized too late he had gone too far in reassuring me, and Gin gave him a big nudge. Gin is always subtle. Hoot blushed to the roots of his hair. "But, I didn't mean it that way—just that he likes you an awful lot and you don't have to do anything special to make him like you."

When we got home, I gave Gin a kiss and Hoot a hug and sent them back to get you through the rest of the day. I trust they found you.

Verge

12/15/83

My Sweet Verge,

I have just reread your answers to my wondering questions. I had to pause a few times like a teenager who is smitten for the first time, and sigh a deep sigh. "Here," I had to say to myself, "is another reason why I love this woman. She talks to me like I am a grown up human being, straight across, human-to-human, with mutual respect understood. No frills, just talkin' to me what her head says." It was nothing that wasn't already in my head in bits and pieces, but the way you say things pulls them together for me and gets me to see them fresh and say, "Oh yeah, it makes sense that way." All the while you are letting me know it is cold out there for everybody, that we are no exception, except we have got each other to hold on to as we sail, and search, and hope.

I have become increasingly aware in the last six months of a sharpening of perceptions and feelings. Remember last summer and fall how I remarked on the vividness of flower and leaf colors? I also notice, especially with the holiday and its deckings, a greater appreciation of the festivity and good will. I am even forced to admit to flashes of a kid-like feeling as the holiday approaches. There is never a second when you are not with me in spirit.

I finally got a response from Eric. About my saying he is in my prayers, he said he would rather be in my car. His letter made me feel sad and a jumble of other feelings, but to keep to maximum honesty, I confess there was a certain feeling of relief mixed in. Maybe I am anxious to end the relationship. The adult way would be to tell him that, but I have not reached that level of maturity. Sometimes growing up looks like an endless, futile battle with the old one step ahead, two back.

Michael

12/31/83

My Michael Man,

Thank you for calling last night. From the depth of my innards I desperately needed to hear your voice. Today I can hardly move from the cruel hurt of being torn away from you. Will I never get used to parting? All that I said on the phone about gotta live this day and get out of it all I can...yes, well, BUT...as Gin would say, if I weren't holding my hand over her mouth, "It's like toast without butter, and definitely NO JAM!"

As you know, Eric picked me up from the bus and gracefully left me at my doorstep. But then he called me at 4:30 AM saying there was no heat in his room and could he spend a couple of hours at my house as he was freezing. He said he was stone sober. Man or beast, what could one do with such a request? So he came over.

Upon interrogation, I found out he had not notified the person who runs the motel. He said he thought nothing would be done until morning, anyway, and there was only one other person in the unit. I told him he had rights as a tenant, and if it was a problem with just his wing, they should put him up in some other warm room for the night. I also asked about a space heater he said he had borrowed at another time. He said he was afraid if he ran it the electricity would go off and he would be blamed. This conversation was conducted through the bathroom door, while he was fixing a cut he said he got on his car door because it was so cold. I was furious that some motel owner was peacefully sleeping in his bed, while I had been so rudely awakened from my own for his problem, and I told Eric so. He got pissed at that and left. I have to view this as a situation of my own making. Got a problem? Verge will fix it. I do feel awfully sorry for the man, but I can't keep getting in the way of letting him solve his own problems. It seems every time I act a little human toward him, he jumps in with both feet demanding more.

This morning the wind was down and the sun was out, so to get out of my lethargy I took a walk on the ice over to our swamp haunts. To my private self I said, "Oh, Michael would really love looking through this black ice and seeing the duck weed flow with the stream underneath our feet." As I passed an uprooted tree I thought, "Michael would turn to me just here, with all that laughing love in his eyes and kiss me in the shelter of the root system towering over our heads." And watching the stately Hudson River iceboats skimming along the ice, I thought if you were here, you surely would make friends with one of the owners and hitch us a ride down the lake.

This newsy stuff is just to avoid telling you my heart is all over an ache. Wrap your arms around your body and give yourself a real tight squeeze, 'cuz that is me hugging you all over.

Verge

P.S. Gin has a note for Hoot.

Dear Hoot,

Thanks for the ribbons, the barrettes, and the comb. They are awfully pretty. You must have felt real dumb buying them. You did it anyway. I hope nobody saw you or laughed or anything.

Your best friend, *
Ginny

P.S. I wore the barrettes today.
P.P.S. *You said not to write about I love you in writing in case somebody saw it, even if I do, and I do, so did you notice I didn't write it?
P.P.P.S. That is a funny looking comb. Is it for my horse? Ha, ha, ha!

1/5/84

Dear Verge,

Now the hoopla is all over. The only thing that makes me sad is that my Verge had to go away. It was lots of fun getting ready for you and as usual the reality far outclassed the anticipation. I love the way you think about picking out gifts.

My mother has had several episodes recently and her nurse says she thinks she has to bow out. She thinks Grammy should not be left alone, that she should be in a nursing home. My brother did not turn in an application to the home because he said he wasn't sure how I felt about it. It will take months after it is turned in to get space. I am not sure how things will proceed, but I am valiantly taking them one day at a time. I hate to see anyone confined to one of those places, especially one so active and self-sufficient, but her dizziness and confusion and wobbly legs indicate that some steps should be taken.

I got your letter last night, and I have a message for Ginny from Hoot if you will relay it to her. I told him to send his own message, but you can physically sit that boy down, actually put a pen in his hand and he will still sit there for hours daydreaming—anything to put off the transferring of thought (if any) to paper. Worse than an old never-start car I once had. Kick it. Cuss it. Push it. Wouldn't start until it was ready and then it was begrudgingly. The effort required to get anything out of that lad makes me wonder if he is retarded, or if there is nothing in his head to begin with. Sooo, in the interest of communication, I'm sending Ginny his message, whatever it means, verbatim:

Gin,

Whadaya mean you ain't gonna tell me about that I love you stuff in writing? YOU JUST DID! You wrote, I love you, and then you said you didn't write it. PS's are the same as writing! It's down on paper where everyone can see it. Why don't you just stand on the street corner and holler it out so everyone can hear it. You did too write it!

Hoot

I don't even pretend to understand all that. If anyone qualifies for duncedom, it is that boy, I swear. As if that silliness wasn't enough, he acted all steamed up, although I could tell he wasn't really steamed up. He took the very same letter that precipitated his outburst, read it again, and started laughing and burbled something about the lady in the hair shop told him that comb was good for snarled up ponytails, but he didn't think she meant for real. "That Gin is a side-splitter...for her horse? Ha, ha, ha." He kept laughing his ass off, and then as he left the room, he said something as if I weren't even there, "I love her, too." And Verge, I love you, too.

Michael

1/7/84

My Sweet Michael Man,

I adore the way we give gifts to each other. I am glad to be part of the impetus for you to discover the imaginative act of gift giving—caring about someone, picking through your recollections of the person, finding something that is a statement to the person that she is visible to you, then watching the person be delighted with your choice. At every turn I find an imaginative you waiting to be tapped, encouraged, and appreciated. It is as if, one day long ago, you decided to dam your creativity in a secret place, perhaps because of someone's callous response, or maybe out of spite, when you decided your tender imaginings were too good for the cold world. Probably much of it is in direct proportion to your drinking, or so I have come to recognize from my own self-searching. You have taken every means of expression we have explored in the last few years and run with it as though the floodgates opened and you flowed out. It is exciting to watch.

That is what I was trying to tell you about my observation of you at home with your own family. I have come to know you as a person released, with a variety of ways of expressing yourself, physically, emotionally, and verbally. In the last year I have mostly seen you alone. It came as a shock that the unrestrained, boyish, happy person I know is not necessarily the person other people know. The only other time I have known you to be so somber was that first, non-drinking visit when you came with Doreen, and the three of us were adjusting to life bereft of liquor. We all were terribly sensitive and ill at ease. Eric was making everyone jumpy by constantly egging us on to drink with him and it was the most peculiarly disjointed time I have ever had with you. Since that major hurdle, between us, your spirit has been on the soar, going higher up and further out, soul diving and star swinging. I had almost forgotten your shell, and was bewildered to see it so intact.

I know I still have mine kicking around, too, and that it comes down like thunder when I am in Eric's presence. I'm slowly learning to keep it off for longer periods of time, in direst proportion to not having to deal with him. I like our selves with us a lot more than our selves for the world to see.

Verge

1/12/84

My Verge,

I marvel at the fact we can still be shy with each other at times. Not that being shy is any accomplishment, I have been enough of that throughout my life, but after all this time of knowing each other and learning about each other, we have not nearly reached a stage where we take each other for granted. Whether we are shy because we are uncertain about a situation, as you indicated on the phone, or because we have found a new something about ourselves, or just because that is the way we feel at the moment, doesn't matter. The beauty is that we are fresh enough, have stars in our eyes enough, respect each other enough to occasionally be shy in the face of it all.

It is not uncommon, in fact I think it is the rule, for people to take each other for granted, or take advantage of each other, or even harm each other, once they get any amount of intimacy between them. Feel shy about something? Unheard of. I even believe some people get pleasure from the hurts intimacy can inflict, if not treated gently—both from hurting the other and being hurt. It makes me feel good that we can still be shy with each other.

My shell—I had to pause before I wrote that, just as I had to hesitate when early on in The Program I first said, "I am an alcoholic." My head said it a lot, but saying it aloud was a different story, and not easy. It felt funny to write, 'my shell'. I understand what you mean when you say you were shocked to see the shell so very much intact. I was shocked to see it in print, or out in the open, myself. It is not that I didn't know it was still there. I just didn't pay any attention to it. Joy and exhilaration reside where the pain of having isolated or cut myself off should be. I understand your shock, because of how I would feel a stranger when you put yours on with Eric. I would know what was going on, but you would be so different from who you really are, that although necessary, it was chilling.

When I think about it, I find myself feeling pity for those being cut off. I don't feel indifference toward them, for they mean a lot to me, but I feel like they are way back there, or down they're someplace. I can't reach them and I don't care because the beauty and joy is too great where I am. Somehow it doesn't sound too healthy, but my state of mind is too joyous to pay attention. I know I don't have a very good handle on this, yet. I need your feedback. The way we are, there doesn't have to be a right or wrong; just talk. As we talk without judgment or conclusion, things slowly unravel. When I am tentative and afraid, I am still able to talk openly with you.

Michael

1/12/84

Dear Michael,

You really went and did it this time. When I read the letter you sent with the message for Ginny about Hoot, I was plenty upset with you for all the bad-mouthing you did about the boy. There is nothing wrong with being a dreamer, and you know dog gone well that he is neither retarded nor empty of thought. Whatever possesses you to say such things of him?

Well, if you think I was upset, Ginny got all excited when I read her the message from Hoot, and she just snatched the letter out of my hands, starting to race through the first part to get to the part about Hoot. I tried to keep her from it, but she was too quick for me. You could see her hair just bristling, "Why did he say that? Why did Michael say that about Hoot?" By the time she got to the part about retarded, her face got all red and great big tears rolled down and plopped on her shoes and there was fire coming out of her ears. "That's not true! That's not EVEN TRUE!"

It was as if you had betrayed her or something. I had to get down on my knees and give her a hug and say, "Michael didn't really mean it. He just worries about Hoot and all the hurts he is going to get because he doesn't act like other kids. We all know that is what makes him special to us, but it is going to make him hurt a whole lot out there in the world. Michael knows that, and he can't make Hoot be any different, so he sometimes says hard things to cover up how he feels. Maybe you could write Michael a letter telling him you understand why he says what he does, but it hurts you and ask him not to, because Hoot is very special to all of us. He probably won't be able to stop instantly, but maybe eventually he will realize that Hoot has to hurt a lot to become the beautiful, loving, caring person who is Michael."

I wish I were a gambling person for I would have a heyday with a dream I had last night. When I awoke, I was desperately trying to hold on to a poem I dreamt. Although I feel there was more to it that faded before I could write it down, here it is:

Men there are, born to thrive.
Then there are the thirty-five,
Men there are, born to die.
Born to marry.
One there is who will not die.
One there is who will thrive.
One there is who I
Will marry.

Profound it is not, but curious in that I never remember dreaming a poem. I have dreamt paintings, and pieces of music, and that I was writing, but never before the words I had put down.

It snowed last night, and at 7:30 this morning, Mr. Mowing Man came up with his little tractor, now with a snowplow attached, and cleared the snow in front of my garage and up the walk to my door. Actually I had rather looked forward to the little exercise shoveling would have afforded me, but I graciously accepted his gesture.

This morning I took my car to the garage for a 30,000-mile check and after I stopped with Elle for breakfast, she brought me back home. I had fourty-lebbenty things I wanted to get done today. When I got home I read the paper, got into a book, and the day petered away. Before I knew it, it was time to get my car, cook dinner, and go to a meeting. I hope I am going through a temporary state. I seem to have no energy to do anything constructive, just dream and fritter away my time. It is getting to be a bad habit. Although I don't feel depressed, it smacks of depression, and I don't think it is healthy to continue on this way. I need some sort of exercise program to get my energy level back up. As they used to say in my childhood, "I'm waiting for the spirit to move me." It better be soon or I will turn into a blob of protoplasm. Ugh!

I can feel my head trying to worry about my work situation, and I am not getting any answers. I was just beginning to cope with the classroom stress, and feel better about it, but now, in the interest of looking good, the new program director is beginning to shake up the department. I am not saying the department doesn't need revitalization; I would doubtless do the same thing. I just don't know if I am mentally at a point where I can cope with it. I have to get out of this junior high position, one way or another. I am doing my job adequately, but I am not over excelling, shall we say, and I had hoped to slide quietly through the rest of the year this way. Now there is pressure to excel, if I want to move to the high school. The program tells me to turn it over. I know I am projecting, but I can see the predictability of the situation.

Love,
Verge

1/14/84

Dear Verge,

I apologize to you and Ginny for my ill treatment of Hoot. Please tell Ginny that the things you said to her, when she was crying, were true; I would have explained my behavior in the very same way. Often we become so concerned for a loved one that we forget their feelings and those of others who cherish them. Thoughtlessly we lash out, when our only intent is to protect and guide. We end up bruising the dignity of the party, and of those who are a part of him/her. I am sorry, and I have told Hoot so. In the future I will show restraint when my concern overcomes me.

I did like the way that incident brought you and Ginny together. I was touched by the picture of you on your knees hugging and explaining to her. That made me smile and feel warm. You know you haven't been all peaches and ice cream with Ginny, either. Maybe we will both learn something, eventually. Did she really stomp around with that hen scurrying in the dust at her feet? I wish I could see that.

Just one more word about this shell I carry around. I guess most people have one in case of emergency. As I roam this world currently, I find that I am able to set it aside with more ease. The big "us" seems to give me new confidence and support. Unfortunately, I find it still necessary at home. I am tempted to say many of the reasons lie with the others. In fact, I was going to say that, but brought myself up short, when I heard how it sounded, and considered the possibilities and the logic. Part of it is true. Things that work for me "outside" throw Doreen and the girls into confusion, or at least create an air of misunderstanding and then non-communication. For some reason that makes me feel dumb, and I hasten to throw on the shell. Sometimes I leave it on for days at a time—without washing it or anything. Geesh, folks run!

I think much of that is a result of me turning in on me. I know down in me I harbor a lot of guilt and self-pity stemming from the past. People can pooh, pooh it and say, "Oh, there is nothing so bad you should feel guilty about, as far as your family goes. You weren't that bad." Often, I am taken in by that, because it is easier on me and I can cozy into it. If I am real with myself, I know better. It is apparent that I am ready to do the Fourth[10] and Fifth Step,[11] if for no other reason than to be rid of all the guilt and self-pity. Maybe that will make me feel better and then I can grow some more. I'm not suggesting that it will solve all the problems and feelings, but I'll feel better for having tried to solve them. Sounds good. Now, to do it...gulp!

I also have experienced dreaming that I am watching myself writing, or composing, or choreographing, and saying to myself, "Holy Cow! (Exact words—learned them in Boy Scouts.) I didn't know I could do that." It is a very weird feeling. Then, I would watch or listen very intently. The words would be going on the paper, the dance would be flowing, or the music would be swelling, and I would think, "I'm pretty good at this. I

---

10 Alcoholics Anonymous Step Four: "Made a searching and fearless inventory of ourselves." Ibid., 42.

11 Alcoholics Anonymous Step Five: "Admitted to ourselves, and to another human being the exact nature of our wrongs." Ibid., 55.

must remember how it goes, so when I wake up I can jot it down." When I awoke it would all fade away so fast I could never remember more than what I just told you. The fact that you remembered the actual words long enough to get them down is fantastic. A message directly sent from your subconscious. What cryptic, symbolic meaning is hidden there?

Michael

1/17/84

Michael, My Love,

I have just read the second installment of your response to the "shell" letter. I awaited an answer with some trepidation, wondering if I had offended you, gone too far, misread what I saw. I am glad you were able to think on it.

"Hi Hoot." That was Gin passing through. I guess you were right that I ride a hard hand on that girl, too. She is such a spoiled brat that I am afraid to encourage her ways. She can be an awful lot of fun and often I can feel sympathetic toward her, but she just can't expect to have her own way in life, especially when she wants everything NOW! At very least you have to learn to dissemble about both of those desires, and hopefully you mature to where you accept that things happen in their time and in their way, and not at your command. I despair that she will ever grasp that idea, even though I try my best to get her to see the light.

Your interpretation of shyness and what it means to our relationship is something I hadn't thought about, but I have to agree; in that perspective it is an exciting element. Sometimes I feel like a first time lover, eager to find out about you, to find where we fit and where we disagree. When I feel that way, I privately have to laugh at myself and say, "You have known this man for 24 years and at least 14 of them intimately; how can you feel this way?" It is no secret between us that we have invited each other into our deepest depths. We have done away with masks, false modesty and pretense, revealing to each other the self we are when we are alone. The more open we are, the more apparent it becomes that we can never be satiated.

I think hurting with, and being hurt by the vulnerability of intimacy that you talk of, comes when one is dominated by a stronger personality, or is sickly dependent. The rare part of our relationship is that we have always envisioned ourselves as equals. The differences we do have only enrich our body of experience. We each have areas in which we are more skilled, but the other is glad to stand by and cheer or help if it is in order. We are never in competition. Intimacy has never been a point of power between us.

Verge

1/21/84

My Sweet Verge,

Since we have let our love out of its cage to fly, I am hard pressed to think of anything in life that bores me. You talked about how we grow together, never in a way to consciously accommodate the other's changes, but the natural course has led us both in the same direction and at about the same rate.

One of the changes in communication has been between Hoot and Ginny. It seemed important at first to relate adventures between them in a suspended time and space. On its own, their intricate relationship grew. They learned and we learned. We grew to know, like, and love each other in different and deeper ways. Then, without a signal, the stories faded away and the communication continues in a more direct way between them and between us adults. It is as if they are slowly being incorporated into a whole, being more and more grown up, and more us. What made the child, no longer stands alone, but is now part of the adult in a congruent way. In retrospect, it is fun to see that evolution. It is amazing, the way it happened to us in the same flow as if on its own without adult interference.

I enjoy thinking of Hoot and Gin walking through the woods together. If they run into an obstacle, one or the other will give a leg up, or crossing a brook, will reach out a hand to help jump to a stone. They do it without thinking, an act as natural as scratching.

Michael

2/5/84

Dear Michael,

Today, during lunch-break, I got a call at school from an official asking if I would put up bond to release my husband from the county jail in Goshen. Eric was picked up last night for driving while intoxicated. Al-Anon preparation spoke in my ear saying, "Natural consequences are the best medicine for denial. Do not try to keep the alcoholic from his consequences." I found myself saying that we were separated, and I was not legally responsible for him. I said I was at work, and I could not pick him up. The official sounded peeved at me, but I ended the conversation. Of course everyone in the teacher's lounge looked curious, but I just walked out without explanation.

I just talked to you on the phone. Thank you for telling me what I needed to hear, program stuff, heart stuff. Thanks for not judging me about not being able to leave Eric there, as you pointed out Al-Anon would probably suggest. Tomorrow I will call, agree to put up bail, and bring him back to Newburgh. No busses run from there, and he surely cannot afford a taxi.

There is a biological theory that people have a predictably cyclical ebb and flow of energy. If that is true I must be on the upward swing of my cycle. I told you a while ago how lethargic I felt. I gave myself one month before I would begin to worry. Either I scared myself, or the theory is correct, because since you were here I want to go out and get both feet into the world up to my elbows. I have just applied to that alcoholism-counseling course I told you about, held on Thursday nights and Saturdays, and I am thinking of enrolling in an in-service computer course held for two hours after school on Wednesday afternoons. (My justification for that being the more skills I have, the more marketable I might be.) With those, my Tuesday home-teaching job, my regular job, and my AA and Al-Anon meetings, my week is sewn up. Also, I have been asked to hostess one day in May, at an Al-Anon convention at Terrytown. How is that for lethargy?

Come snug with me,
Verge

2/7/84

My Verge,

The "kick in the stomach" came a little late this time, sort of a delayed reaction. My daughter and her boyfriend picked me up at the airport, and we got home to the usual busy stuff: the grandbaby with a cold, car covered with snow, Doreen home, and so forth. It wasn't until I awoke to go to work that I felt that hollow, thud-like feeling. How could I be so exquisitely happy and complete, and in a wink whisked away into another world?

You said several times that you liked the way I just naturally fit into a new situation, without seeming to exert any effort. That is curious, because all through my life I have had a hard time feeling I fit into much of any situation. Just below the surface I always had an edgy, unsure feeling, even with Eric, with myself, or with family. I got pretty good at making it look like I was cool, so as not to draw attention to myself. Attention meant I had to perform, and performing meant potential failure. (Stage performance was different, because I could hide behind the character. All I had to do was prepare to be acceptable in the part so no one would pay too much attention to me. Mediocrity allowed me the fun and the fringe glamour of the theatre without the attention and responsibility.) Having lived with that tension through most of my life, it became second nature. But give a person one breath of relief from that feeling, then put him/her back in the tension machine and it changes everything.

That is what happened to me when you opened the door at Eric's apartment, all those years ago. As we talked and got acquainted I had the first time ever feeling of weight lifted from my body, our very first "click". I felt safe with you. Since then, being with you has always been an easy, fall in with things time for me. If I have a glimpse of you, or feel your presence, I get that belonging feeling. You said there are no secrets from me in your house. I have been thinking about that ever since. For some reason that seemed so strange, yet something we always knew. It took on a therapeutic dimension, as if saying that your life has no secrets, set you free. Your saying that made me able to begin a search of the closets and hiding places in my life.

Of necessity, both of us kept secret places in our lives from those we live with. Those places were partly for refuge and defense, and partly to build our ego by retaining an unshared self. The thought of letting someone in seemed the antithesis of freedom. The miracle is that we found letting each other in was freedom. How right it feels.

Hoot is pretty excited about seeing you both soon. He is very anxious about a possible surprise he has for Gin. I have to watch him, because he will be crushed if it doesn't work out. He made me promise not to tell; in fact, he was a little upset with me for the hint I gave her. Just tell Gin to wait.

Michael

2/11/84

Dear Michael,

The next time Hoot has a secret, I hope you keep all the clues to yourself. Gin said she isn't going to go to Cleveland, 'cuz Hoot is going to laugh at her for not guessing. I told her of course she is going; look at all those cookies she baked for him. She said, "I'm going to eat them all up, myself, and then he will be sorry!" I said that I was going out to see you, and if she didn't come along, she never would know what the surprise was, that Hoot was only keeping a secret because it might not happen.

Later, I heard her talking to her chicken out on the porch. She was saying something like; "I guess I'll have to tell you all my secrets from now on, Chicken. Just wait, you and me will get us a big, FAT secret and not tell Hoot, and see how he likes that. You don't eat cookies, do you? I guess I will just have to take 'em to him after all, or they'll all go to waste." She wandered away grumbling a mile a minute to the chicken that kept tipping her head sideways and fixing Gin with one eye, as if she was trying to figure out what that girl was steamed up about this time.

You have said, on several occasions when you have had a busy night that you are just writing me a note, because otherwise your love would build up and race on so fast you would never catch up with the telling of it. That is how I feel on this Sunday night. Elle came over for supper. I've been so busy we haven't had a chat in days. Thursday night I went to a district Al-Anon meeting in Middletown, as our group representative, a position I newly accepted. I rode with the head representative of the district, so I found myself trapped into staying longer than I might have and did not get home until eleven. Friday night I shopped and went to my meeting, and Saturday I got up early, but my day disappeared doing chores and schoolwork.

The alcoholism-counseling course has green imp and H. P. written all over it. I found out about it at an Al-Anon meeting, when a woman I did not know came in and put the flier announcing the course on the table in front of me. She has a counseling practice with the man who is running the course, and she just happened to bring some fliers in case someone might be interested. I just happen to be looking for alternative livelihood and counseling was an avenue I was already thinking about.

Recently I had met a person at an AA Meeting who had just received his accreditation as an alcoholism counselor. He is a school principal, and is starting a program in elementary school for alcoholism awareness. He is working on developing one for junior high. I know him slightly, as he had come to the house a few times with one of our theatre friends. Eric rode him unmercifully because he didn't drink. I might be able to interest my school system in his program and certainly they would need a qualified person to run it. Perhaps that would fulfill the counseling accreditation requirement for one year's work in the field. It all fits together, in a more than circumstantial way, as many things seem to since I have become more receptive to new ideas with the help of The Program.

Sometimes it feels eerie, but it has happened to my benefit enough previous times that I feel assured all is happening as it is supposed to. All I have to do is the work involved. The road and the way seem to be revealed when I am ready for them. If I trust and try them, they work. It is foreign to me to trust that much, but I am feeling optimistically anticipatory in this case. Perhaps it is a way out of my dilemma at work. If I like counseling as much as I think I will, it would give me flexibility and mobility. As it is now, I could never move from my school system, because no school would pay for a senior art teacher when they could hire one just out of school for half the price, unless that person has some other specialty to offer along with the teaching. On the other hand, my teaching experience could be a plus if I were to work with kids in an institution.

I have a whole bursting of things to say, and my pen cannot keep up. In five days I will be with you and can just say them in your ear.

Verge

P.S. Good ol' H. P. had his laugh once again. Can you believe, when I went to pay Eric's bail and to take him back to Newburgh, he said the judge was going to let him go anyway, without bail, if he would agree to attend AA for a month and get a paper signed five days a week? I interfered with the process. Damn! He says he is still going to try it out. V.

2/24/84

My Michael,

I find myself calling you Hoot, more and more, as an endearment, the most intimate of intimates, to be used at private times just between us two. I cherish it because it evolved out of our imagination, as a kid's nickname. I have read that some psychologists say nicknames are important to a child's development, giving a sense of belonging. Even an unflattering one is better than none at all, because it marks an acceptance. You are the only person outside of blood relatives that calls me Ginny or Gin, and it, too, has a whole body of fond memories between us since we dug it up and brought it to the present.

This last time we were together, you talked about "finding our relationship becoming increasingly spiritual in nature." Of course The Program makes us aware of a need for a spiritual search. I opened myself to being a little receptive as I started to hear an accumulation of "coincidental happenings" for the good, in the lives of people in The Program. They chose to call them miracles, and many even say there are no coincidences. For the same reason you were also open to allowing things of a spiritual nature to be that. Our minds are in a climate of accepting things we cannot logically or intellectually explain, willing to explore them, and daring to at least talk around the edges of miracles and spiritual things, without fear that the other will ridicule or laugh at considering such possibilities.

Because we do not shut our minds against anything at this point, we could admit that something happened between us in sleep. If we had pooh, poohed our sleep communication when we first became aware of it, it might have died of closed brain. Instead, it increased as we became more welcoming of it. Simultaneous dreaming was an interesting development. When we shared a part of ourselves we had no control over, even when there were elements we were not particularly happy about, we found we dreamed uncannily similar dreams or variations on the same theme.

We both have come to a point of letting events happen as they will, instead of trying to shape them to patterns they do not fit, as we first did. It seems that as we become more receptive, more happens. Perhaps, between us, we will figure out the meaning of life. Better start scouting around for a mountain for us to guru on! (Please be sure it has a nice flat top for rolling around and preferably not located on a known fault.) I love you by leaps and bounds.

Verge

2/24/84

My Verge,

Even though I spend my waking and sleeping hours missing you, and it takes a mighty effort to sweep that feeling behind me before it cripples me, I walk tall, and proud, and happy, and repeat "things are unfolding as they should," [12] over and over, and even get an occasional feeling of believing it. In with all that joy is a touch of serenity. What we are and how we are with each other fills me up. That feeling is a great encourager, healer, restorer, and soother.

I love the way we are kind to each other. When human stuff runs smack into one of us, leaving us feeling weak, and afraid, and intimidated, the other, without needing to know why, is there with a soft touch, a nod, a boost, or a prod. It is never done in a condescending or impatient way. We are automatically able to let the other know it is a tough game, and being imperfect is not a big deal. We are kind to each other without all those complications sometimes associated with kindness, like martyrdom and resentment. These thoughts are elusive, but someday I am going to capture one, get a good handle on it, and send it straight to you—a gift of my love.

This is an anniversary time of year. Remembrances, that started three years ago with putting down the drink, fill up a lot of reflective time. I am smiling now thinking of some of them. Also, yesterday was my fifth month anniversary of not smoking. I have been preoccupied with that for the last few weeks. It feels unreal. The whole experience has been strange from the start, maybe because I had been smoking for so long and had dreaded the pain of stopping so thoroughly that I never thought life could continue with that part of me cut out. Since I quit, there has been this little glowing ball of unreality drifting through my life. It is as if I am standing back watching someone else do it. The relatively abrupt decision (for me a few days or weeks is abrupt) and swift action left me feeling I never caught up with myself. Sometimes

---

12 Reference to *DESIDERATA, a poem by Max Ehrmann*

when you mention it, or it occurs to me, it comes as a big surprise that I don't smoke. Sometimes I expect the cig pack and lighter to fall out of my shirt pocket when I am working around the machines as they used to, as if nothing had changed. When I stopped drinking, every day was real, it was measured by meetings and talk and Steps. People were progressing along with me. The reality of the disease and its progression was obvious, and the getting better part was shared. I think that gave the process an anchor. Shaking the smokes remains nebulous. I needed to sift that out and share it with you, my favorite sifter and sharer, 'n everything, Gin. I love you.

Michael

2/28/84

Dear Love,

Michael, I have three fears: One, that you might open your eyes one day and look at me with blame for having precipitated you into unhappy change. Two, that somehow our love is made to look shoddy in the eyes of a beholder dear to us. Three, that I lose your love. I have had a two-year wrestle with myself to not say what I am about to attempt.

I made a decision some time ago that I was willing to take your love any way I could get it, because it is quality. It is so many things more than an *affaire de cour*. It is life, and unless I wish to give up breathing, I see no way to quit. I never thought of us as having an affair. I had no chance to plan on falling in love with you; a door opened and it always has been so. Our love was often survival to me, and never once could I think of it as bad, wrong, or improper. It isn't and never was.

Hoot captures an elusive thought

You know what is in my heart, Michael. You know I want to share every waking and sleeping minute with you. Because of that, I have feared and hesitated to speak, wanting to be awfully sure it wasn't the heart talking, and fearing it wasn't my business, that I had no right to say anything. But I do have a right, Michael. I have twenty-five years of unselfish love behind me, and I have to trust that you will believe I say this in the same spirit of unselfishness. I do not present this with the expectation that you will act upon it—just that it is a side I don't think you have considered.

You and I are not suffering. We have never suffered since I forever swept away any question by declaring out loud my love for you. Whatever pain and sorrow we went through, or are going through, we always have that life-giving, joy-giving balm against loneliness—our love. We need nothing. It nurtures, it soothes, it makes sense of all life's nonsense, and it gives us courage to grow on all levels.

Michael, other people may not need (or want) as intricate a relationship as you and I have, but if they are married they usually do expect more than a brother-sister relationship. I know. I lived in one, back when I was trying to make my marriage work. It is painful; it is devastating; and it corrodes self-esteem. If a relationship has come to that, it is time for change. Either it should be honestly worked out, or the people involved should be released and made free to find a new relationship in which to grow.

Knowing the mental anguish it causes, I feel compassion and pity for Doreen, and also for you in this situation. When I finally came to acknowledge that drinking had dissolved my marriage and realized how dependent Eric had become on me, I knew I had to leave him before we destroyed each other. Monogamy makes a great deal of sense during the child-rearing years. Not too long ago that was the usual life expectancy of a person. But now, there may well be 30 or 40 years to look forward to at mid-life—time to have a whole other life. People change; circumstances change; people grow in different directions. It is not a mark of failure that relationships change. Does it make sense to stay in a relationship where both people are unhappy, when there is time for a whole other life to evolve?

As it is, you and I aren't going to suffer. We win either way. We can wait for death do us part, for the other person to get tired and perhaps terminate the relationship, or for the almost inevitable disclosure of our relationship and the ensuing scandal, and then either you will give me up or you won't. Last Saturday, one of the counselors said, "People will go to almost any length to not change. In the face of devastating evidence they resist it." How very well I know that. I wish I had five cents for every time I said to myself, "It will go away. It is getting better. This time it will be different. I know it can't happen again." It didn't. It didn't. It wasn't. It did. When the change came, it was almost the way you stopped smoking. It was as if I were being steered through it by some power greater than my indecisive self. I felt like a bystander to the event of a major change in my life. It hurt. It did not come easy, even when I knew it was inevitable and the very best thing for both of us.

That is it. That is all I have to say on that subject, except for the semi-annual offer—If you need space and time to work out your marriage without my influence, ask. I would do my best to acquiesce.

I do know what you are saying about the unreality of not smoking. It is a very lonely thing to quit. Nobody much remarks on it, so you have to be motivated by the personal conviction that you must. No one else seems to care, other than an occasional, "Didn't you used to smoke?" said with a thoughtful frown. You have to keep reinforcing your own reason for quitting like, "I want to live to be 105 so I can get to live with Verge someday." I love you beyond life.

Verge

3/2/84

My Sweet Verge,

You remarked on our open-mindedness toward spiritual matters. At first my mind was very busy quarreling with itself, over risking exposure to even the possibility of thinking such thoughts. A lot of my hesitation was due to Eric's influence. Don't misunderstand; I am not putting my thinking in Eric's pocket. I took on what I wanted to hear during all those years of listening to and agreeing with him, and that became my own philosophy. I could hear myself saying to me (and to Eric, even in absentia) "Hey, are you getting soft in the head? What in hell are you doing with those mumbo jumbo thoughts? You are hiding behind unreality just to escape, because you are weak, can't drink anymore, looking for replacements, (milk sop things that can't hold up under the tiniest bit of scrutiny.)"

I was timid at each new step and way over sensitive. Anything that hinted at dissent sent me scurrying behind a boulder to peek out and watch what would happen as a consequence for saying or thinking such dumb thoughts. I am slowly getting some confidence from seeing other people search for and deal with "strange things that cannot be explained." They haven't been sent to Siberia. Then I see and feel what we have experienced, and I watch you and listen to you. With each experience and each new sharing, I feel a little more confident and more receptive. You are right; the more receptive I am the more I experience.

So, we touched each other's souls and dared to look. Taken symbolically, that seems casual enough, nobody thinks of actually doing that. Really looking delves too deeply into the personal. Isn't that where all the secrets are stored—where the demons live? To look risks letting them out. But we did. We trusted each other even if we did not trust what we might find. We found it was beautiful, not fearsome.

I have started to search around to find out what this spirituality is that the program is always talking about. I've read some books on spirituality and the paranormal and have checked into a few ideas of what other people think it is. As near as I can decipher, the pie in the sky is belonging to the great WHOLE, and knowing that you do. I am not going far out, just staying receptive, and open, and glad to have you to nose around with.

No, I am not sick of hearing about counseling. I think it is exciting that you found you were in need of a new direction at work and are exploring possibilities. It's exciting, and brave, and very healthy. Many people just plod along in resignation and unhappiness at their job. I share your thought that a job one loves isn't work. I felt that way working in the theatre. It was just steady dedication and pleasure. Nothing was too menial or too hard to do, and the hours melted away. I am glad to think that your vocation can be brought back to joy by working counseling in with the teaching, as you mentioned.

Hoot has a message for Gin: 9/ 12-9-11-5/ 25-15-21 a lot, Gin. 9/ 5-22-5-14/ 12-15-22-5/ 25-5-21. Whew, I'm glad we have our new decoder rings! I'm sorry I had to keep them secret. I wasn't sure they would come in time.

12-15-22-5,<br>Hoot and Michael

3/7/84

Dear Michael,

Today I was notified that I am enrolled in the computer course. I hope it has no homework for I don't know where I can squeeze any more of anything in. I'm supposed to get some reading done tonight, and what I feel like doing is snuggling in with you in my head. I have two books to read by next week when I have to give an oral report to the counseling class on the history of AA.

After school, I stopped at the judge's office to pay Eric's fine. It is just down the road from my house; so stopping was no particular hardship. According to a conversation I overheard, between the judge and the district attorney, I believe the charge will be driving while impaired. He has to go back in April for the conviction. I think it still entails an enforced attendance at AA. Please?

While I waited for the judge, the legal secretary (dragon lady) treated me like some low life scum. I was being polite, using my best Michael tactic of smiling and talking pleasantly, but she was curt and unresponsive. I do not view her job as highly stressful. It is a small law office in a town judicial district that doesn't exactly have murder and mayhem on every street corner, and I was the only person in the office. Why would she treat me as if I consorted with criminals when I only came to pay someone else's fine? By the time the judge was free I felt like giving the woman a lecture, but instead I did a Michael and gave her a smile. Gin was only holding back because I had a firm grasp on her pigtail. I just know she turned around and stuck her tongue out, as we went into the judge's office, but I chose to ignore that. The judge, himself, was a warm sympathetic human being.

In a recent letter you told me how you admire me learning to be me. The tone was so sincere; I felt it was observation rather than flattery. I like knowing how you look at me and see change, and how you approve of the changes. It does not feel like conceit or an insecure need for encouragement. Rather, I am trying to grow and become different, and I cannot always see it happening, so I am glad when you reflect it for me to see. You never make me feel self-conscious, but you do have a lovely way of making me conscious of self.

Verge

3/13/84

My Verge,

I'm just plain feeling crumby tonight. I have gotten myself into such a frame of mind that nothing could be right even if it tried. I feel like everything is conspiring to bug me. Funny how that works, no matter how I tell myself what is happening and how I explain it to myself, more just keeps piling on, almost as if I wanted it to.

I asked myself, "Well, self, what will it take to make me feel better?" and self said to tell Verge about it. So I am. I told you on the phone this afternoon that I had the car situation under control. I thought I did, but tonight it is there bugging away at me, and it makes everything else look like a bug. I am sure I am missing something. It is probably not just the car thing that set this feeling off, but that's what it seems to be, so I am blaming it.

Funny how things snowball once a foothold is secured. I start grinding about the car, then I commence to build resentment because daughter's wedding is coming soon; that leads to another resentment that the house definitely must be wired this spring, and these all require money from the credit union. How will there ever be enough money for all that? Oh yes, gotta paint the house this summer—and still buy a car? All that means I must have an ill feeling toward the credit union. I start getting edgy about the job—the boss gave me a lousy assignment. Then I jump on myself because I haven't written to you and I start fuming, calling myself a lazy, worthless bum who doesn't know how to do anything but vegetate, who can't even make a decision about a dumb, beat-up, old car, and I am back to that, but it has grown since I was there before, and the cycle starts again only bigger.

Along about this time, not long ago, I would have settled myself into a very deep funk, not even wanting to get out, just wanting to suffer. It would last—who knows how long? I would be brave and tell no one, pretending I was fine. But today, I can figure out what's wrong with me, (yeah, I need my Verge) talk about it, pray about it and get the wallowing over in a short time. When I do that, then I can act. I am not crippled. I am deeply in love with you.

Your Michael

Thursday, 3/15/84

My Verge,

I walk around this night being furious. I don't know why I am furious. I am not furious at any special thing, just everything—that steel girder in the way, that fellow worker who wore a black shirt tonight, the boss for giving me an assignment, the machine for making a funny noise, just anything and anybody. I can feel the rage boiling around inside. It is a new feeling—well, not new—just new being this big. It is scary because it precipitates all kinds of funny thoughts, not funny ha, ha, weird funny.

You would laugh to see the tug-of-war I have going between old H. P. and myself, "You've got it; no, I've got it; no, you've got it." I can't specifically pinpoint where this is coming from, but I suppose it is a culmination of things. Mostly I feel impatient with myself. I call myself dirty names and cook up wild solutions to my troubles—all of which if carried out would punish me.

I think patience is the only line of action for me right now, but I tug at myself and tell myself, "That is only a cop out. You must charge forward; take the bull by the horns." Voices give occasional prods in my ear to take action and make the changes that are indicated and necessary. "Oh, yeah. Yeah." I say on one side, then, "Yeah, yeah," on the other. Doubts grow bigger until I can't see around them. This indecisiveness is driven by a realization that I never have handled my relationships with others well whenever there was a strain or a crisis. My reaction would be to hide away or run as fast as I could, never facing problems squarely for the sake of some resolution. Pieces of that knowledge were there, but I never saw them in perspective until a recent moment of insight. That knowledge is worrisome, not only because it does not speak well of my past behavior, but also it could still be lurking around waiting to strike again. That it is not a healthy way to deal with problems or people, for sure. I have the resources to help me, but have I grown enough to take advantage of the help, and am I strong enough to avoid being sucked into old ways?

Michael

3/18/84

Dearest Love, My Michael,

For class this week I had to list all the minutiae of my life—organization memberships, magazine subscriptions, what I do with my time, where and on what do I spend my money (look in checkbook). It is amazing how the trivia of one's life reveals the principles a person lives by. I also have an oral report due March 31, and a ten-page autobiography due before Easter.

Thank you for confiding in me about your bad time. I feel like you allow me to see the whole person who is you. I know I can't take any of it away, but I also know, when I had troubles talking to you helped to put them in perspective. Once I was able to identify all of the problems, resentments, or fears and label them properly, then I could look them dead in the eye and they diminished in size. I found when I got into one of those nagging, rotten times, if I listed (actually wrote down) all of the things bothering me, then prioritized them starting with the most critical, it helped me to see what I needed to deal with first. The other things could wait.

When you said you felt nothing, I understood how that was. Sometimes when I jam my circuits with too much, I get immobilized. (That is new since being in The Program. Previously I would scramble in 40 directions botching everything.) It seems to be my rational brain saying, "Wait a minute!" Sometimes it lasts for longer than others, but once I get straight in my head what I have to do first, it all falls into place. I am not saying that all goes necessarily to my liking, but it does proceed without panic. It is the panic I can't handle.

If you do try making a list, you may find you are a touch resentful that I am taking this class. I told you that I was feeling some resentment last summer when you were taking your sailing course. My rational head said that was silly and it made me squirm to find myself reacting in such a childish manner. Nevertheless, that is how I felt. I was glad you were having the opportunity and the joy of it, but I wanted to be part of it, too. I am still working on growing up.

Last Friday when I did my grocery shopping, I bought a small corned beef, so I invited Elle over for corned beef and cabbage on Saturday. She made Irish soda bread to go with it. She knows enough not to linger, with my tight schedule, but it made a good break for both of us, as I hardly see her for more than a couple of minutes at a time all week.

While she was here, Eric called to ask if he could use my phone tomorrow. Apparently it is about a job interview and a coin phone would be too distracting. According to him, he went to his first AA Meeting and, "It wasn't as bad as I expected." There are miracles, Michael, and for him to go on his own to even one meeting is a miracle! It is a far cry from being a member, but now I truly believe he has found the tool to rejoin life if he wishes to and choices are available to him. He said he asked someone how to get a sponsor. I have a peace about him now, and I can relinquish him to his choices.

You do understand, Michael, that no program could ever give me back the boy I loved to my fullest capacity of the time. I am not the girl who lived then. Nothing could make Eric and me more than strangers with a crossed history and a shared progeny. Sobriety might make him into a brand new person—as it did for you and me—but the gap between us is too cavernous to cross. My peace is that now, if he wants to, he can get out of that torturous, black place and maybe fulfill some of his potential. I would never say his life has been wasted, for his example has been the catalyst for several people to examine their own lives and make changes. Now I wish some good for him.

Verge

3/19/84

Dear Michael,

I just got your angry letter and Babe, could I ever identify with that kind of anger that comes up like thunder and seems directed at anything in your path. It seldom happens to me like that anymore, but when it first began, it scared the hell out of me because I never thought I could be that angry. It was the most unpleasant step toward a return to mental health that I experienced. I have read, and I have been told that it comes from years of repressed anger. I learned while studying about children of alcoholics that they repress anger for fear that the people they need or love will reject them as bad persons if they express it. If anger is not accepted as a normal emotion, a person grows without learning how to acceptably express a huge energy force that can build until it wants to destroy things. Anger turned inward makes us sick, so it is healthy to learn how to appropriately express it.

They say in The Program that we don't get anything we are not ready to handle. I thought anger was going to blow me up. Thank God it didn't come until I had been sober for a while, not until I had some tools to deal with it—like talking to people. It can be a useful force that provokes change. It can force the body, immobilized by indecision, to do what it knows it has to. For myself, it forced me to deal with things I was frightened to do, like talk to Eric. I told you about several occasions when that happened, but you had no way to understand just how explosive that anger was. It was a tornadic force inside myself that propelled me to do something I could not get myself to do, no matter the provocation.

I'm not saying yours will necessarily do that, but it might. In any case, it is part of the healing process, no matter how out of control it makes you feel. It will calm down when you get done with being frightened by it. I find that if I look it in the face, tell myself what it is, talk about it, and ride it out, its force dissipates. Ignoring it is not the answer. I used to drive in my car and scream a lot, at first. I'm certainly not proud of it, but when it really shook me to my toe bones and I didn't know how be constructive with it, that kept me from doing violence.

Not too long ago, I would have sneered at this as two-bit psychiatry, but when you have really been down and out, you will try anything that comes from people you have some faith in. I have faith in AA and the Al-Anon Program, and what I see working for others, I am willing to try.

Isn't it strange, with all our love for each other, I know that I cannot help you in this lonely process of healing up? I can only stand by and empathize. I feel honored, though, that you let me see you hurt—let me in to that old wound-licking place you have always before gone to alone. I can't make it go away, but I can share it with you and not feel shut out. Thank you.

Verge

3/20/84

My Verge,

I know I am not going to feel anywhere near better until I write everything out, telling you about it. But I feel funny doing it. Funny because I am guilty of not doing it sooner, funny because it just doesn't seem fair to make you feel bad, and funny for saying that because I know you want to be involved just as I would if it were you. I feel confused and bothered about everything. I feel like I have lost everything I have built up for the past three years. Poof! Just gone. The straight thinking, the faith, the joy, the feeling experience—everything! It's like a big steel door slammed shut, cutting me off from what I was gathering as life.

I can't stop wondering how that can be. It is not like I caught a germ that attacked a group of cells, or that I had surgery, or broke something. I just turned around one day, and here it comes as a surprise, whatever it is. By the time I realized it was upon me, it was too late, like throwing up my hands to stop a freight train. "Aha," I said, "I have all the tools now to stop this." Wrong. (Maybe not wrong, but somewhere I seem to have lost the knowledge of how to use them.)

The program advises me to have faith, pray. The best I can make is little tentative whispers, because frankly old H. P. scares me to death these days. I feel like he set me up and got me. Silly, I know, but that is where I am. Talk to other people. I know that, but the best talk I can muster is surface, or feeling out talk. When I start to go deeper I perceive the people as backing away, and I run and hide. I can't seem to push past that.

I have been told and I have read that it is a test. Well, I flunk. Call off the test. I acknowledge flunkhood. True, I have not taken a drink, but it has been a mighty battle, believe me. I make myself go to meetings and say what I can there. So far that has saved me, by holding back completely immobilizing fear and despair, but it is your voice, the knowledge that you are encouraging me, that keeps me doing the things that are right to do if I am ever to get out of this alive.

You say, "If only I could think of something to help you." You don't know it, but in this painful time, you give me the straw of sanity I am holding on to very tightly. I hear your voice, and your suggestions, and feel your love through the day. I try, however feebly, to follow your suggestions, and I think about them even when I don't do them. That is what I hold on to. Thank you for you and your holding place.

Michael

3/21/84

Dear Michael,

Remember a couple of days ago Eric wanted to use my phone? Would I leave my door open so he could come in to call about a job—incidental talk about AA thrown in? I agreed and spent some time Eric-proofing my house by putting away personal items. The next day he called me at work saying a tire had fallen off his car on his way home and could I pick him up on my way home to let him use my phone again?

You know, Michael, I sometimes watch myself being sucked into the alcoholic web in slow motion. One show of humanity to the alcoholic seems to set up a pattern of suck as much as you can get before the suckee comes to her senses. Granted he did take care of calling someone to tow the car and to fix it, but yesterday I found myself taking him to the garage to pick up his car in the precious few minutes I had between school and teaching my after school student. You know, Hoot, that is an awful lot of mileage out of going to one AA meeting. The aggravating thing is that it is never just one thing! How he can collect such a variety of miserable happenings, I don't know. Drinking did not cause his tire to fall off, so I can't blame everything on his alcoholism. Will I ever get bright? Underneath it all, I know I allowed myself to get pulled in again so I could shoot off my mouth about AA and try to push it. I get so mad at myself I'd like to beat me up! Just a few days ago I told you I was at peace relinquishing him to his choices, and it is almost as if this came along as a test.

Speaking of beating ourselves up, Michael, easy Love, take it easy on yourself. You are way, far too hard on you. Lighten up! You know, when you were heavy on Hoot, Gin got real upset? Well, when you are heavy on Michael, Verge gets upset. This growing up stuff that should have been done over a 35-year period or so, is getting done in big chunks in three. It is not easy. Not making any decisions at all right now can be a form of choice. No choice has to be made instantly. Saying if you get through this you will never let yourself get happy again is probably the worst example of alcoholic thinking you could come up with. That is like saying I won't love anyone and then no one can hurt me. No one would have to, because you would be hurting yourself far more than a lover might. Grab the happy, Babe; it helps to buoy you through the pain parts. I can see your look of disgust right now. But it really is true. I'm laughing, because I can remember, easily enough, my own cynical ear that message fell on, a year ago. "Piffle, too childish for my predicament! How could anything so simpleminded even approach this huge pain?"

I have come to firmly believe it will and it does. You can find your way through the maze of your pain if you take each simpleminded tool and apply it. The pain has rewards afterward that you cannot dream of while you are in it. You sounded so hurty on the phone this morning. I felt frustrated because I know little I can say will be welcome, as most of it sounds too simple to apply in your situation. It is hard to sound reassuring without sounding like a pompous know-it-all. I could shut up, but one thing I have learned, above all, in The Program is not to shut up. As impossible as it seems to say stuff, or as silly, or as selfish, don't shut up! If I step on your toes or your feelings you will just have to tell me that in words, too. More than life, I love you. Please take care of you. Grab someone and talk and keep grabbing someone until the crazies go away. I love you in a new allowed-to-be-part-of even the bad stuff way.

Verge

3/26/84

My Verge,

What to write? I feel kind of sheepish after not writing for so long. Truthfully, it makes me angry with myself that I have been unable to write or do much of anything. It bespeaks a huge ego too much preoccupied with self to be able to reach out to share or seek help. I think that little is served by dwelling on the past, except I have never experienced such a crushing feeling. I feel anger right now for not being able to form thoughts into words. I don't know if I am being dramatic, but I feel like I will never be the same.

This is the first time for me that self-destruction appeared a worthy alternative. Somehow I never really understood how well you know what it is all about, until I was able to share some of it with you. I never realized, at the time you were writing it to me, how devastating an experience you were having. Your telling me again in small pieces in recent letters and on the phone opened my eyes. In talking to other people at meetings, I also learned in bits and pieces that they, too, have been through similar experiences. It is as if it was all locked away until I went looking for it. I don't think this anger is going to go away until I take some action, like doing the Fourth and Fifth Steps.

I felt it coming back again this morning while I was in church, and I got scared. That panicky feeling started moving in. I just mentally crumbled and said, "I have got to leave this right here. There is nothing else I can do with it right now." I walked out without it, so far.

Thank God for you, Babe! Without you reaching out your hand to me and guiding me through, I never would have been able to talk to anyone. You saved me. It was your kindness, patience, encouragement, and love that saved me. I don't feel beholden, just much closer to you than ever before. Who could believe that would be possible? I can't explain the comfort I felt that you could help me without being drawn in too. I could feel your health, and it was very reassuring. I love you beyond any words I can form.

Michael

3/28/84

My Love, Michael,

Thanks for calling me in the middle of the day for a little contact chat. I don't take you for granted, but everything about us seems natural, including an afternoon "Hi." Thanks, also, for telling me that you didn't feel beholden because I shared your recent pain. Intimate pain, like sex, defies being prettied up. It just is. When you are in the middle of it with a person, you find the essential elements of that person. It is beautiful to find that you can love the unprettied up person even more than the one you usually see. To me you are the most beautiful human being ever invented, and I feel deeply honored and moved to be allowed inside your pain. Every time I find myself in love with you more, I feel like a pre-speech savage uttering grunts and whistles trying to get them to tell you about this beauty that mortals have not invented words for.

I surely know what you mean by self-destruction being a worthy alternative to pain. It still can be a very seductive idea, when I think I can play God and help other people straighten out their lives by my non-being. But, just as with the bottle, you always take people with you when you go. Unless it is to end the unbearable pain and indignity of a terminal disease, someone is left cleaning up the emotional debris and guilt for a far longer time than with ordinary death. Although I still reserve my right to do it, today I have to admit to a great deal of curiosity about how it's all going to work out. I'm becoming aware that little of life is boring. As my self-assurance increases and I become more curious about how this old world ticks, I am able to take the focus off my own discomfort and look for the unique, even in situations that I might find threatening. I no longer stereotype people so readily. If all else fails, I have the option of amusing myself in my own head without the panicked feeling that I must flee. What is the master plan? Tune in tomorrow to "Green Shoots and Dead Branches."

Can you believe it is snowing outside like a major winter storm? It is not a good night to go for crab legs as Elle and I had planned. It is a perfect night to curl up with you. I know without question that my love for you is a green shoot!

Your Verge

3/29/84

My Sweet Verge,

It feels like my self-esteem has slipped (not that it was ever that straight, but it was getting there.) I know you were in a scary position when I was so depressed, probably filled with anxiety and doubt about doing the right thing, but you stuck right there with me, reaching out and sounding unafraid. You didn't let the muck and mire draw you in so we would both be sitting helpless together in that old "slough of despond" they tell of in The Program. You helped me by guiding me along a way you had traveled, sharing the falls and traps you had found. It was not like you were leading a child that didn't know anything, more like a co-traveler. You had climbed to the ledge above me, and were reaching a hand down, explaining the terrain and how I could avoid problem areas to get a foothold, so I could stand with you sharing one more growth adventure.

The way you were felt good to me, and you said things in a way I could listen to without resentment and could try to do. Except for you and people I talked to at meetings, everyone else seemed in a quandary about what was going on with me and said all the wrong things, causing me to feel even more resentful.

One of the problems with trying to tell about anger after the anger has faded, is remembering just what the anger was, where it was directed, and why. I hope I learned to vent without waiting so long. Superficially, I did to you and at meetings, but the deep inside anger was too scary and I held it in not wanting to bore anyone with it. I could feel it turning on me. It involved guilt about my neglectful and turning aside ways that I knew hurt people close to me, who depended on me for more than just physical sustenance. The realization would flash in front of me, and guilt would come down so heavy I would physically cringe. I felt so angry at myself; I literally despised what I saw in the mirror. Funny, I never felt all that hate, and guilt, and anger when I was in the process of creating the circumstances of it.

Before I fell into this funk, you told me Gin was being a handful. It would be all right with me if you sent her over here. I know Hoot would stumble over himself if I told him she was coming. I understand about her looking at herself in the mirror and acting funny. Isn't she getting to be about that age? We will treat her gently.

Michael

4/3/84

Dear Michael,

Tonight I went to the door to let the cat in, and guess what! I heard spring peepers for the first time this year. That sound always makes my heart leap. It's spring! It is time for Michael to come!

Last night, Gin came in to give me a letter for Hoot. She had the letter in one hand and several pieces of paper taped together to make a long scroll in the other. I asked her what that was. She said it was stuff she had to do. I didn't even bother to pursue the matter. There is just no understanding her these days. Yesterday, when I asked her if she wanted to go stay with you and Hoot. She yelled, "Yes," and went running off. Then a few minutes later she came back with a long face and said she didn't know if she wanted to go. "How soon do I have to tell you?" I guess if she doesn't have more interest than that we can forget the whole matter, and I'll just muddle through with her as best I can.

Just before I sat down to write this, I walked into her room to check on her. I could hardly get the door open. On the floor was a huge roll of papers taped together. Taken aback I looked in around the edges and this is what I saw.

1,538: Clean out chicken coop

1,539: Put in new straw

...and skipping along...1,550: polish all my fish hooks...1,551 pick dead worms out of tackle box. Can you figure out what is wrong with the girl? I'm at my wit's end. Hoot seems to be having his problems, too. Gin said he never could tell nothing without a program and burst into tears again for the lebbenty-fifth time this week. She is getting to be a hazard to our already flooded lake area

Verge

Dear Hoot,

Verge says I can go out to stay with you and Michael. I said I didn't know if I wanted to or not. Hoot, I don't look like I used to look. I mean I'm the same only different. Maybe you won't like me any more. Also, do you have a girlfriend? Maybe I would just be in the way. I mean maybe she wouldn't like me following you around on a date or something. Hoot, why isn't everything just yes or no, like it used to be? I don't want to come unless you want me to. I've got lots of stuff to do, if you have too much stuff to do and don't want me to come out, or anything. Hurry up and let me know fast, so I will know whether I should start doing all my stuff, or not. I mean, I don't want to be in the middle of something and find out you want me to come.

Your friend,<br>
Ginny

P.S. Of course I like Michael a lot. Maybe, if you are too busy, I'll just come see Michael, and I won't bother you and any old girl or anything. I could play with your dawg. Hurry up and let me know.

Gin

4/7/84

My Verge,

Hoot asked to enclose his letter for Gin. Please pass it on to her. (He is making out like I made him write, but the truth is he couldn't wait to get off and answer Gin's letter.) Please send the girl on. We are anxiously waiting for her.

As I jotted down the date at the top I couldn't help reflecting on Eric's birthday—couldn't help remembering some of the birthdays we spent there all together. It marked the end of a very long winter of not seeing you and barely communicating. How readily we would fell in together, right off at the kitchen counter. I thought of all the carrying on, with champagne and what have you, later in the candle-lit, music-filled room. Good fellowship, love. There were indeed some fine times mixed in with the non-fine. I was pissed off and resentful for a long time about Doreen's attitude toward going to New York. Although she never came out and said so, I could feel her negative vibes about going there and I would purposely ignore them, because it wasn't going to stop me anyhow. It was a run-to place, with people who understood and shared my values and attitudes, and I determined to shut out any factor that threatened it. I think Doreen knew her protests or refusals would bear no fruit, so she came along and convinced herself the drink would make a good time of it all.

I denied that anger I felt, along with all the other troublesome problems I thought I should be strong enough to bear, and stuffed it down inside. If any of them threatened to come out, I stuffed them deeper until they disappeared. I knew what psychologists said about the danger of doing that, but I never believed it. I believed that feelings, ideas, and thoughts have no substance, so they could have no effect on substantial matter, like my body, especially if I willed them out of existence.

One thing I learned out of these latest growing pains is that it is OK to be angry with someone or something, but it does no good to blame them for it, and whatever you do don't store anger inside. Don't make yourself the goat for everything.

Michael

13-25/4-5-1-18/ Gin,

Hey, Gin, why don't you write this out in code yourself and then decode it. This decoder ring is a pain! Wow, it sounds as if you are very busy! Michael and I think it would be nice if you could save all the stuff you have to do for later and come to be with us for a while. We sorta need you around here. Things are kinda upside-down, and we know how good you are at getting stuff straight again. I tried to get Michael to write this, but he made me do it. I hate to write.

I went out with a girl one time, a few weeks ago. It wasn't any fun. She didn't even know anything about fishing or dawgs or hens or anything. I'd like to show you my new lure. Hurry up. Gin, how come you're different? Did you go to dancing school or something? I hope not too different. I kinda liked you the way you were.

Your friend,
Hoot

4/9/84

Dear My Michael,

Did you ever think you would see April this year? I thought for a while someone had stopped the time projector (as in old home movies) and I kept expecting to see the film melt away to a black hole. Whew! Am I glad it didn't happen, 'cuz I've got a few frames with you left, to add to this movie.

I feel guilty, because I received your letter today, and I have been remiss in my letter writing because my autobiography and other papers are due soon. After reading Hoot's letter, Gin went right off to pack and is heading out. I'm sure she will precede this letter. A little while ago I heard, "klunk-a lunk-a lunk," from her room and out the door. I couldn't figure out what she was doing so I peeked out the window. There she was rolling this huge scroll of paper (grown since I looked at it in her room the other day) out to the garbage pick up point. She even set the garbage can beside it so the truck wouldn't mistake her intent. She had a wicked grin on her face and she picked up her chicken by the heels twirling it around. Chicken was squawking and grumbling. When Gin stopped, realizing what she was doing, the chicken shuffled itself together and stomped off in a huff. Gin just giggling! I had to take her to task and she said she wasn't hurting Chicken—just rumpling it up a bit. You are a brave man, Michael to take her on. I especially feel sorry for Hoot, for I am sure he will have his hands full with her.

I love you,
Verge

4/10/84

My Verge,

I am beginning to feel some angers and resentments sneaking in and they are threatening to turn into poor me's, so I am not going to fall into that trap again. Where to turn for instant cure? Why, to the miracle of my life, Verge. Why am I stuck with all this stuff concerning my mother, me, the one who couldn't care less about the mother-son relationship? I do believe in humane and compassionate treatment for fellow travelers in this life who are stuck and cannot fend for themselves, but I have never fallen for the dutiful son, I owe my life to my mother syndrome. Suddenly, I turn around, and I am playing that role. Everyone is watching me, and as they watch they are tippy-toeing away leaving me on stage by myself.

Every now and again my younger brother makes noises like he is helping, but then he falls over drunk someplace and forgets. My oldest brother is around at Xmas, and then rides away saying over his shoulder, "Whatever you do is fine with me." My next oldest brother makes valiant efforts, because his conscience hurts so badly that if he doesn't Band-Aid it, every now and then, he would bleed to death. I guess he has decided to risk even that now, because he told me last Friday after taking her to the doctor that he and his wife will be gone for a month. "Is there someplace I can reach you if anything happens while you are gone?" He said no, there was nothing he could do anyway. That sounded like a sign off to me.

I have been asking, even semi pleading, for some one of the female members of the family to pick up some of the female type chores connected to her needs, which are hard for me as a male to do, and which truthfully I am loath to do. Even if they would pay her a visit, to spell me somewhat, would help. No response except, "Oh yeah, sure." The end.

Stuff comes up which requires decisions and it would be nice if I could call someone to help me make them, or at least some backup, or an, "I'll stand behind you old pal, because I know it won't be easy." When I got up to go to work last night, I got the word that the nursing home called. They have a vacancy they will hold for her if she will sign the papers. She has been doing a "yes I will, no I won't" about signing for the past three months. She is going to have to make that decision herself, but the episode is going to be a great emotional storm on me, whichever way it goes. Not a soul to help or support—it pisses me off. How did I get to be such a softy?

I know I have no one to blame but myself, and I know I would have to do the same for anyone who was more or less helpless, even a bum in the gutter (maybe especially a bum in the gutter). All those other people surely did a fast shuffle, though. I know I could scream a lot and force the issue, but I am not sure I have the energy. Maybe I am pulling for a martyr star. I hope not.

Love,
Michael

4/12/84

Dear Michael,

Look at me—playing truant—skipping my Al-Anon meeting. Since I last saw you, I've been running so fast that I haven't had two hours free to loll about without feeling guilty. Busy as my days have been, I have liked them all, except for my seventh period class. I still adore my Mechanical Drawing class. It is such fun to teach a whole room full of reasonable, intelligent, hard working, humorous-without-being-mean kids. But can you imagine, my most draining class only has nine pupils in it? There are four boys, heavy into the drug culture, two girls, periodically swayed into that corner, and three interested and reliable students. I have all I can do to tolerate the boys' behavior in the classroom, because I have seen it all before. They cannot concentrate, their attention span is roughly two minutes, they have no motivation, and they exhibit no understanding of their own feelings or those of anyone else. These kids are roughly fifteen years old talking about being "burnt" (mentally effected to where they are not functioning due to drug use) as if it were a rite of passage. They are brazenly open about it, yet I can't tell you how many incidents of family denial I have heard in their conversations this year. Society itself seems to be in denial about these kids. I try not to feel panicky about them, but one has to be blind not to worry about where they are going. They are crying out for some attention, but I was told that to suggest a kid has a drug/alcohol problem without proof runs the risk of a lawsuit.

I can see there is a great need for drug education in the school, both for the parents and the kids. Maybe that will be my niche. Right now my eyes will not stay open, so I think I will go find my niche right up next to you in my dream.

Verge

4/13/84

My own Verge,

I picked my mother up at the hospital this morning, and, after she was tucked into the car, I let her convince me it would be fine to go to the nursing home for an inspection of the premises. My weird mind congers up a picture of rows of old folks sucking on huge mammaries protruding from the walls at regular intervals. That makes me laugh.

Grammy appeared to be impressed with the place and made up her mind to move in. Whatever was going on in her head remained well hidden. She did say that it made her feel blue, while we were waiting for the interview, but lost that as soon as the nuns came for the expedition. She is very impressed by nuns. She kept trying to foist the decision off on me, but I kept throwing it back to her. She is still a clever, conniving old fox, for she skillfully kept twisting and bending and tossing it back. The only way I could handle it was to ignore the trickery and keep repeating, "It is your decision. You are going to live here if you choose, not me." She ended by signing the papers, but couldn't seem to bring herself to choose a date—tomorrow, next week?

This whole episode, these last several months since I have been more or less on my own with my mother, whom I don't really like, let alone love, have been quite an experience. An eye-opener, in fact! I have often let my ego try to take over H. P.'s job by wondering what the sense is behind all of this. Is it just to harass me? What purpose can be served for this woman to live so long? Is it a test? I am stuck alone with all this, why? Very selfish, egotistical thinking. I don't mean I walk around with this chip on my shoulder all of the time, but those thoughts do sneak in.

I find since I have been able to let out some of my anger, by talking about it to you, I am more able to come to grips with my feelings toward the woman and accept her as another human. That feels liberating. My capacity for compassion and understanding seem to have increased. It seems there has been some personal growth in this, as well as a chance to be of service to someone who needs it.

This afternoon I overheard Hoot talking to Gin:

~

*What'cha doin', Gin? I saw you sitting here on the back stoop throwin' stones when I came up. You were throwing them harder than usual; are you mad?*

*OK, OK, you don't have to be mad. You can throw all you want.*

*Well, I have been watching you close for the last two or three weeks. Yeah, Ginny, I mean like you watch me. I like to watch you, what does that hurt? Do you mind if I tell you something?*

*I'm not trying to be mean, I'm trying to tell you that I understand about how you are trying to grow up, how sometimes it is scary, and sometimes you get feelings that make you mad, and sometimes it feels as if no one cares or understands. It's like grownups think that a kid is all of a sudden plunked down one day and he or she is a grownup, too; they forget that ain't how it is.*

*Yeah. Yeah, that's it. Well I just want to let you know that I know, too.*

~

I love you,
Michael

4/16/84

My sweet Honey Man,

I am proud of you, just standing up on all your new found strength, writing straight out honest and caring stuff to Eric, telling him that even if he comes to Cleveland you will not be able to spend time with him as long as he is drinking. I know the cost, but I know it is a burden lightened. The first time I told Eric a flat out, "No, I won't," I thought I would shake apart mentally if not physically. A couple of old friends had called to say they were in town and were coming by for a visit. Eric was in a dry period stemming from my saying I would not be in his presence when he was drinking, as I felt it was dangerous to me mentally and physically. He asked me to go buy a bottle of wine, and I refused. He stared at me in disbelief and said non-threateningly, but as if the wind were blown out of his sails, "You are saying that you won't get me a bottle of wine?" I restated calmly, "No, I won't."

He slammed off to his room, and pouted, and would not come out to see our guests, but he neither tore me apart limb from limb, nor did the sky fall and the roof cave in. That was a thunderous victory over my fear and awe of the man. It was like the key discovery a child makes when he first says to himself, "What is the worst thing my parents can do to me?" and nicks the seemingly impenetrable wall of parental authority.

I have since heard other people in Al-Anon try to express the way they felt when they first refused to jump, when their buttons were pushed. A calm refusal creates the release, the bursting of bonds. Joy seems to be the universal response. I don't know if it will happen as dramatically with a letter, as it does with a face-to-face confrontation, but I think you will find similar results. No matter how hard the person tries to manipulate you again, it is never the same.

You wrote, that talking some of your anger out increased your ability to feel compassion and helped you resolve some of your resentments against your mother. Somewhat in that vein, we were talking in class about occasions when a counselor feels a conflict or a dislike toward a client. The instructor said, "At that point the counselor needs to look to himself and see what is wrong within." Boy, did that statement give me the "Yes, but's. I did not like that concept at all; thinking what if that person is just plain rotten, and nobody likes him, and so forth?

As time has gone on I see that the instructor meant a counselor cannot be helpful if he sits in judgment of a client's values or feelings. Values and feelings are not good or bad, they just are. If some values and feelings cause conflict within the counselor, he better resolve them with his colleagues, or they will be a drawback every time he has to deal with that combination of traits. It is a refinement of the concept espoused in The Program that nobody, place, or thing hurts us, unless we allow it to happen by giving them that power. I didn't care for that concept either. It took a lot of work on myself to accept that idea. I see you making big strides of growth in this area.

Milo called tonight after I spoke to you. He has decided to wait until June to come out. I couldn't help but ask motherly type things, like was it worth losing his apartment and his job to take this trip? He said it was his dream, before he got settled, to see the United States and Europe. His new motorcycle has a warranty, and he has figured mileage and gas and camping out places. So be still my mother's heart, and just turn this right over and leave it, because I can't even pretend to have any control over any of it, nor do I really want to. I wish him a happy trip.

I love you and I wish you a happy trip, soon,
Verge

5/5/84

Dear Verge,

My head feels all swirly, like it does before I'm coming to see you, only now it is full up with the remembering of the marvel of us together. Didn't it feel like a gala celebration?

I was surprised when you asked me to say grace before dinner, that last day, only because we are still not sure where either of us are coming from, on the religious or spiritual side of living. To be truthful with you, I am no longer too sure from whence I come, as far as religion goes and not real clear about the spiritual, but I do feel convinced that there is something going on out there. I mean we are the goldfish. One thing I am sure of is that old ways and ingrained behaviors die very hard, especially in this area. I haven't confronted the dogma I have been threatened with since infancy; that will have to go on my prescription-for-growing list to be tackled some day. I think I will be able to keep some, and throw some away, but I haven't gotten around to deciding which is which. Your thoughts on formal prayer made me stop and think. I believe praying is sort of like "acting your way into a new way of thinking". I understand that you are not desirous of a new way of thinking about religion, but it might give you a chance to do some exploring of program suggestions.

Eric's answer to my letter was classic. He started it by saying that he could tell I was nervous and undecided when I wrote to him. He is a master at making attack his best defense. The whole letter was a textbook example of alcoholic manipulation.

Do you feel any different, now that you know he has left town? Less threatened? Less inhibited? It is weird, but I can feel his presence here in Cleveland, even though I haven't seen him or talked to him yet. When I can feel that power gone, even though he isn't, then I will know I have taken another giant step in growth. I wonder if Julie knows what she has gotten herself into? She hasn't seen him for a few years. Of course she, herself, always had a wee drinking problem, too.

Michael

5/11/84

Dearest, My Michael,

Spring has finally come to Newburgh. You remember our local eccentric that I call the Mountain Man, who plods along the roads checking out cast off cigarette packs and the store dumpsters? This morning, on my 7:00 AM way to school, there he was in his usual garb with a stick in his hand popping flies with stones. When baseball comes to the Mountain Man, surely spring has come to town.

I got back the paper I turned in Saturday when you went to class with me. The instructor wrote on it that she thought that you were a special person, and she hoped you enjoyed your day. Several other people made complimentary comments about you. Our last class ended up being a rather emotional day. Everyone commented on how close he or she felt to the group members and what a unique experience that was. From the beginning everyone participated on an extremely personal level. Even the most competitive people found nothing to compete against, for we were only called on to share an internal examination. No one felt intimidated, as there was no right or wrong, only a pool of personal experience from which to learn. Between us, there was a mix of all sides of the alcoholic problem. I came away from the course convinced of the concept that alcoholism is a disease, with any shred of reservation gone. Also, I have come to understand that the alcoholic can successfully be brought to treatment through intervention, as well as by reaching a bottom.

I used the course for two personal gains. By finally believing in the disease concept, I can stop letting some of the devastatingly painful things that happened to me, hurt anymore. I finally understand them as symptomatic of the disease. I also am able to leave the last vestiges of guilt about leaving Eric "sick and helpless." His only chance for recovery is to take responsibility for himself. He was too able to manipulate me; I had to get away or I would have been his crutch forever. I have a responsibility to myself, as well. That got internalized through this course. Other than the guilt caused by our living a double life, I also learned that you and I have an exceptionally healthy relationship.

You asked me how I felt now that Eric has moved to Cleveland. I'm not sure my brain really believes it yet. I drive by the motel with the half fear of seeing his car there even when rationally I know he sold it. There is some piece of me that still wants to be concerned about his welfare. I have to recognize that as being part of my co-dependency and keep working on getting well. I have never found a way to make an intelligent human ending with him, because he is not a rational human being. I would like to convey to him that I am over bitterness, that I never did hate him, and that I sincerely wish him well. I am grateful for many things he gave me that I have integrated into myself and wish to keep.[13] Most of all I am very, very grateful he gave me Milo and you. I don't guess I will ever be able to tell him any of those things—certainly not in his sickness because they would just be warped and twisted against me and not understood in their purity. That makes me sad.

But, yes, I am relieved that he no longer lives around the corner. I feel the umbilical cord is finally severed, and now we both can get on with our lives. I certainly know what you mean about that feeling of his presence, his power, even when you have not had contact with him. I don't envy you. I found I had to keep reminding myself that he had no power over me if I didn't grant it. Somebody said at a Meeting, "You can't have a king if there are no subjects." That hit me at one of those receptive times when its simplicity bespoke truth to me. It certainly is an imperfect control I have over myself, as witness my reaction the morning he came to the house to ask if he could leave his trunk in my garage. Despite that, I am getting better.

No blood, no certificate, no family, no dawg or chicken could make me feel more solemnly or profoundly attached to you, or more committed.

Verge

5/16/84

My Own Verge,

Thanks for telling me how you feel about Eric moving away. I never would be able to tell those thoughts to another soul. I would carry them around as my private burden and never be able to give them away, no matter what or how heavy, so I especially thank you for telling me.

It seems that old H. P. is trying to catch me up on my honesty at the job. You know, make up for all those don't wanna, ain't gonna do nuttin' on this dumb old job nights. Except he/she seems to be doing it in one big swoop. That's OK, though, as long as I get a few minutes to talk to my

---

13 Beginning to explore Al-Anon and Alcoholics Anonymous Step 8: "Made a list of all persons we had harmed and became willing to make amends to them all." Alcoholics Anonymous, *Twelve Steps and Twelve Traditions,* 77.

Baby. Tonight we have to change a motor in a machine, so I am rushing. Let me just take a minute or two and sow a few seeds of thought. Soon we can sit crossed legged in front of each other and discuss them face-to-face long into the night. I believe that the joy of life and its humor that you talked of comes from what we give each other. We have blossomed, because we encouraged each other. Do you think our common heritage of Eric was a factor? We were brought together by him, intimidated by him, and shared a sickness with him. We both loved him and probably still do. But then, as we giggled and conspired, we wiggled the lid off the jug we were stuck in, ever so slowly, until poof! We were free and found that the joy bubbling out of the bottle was us. We were free to create, to appreciate, and to love even more.

I melt when you say nothing can make you feel more profoundly attached or committed to me. There is no word in our language for people who are as close as we are, male or female, same sex or not. Friend just doesn't do it, nor lover, nor mate. It is closer than brother and sister, or twin even. It is closer than any tie one can think of, and sacred. I cannot think of any word to use, but it makes me feel tall, and proud, and joyous.

Michael

5/17/84

Dear Michael, My Love,

No sense in telling you much about my doctor visit, for I am sure you will hear it all on the phone tomorrow. He did have a competent manner, so I am satisfied to have my surgery done by him.

Every time I procrastinate, I swear it will be my last time. It is a true character defect[14] of mine. I could look at it positively and say when I am busy procrastinating I get a lot of other pending things done. I have been shaking myself by the scruff of the neck saying to self, "Do it and stop this pain!" The more adamant with myself I become, the more stubbornly I refuse to do what I have been avoiding. Case in point, the set design. First I wouldn't read the play. I begged, cajoled, and harangued myself to do it. Finally, after I did read it, I procrastinated about making the set.

---

14 Beginning to work on Step Six: "Were entirely ready to have God remove all these defects of character." Ibid., 63.

Upshot was on Sunday I spent the entire afternoon working and barely completed it in time to take to a 7:30 meeting where I had promised to produce it.

I was introduced to the young man who has single-handedly made most of the sets for their productions. He was ecstatic to have a model and seemed surprised that I was going to help paint it. I sympathized with the young man, for I could see myself written all over him. Responsible, hard working, get it done type, but would he ask for help? No! A typical "I can do it all by myself" person, playing the martyr to the hilt, with never a demand or threat that without help the set would not be forthcoming and the play would happen on an empty stage. I did not see it that way when I was in the middle of it, either, but with my fresh new vision I surely do. "Hey, Babe, if you can do it all by yourself, they probably will let you!"

Well, my dear, it is after eleven and I must sleep so I can call you in the morning.

Verge

May 29,1984

Dear Michael,

I wish I could convey the gratitude I have for the way you are with me. A specific example is when I had to go to the doctor and get tests done at the hospital, during our time together. Rather than being annoyed at having to wait around, your attitude was: this is part of you and what you have to do, and I want to be part of it. No one ever gave me the feeling of being cared for, in the way you do. I was comforted by your support and no longer fear the outcome of my operation. It gives new insight on our relationship and a new bond, as if we needed any more bonds! I will be calling on your strength and holding on tight.

Words are poor instruments for my heart's messages, but they will have to serve or otherwise I shall burst of not telling. I love you, Michael, more!

Verge

6/1/84

My woven unto my soul, Verge,

What kind of head is this I am toting around? It is a very, very distracted head, that's what. I am sitting here in the middle of this night with thoughts of you abed in the hospital, moaning with pain and needing help. I haven't heard from you, and my head is cooking up dire circumstances. "I know, I know, self, she is resting quietly and dreaming nice dreams and doesn't need any frantic behavior from me," but my head wants to act frantic. I am not in possession of all my faculties—miss hearing from you one morning and I panic. Maybe it was not hearing from you yesterday afternoon that did it. When you didn't call, my mind went into high gear and it hasn't been right since. I am not making any sense. Wanta hear a Hoot and Gin story?

I was in the kitchen getting some end of the day food ready. Gin and Hoot were in the back yard. They decided to be helpers and get the lawn mower ready to mow. I couldn't help hearing Hoot as they fussed over trying to start the mower.

"It's all right, Gin, I have started this thing a thousand times. You just have to be patient."

"I <u>know</u> the choke position. That is where I always put this lever when it starts cold. Then, when it gets running, you move it over here and let it warm up."

"It should start any time now."

"No, I ain't winded. I'll get it started. ...After I get it going, you can cut grass for a while."

"Wish this thing would start. Maybe it's wet. I'll have to pull the spark plug and check it."

"That's no good! I never did that before. You don't have to move that to make it run." (I could tell by Hoot's tone that he was getting hot, not to mention embarrassed.)

"Gin! Don't move that, you are going to...!" RRRRRRRRRRR!

"Wow! It started right up. You knew about that all the time, huh?"

"I guess I wasn't listening to you. Wonder why I never had to do that before?"

I stepped out on the porch just in time to see them with their heads together and to hear Hoot saying, "Thanks a lot. That'll help next time." They looked up to see me and began to put on a mock squabble so I just went back inside without saying a word. I couldn't help thinking, though, that Hoot has more sense than I do now. Corny, you say? Yeah, but something I've got to chew on. That was woven into all our interactions this time—your much needed help in some of life's basics. I am out of my mind with the joy of you in my life.

Michael

June 1, 1984

Dearest Michael,

It hurt so bad, not being able to call you, before this afternoon. I knew how anxious you must have felt, by turning it around and knowing how worried and upset I would be. I hung on your every word, and still the ache for you won't be appeased. Maybe it comes from feeling so vulnerable.

The first night I was in the hospital, I was amazed when one of my students popped in to see me. On weekends he delivers flowers on the hospital floors, so the hospital staff knows him. He stayed and talked to me for a few minutes without any apparent unease, telling me the gossip of the day I missed at school. I thought it was pretty mature behavior for a 14-year-old.

I didn't go to the operating area until 11:30 on Thursday. I got tired of waiting, because I did nothing Wednesday except needlessly take up bed space. Even with the wait, I never felt nervous, because I could feel your reassuring presence. They put the IV in my wrist and gave me a muscle relaxant. I saw the operating room, and the next thing I knew I was shivering and awakened to my teeth chattering and hearing someone far away groaning. The cramping was bad when I first came to, but they gave me a shot for it, and by the time that wore off I was relatively pain free. It just left me feeling weak and vulnerable.

I called Milo's aunt tonight. She said he got off to a happy start on his trip east. She and her husband went over his checklist with him to be sure he hadn't forgotten anything. His uncle is a little worried about the motorcycle, although it is brand new, because it is not very heavy duty. He loaned Milo a couple of gas credit cards, in case it has mechanical problems. They made him promise to call every couple of days until he gets here, so they can keep track of his progress. She said Milo will still have his job when he goes back, and he has moved his stuff into a house he will share with a couple of friends. She calls it Milo's Odyssey. I thought that was pretty neat.

She says he has really grown up in the last year. Apparently, she mightily approves of him. She said his hair is quite short, and he has grown more handsome with his adult face. I am happy they have had such a good relationship. My only regret is that there will always be something unfinished about my mothering. I would like to have observed some of that transition from adolescence to adulthood. That hurts. However, I am grateful he had his aunt and uncle to support, guide, and encourage him through the rough years in my stead. They both have their heads on straight and have a solid relationship with each other. If I could have picked someone to refine, polish, and influence my son, I couldn't have found a more perfect pair. It is a demonstration of the program saying, "things happen as they are supposed to." They both worshiped Eric, and I think they assuaged some of their pain by having Milo in their life.

Elle found a map of that lake I was telling you about. There are still two weeks in August at the camp that are not taken. When I get home I will discuss it further with you and send you a map. I've been wracking my brain trying to remember all I know about fishing. After all, I have come on as an expert. Actually, other than the little fishing we did last summer and teaching Milo when he was little, I have done no serious fishing since I was 20. I only qualify by being born with a silver trolling-spoon in my hand. I'll have to pick my daddy's brain before we go. If we decide to.

I love you,
Verge

6/9/84

My Verge,

I just want to emblazon on paper that the Father's Day card from Gin is one of the nicest I have ever received in all my years. Not only the cuddly picture of the little girl bear handing a fishing worm to the daddy bear, but the sentiment, "Thanks for being there when things get icky," was very touching. Tell Ginny, "Thank you very much."

I hear a little anxiety in there about the possible loss of your fishing skills. They will come flying back to you, once you get a look in the water and set your mind to concentrating. I enjoy watching you do things you are proficient at. It feels good to watch and have no critical thoughts in my head, enjoy and learn. I look forward to going to that lake with you.

Does the cabin have running water and a bathroom? Just asking so I will know what to expect.

By the time you get this, you will be busily wrapped up with your son. I think that is beautiful. I know just looking at each other and checking each other out will be fine for both of you. I remember how much fun we had together that Xmas visit, and I wish I could be with you guys now. I look forward to seeing him in Cleveland during the wedding festivities. I just plain completely love you.

Michael

6/14/84

Dear Michael, My Love,

Five days have gone by without writing to you. I feel like I am tripping over my tongue trying to tell you everything at once, and I can't even seem to get a coherent sentence out! First of all, this has been one big yell to you. "Look, Michael, see how this is?" When I left my son and his wife in Phoenix, a little over a year ago, I flew to you to tell you how it was, with some reservation and worry. As usual you read between my words and gently told me that worrying would do no good.

This time I could empathize with Milo without getting into it personally. I could take my time and get all he had to give, without projecting into ten years from now and other useless thinking. I got all of the positive stuff, the good conversation, the laughs, the love, the looking, and the touches. Worry and negative thoughts just flew away. I know he does not blame me. I know his attitudes are his own, and will lead him on his own journey. He is neither his father nor his mother; he is unique and will find his own way.

The last time I was with him, I could hardly see him, for seeing his father at that age. I didn't have that problem this time. Things about him that are hardly explainable are totally different. For instance, a motorcycle for Eric would have been about power with a violent undertone. Milo has a healthy regard for the potential dangers of the machine and a practical outlook about it as a mode of affordable transportation. In our conversations I heard no propensity for his father's violence that was evident well before Milo's age. Also, there is a genuine consideration and caring for other's feelings. Milo talked about joking with the staff he works with, to help the new people get a feeling of family working together. It makes his job easier, he readily admits, but also easier in the light of it being a pleasant place to work when people are friendly with each other. He has a kindness about him that I like. I think elements of both his parents came together and reassembled in far better ways in him. I like him a lot. I am grateful that I can see him as his own person and not as someone compared to someone else. I can look at him and have no predictions.

We had quality conversations. I was able to tell him some happy stories about his father and diffuse some of the ogre image into some understanding of the disease, without harping on it. I was able to dispel my own fears that Milo's aunt and uncle might be angry, or resentful, about my leaving Eric and might not care to see me again. Milo turned it around quite simply by telling me about how hurt she was that she had to refuse Eric a place, when he asked to come out there, and that she understood how one couldn't live with him. We talked about Milo's marriage breaking up, and that he feels stronger than ever about the good part of marriage. He seems to have a handle on what happened, and why, and is not a resentful or blaming. I will be sorting this visit out for a while, but I feel released from a heavy burden of worry and fear. I am grateful that you are in my life to share all this sorting out and reassembling of my life.

About that Father's Day card from Gin. I tried subtly to tell her it was not a proper card to send you, but she said she liked it and you would, too. "But Gin, Michael is not your father."

"Well, when I feel fatherless and unfathered," says Gin, "he feels like a father. He is nice to me, and doesn't pull my hair when he combs it, and he gives me great big dishes of ice cream with cookies stuck on top. When I don't understand things, he explains real good and never, ever laughs at me. He asks me what I think about things, as if he really wants to know. He even thanked me when I showed him how to fix things by kicking them three times. He likes it when I tell him about my chicken, and must like chicken talk because he keeps asking me how it goes. Now don't you think that is a good enough reason to send him a Father's Day Card, just to let him know I like him a real, real lot?"

I have to admit she left me nothing to say. Please excuse her poor taste in cards and know I tried my darnedest to dissuade her, even though you say you liked it. I like you a real, real lot, too, and it has nothing to do with Father's Day.

Verge

6/18/84

My Verge,

Feeling. Feelings. Feelings. I don't know what to feel about feelings. It is funny how a body can believe he knows a lot about something and learn he knows nothing. The more I am around this life, one thing becomes more certain—it is good to keep an open mind.

This weekend was a surprise time for me, in the world of feelings. They seemed to be drifting down like pieces of fluffy snow, settling on me in unexpected places at unexpected times, and not always melting, either. I want to share some of them, but they are as elusive as dreams, so if I begin to sound frantic you will know why.

I told you about being shoved back into reality, when the younger folks went off by themselves. Later, while soaking in my bath getting ready for the wedding, I started getting mad. It isn't fair that age should segregate folks, yet that is how it must be. I am mad because that's true, and I am mad that I am age. I can remember and feel exactly as I did when I was at their point in time. The only reason I am now age is because so and so much time has passed for me. I also know that the accompanying loneliness is just a preview of what will be if I live to be my mother's age. No one consciously wants to exclude you; that's just the way it works. One's involvement in the activities of youth (like big church weddings) becomes more and more limited as time goes by. I know that, but it is painful to meet face to face. As I have often said and believed, once past the grandparent stage, a person's grave has outlived its usefulness (except for bike riders such as you and I, who like to stop and read the gravestones and make up stories about how it must have been, and think about them for a minute or two before moving on). The facts of life must continue to be learned, and faced, and adjusted to, or they will sweep you away, and no one will even know you are missing.

I allowed myself a few minutes of feeling some self-pity as I soaked, then let all that go down the drain with the water. I learned from you during this last bad time that if I didn't let it go, after looking it over, I too would go down the drain. The ways of life are indifferent; if I don't adjust and choose alternatives life goes right on by without blinking an eye. The responsibility is all mine.

I didn't have time to feel nostalgic or sorry for myself at the ceremony itself because I was involved and having too much fun watching those two having the time of their life. But at the reception I began to feel surrounded. At one point, as I stood where I could look out over the proceedings, I felt like everyone was making demands of me, all at once. I felt trapped and suffocated. I had a strong urge to settle the discomfort in the way I settled pain or unpleasantness in the past—run from it as fast and as far as I could, both physically and emotionally. There was Julie over there beckoning to me. She seemed to be telling me that having a drink wouldn't be too bad; to remember and slide back into forgetting wouldn't be bad. She represented Eric, as part of the euphoric recall, as if time and the disease had not taken any toll at all. I felt resentful that a huge toll has been exacted and resentful to be reminded of it by her presence. Julie became a threat.

At the same table were some friends dating back to my youth. They were beckoning, seeming to say, "Nothing has changed. We are still like we were then; time went by but forgot us. Come, stay with us." They became a threat. My relatives, my brothers and nieces and nephews, cousins, and in-laws all behaved as if they thought I was strange, when I am as I always have been; only circumstances have changed. They threatened me. And my family, my children and their families, and my wife were all whirling past, and I wondered where they were whirling to, and that was a threat.

I am tempted to say I was afraid, but I really wasn't. I did feel some panic. It wasn't a strong panic, more a continuous series of small waves. Each time, I felt the urge to run, but I didn't. I allowed them to sweep over me, and I held on real, real tight, knowing that I wanted to feel each one of them; I didn't know why. I just knew I had to feel them and not run or it would bring me right back there weaker and more frightened. Like you, I haven't sorted all this out yet, but it has helped just writing about it. Some insight has come with the writing.

Same day! Here's me still writing. Later, as the night was winding to a close, the various traditions began to be played out, the same old bouquet throw, the garter throw. Once again I shrugged off the feeling of panic and became absorbed in watching my youngest daughter and her new husband having fun, loving, bringing all those things they planned for so long, to life. It was hard for negative thoughts to prevail in the face of that.

It was time for the bride to dance with her father. You know, everyone is in a circle and the band plays *Daddy's Little Girl*. I thought of all the times I had sat back at other folk's weddings and played the cynic, scoffing at such maudlin fare. I was little prepared for my reaction to my newly married daughter. I am not totally sure what that reaction was, but I know it was different from any feeling I have had about her since she was born. Firstly, without even thinking about it, the syrupy old song took on new meaning and seemed important. Secondly, I felt unusual vibes from my daughter, as if she also felt that new nameless something, like an understanding or rapport that had always existed between us, but we didn't know about, and it was bubbling to the surface. Holding her as we danced was something special. I could tell by the way she held me, and the way we laughed together, that she, too, was feeling something special and was equally confused by it. I felt as if I should say all the things they say in the movies at such times—about what a joy she has been, how special she is and how I will miss her—but it just didn't seem right, somehow. Maybe that is a cop out. I did want to tell her I love her and didn't because other people had joined in by then. I felt bad that I didn't. Later as I was standing near the bar talking to the photographer, she came over to me, and as if she knew how I felt, or shared my feelings, she put her arms around my neck and said in my ear that she loved me, which gave me a chance to say back in her ear that I love her. Then I think we both felt better. Next letter I will tell you about Milo's visit.

Michael

6/18/84

My Love, My Michael,

I could empathize when you told me, on the phone, about your loneliness after being left out, when the young men went off and doing at the wedding. It was not intentional unkindness, more the generation gap, which made it seem normal to them. Like, you wouldn't have any interest in doing what they were doing anyway. I remember feeling as you did, when I was younger, and the fellows were going off to do male things (you and Eric used to do that often), or after Milo was born, being amassed with the women, who were a bit of a mystery to me anyhow, while the unmarrieds and husbands went off to do—whatever, that being drinking, usually. I used to get some terrible resentments.

This weekend, didn't I run myself right into a similar pity party? Saturday, Elle and Herb came to dinner and we lingered overlong, so I hurried off to the play after they said they would clean up the dinner dishes and lock up after their coffee. The show was a typical little theatre production when no professional people are involved, uneven, undisciplined, and imperfect. The actors, however, were pleased with their efforts and happy to have worked together. There are things to be said for that attitude; after all, it is recreation for them. I have an unrealistically critical outlook about that kind of production, because I was fortunate to work with some very dedicated actors even though it was civic theatre.

Afterwards, some people asked if I were going to the cast party. Because the director, who was throwing the party at his home, did not personally ask me to come, my nose was out of joint, and I hid behind my not drinking as a reason not to go. Not drinking is not a valid reason for not socializing. I know I didn't need an invitation to a cast party—they just are, and all involved assume they are invited. I was just a 'poor me' waiting to happen. All weekend I was feeling blue because I had chosen not to go to your daughter's wedding, and I was looking for an excuse to really feel miserable. I succeeded for a bit. I had myself a good cry, kicking myself the while for I knew I brought it on myself. I knew it wasn't mature behavior as I was doing it. I could have stopped it at any point, but I did it anyway. They say there is nothing wrong with feelings; it is what you do with them that matters. I didn't do too well with mine, but it was over soon.

Verge

6/20/84

My Verge,

Yeaa! Welcome summer, the happiest time of the year. Can't wait to see you! I pained over telling you about my feelings when Milo arrived. They descended on me—plunk—like the other feelings of the weekend, saying, "OK, what are you going to do about me?" Sometimes I phrase things so they come out sounding wrong, and considering what Milo means to both of us, it is important to get everything straight. None of that worry was necessary. After reading your letter, I just flopped back in my chair nodding my head in agreement, because the way you felt fit my head and heart like the same old Verge and Michael glove. You mentioned on the phone that his beard stopped you for a second. Ditto. That, stored away with other mannerisms, facial expressions, and gestures so startlingly like Eric's, produced some confusing feelings for a while.

The night he arrived, we sat around the kitchen table talking, and early the next morning after taking the grandbaby to the sitters, we went off to the motorcycle shop. We had a nice talk over breakfast. Mostly I listened and asked questions. But my mind began to play games with me. I found myself searching for Eric in him. As I said, mannerisms, gestures, his face, things picked up over a growing up lifetime, were exaggerated. When we got home, he went off with the younger folks, and I told you in the last letter how I felt then.

Milo didn't attend the wedding because he didn't have any church going clothes with him. When I got wind of his decision, at the church, I had to grab a quick hold of myself and apply a generous dose of Program to keep from running home and attempting to control the situation.

The next day was sit around day. Milo and I spent most of the time in TV land while the others came and went. I found myself looking for Eric in him, vacillating between believing he was Eric and accepting him for himself. Again I felt threatened. (You can tell it was a very threatening weekend.) I was in turmoil. I found myself confused because the outward manifestations of Eric, which Milo displayed, did not coincide with the behaviors I expected with them. For instance, when Eric used a certain gesture or tone of voice, I expected criticism or lashing out behavior, but Milo behaved with quiet acceptance or agreement—same gesture, different meaning. I was in a state of confusion until what was happening dawned on me quite suddenly (as if Gin had given me a series of ankle kicks). Thank God it was not too late to enjoy the young man's company for the rest of the visit. Once the puzzle was solved, I relaxed and saw things in their true light. Things made sense and I was easy. I began to observe Milo, unique person that he is, and wholeheartedly agree with all the insights you described in your letter.

I can't wait to see you,<br>
Michael

6/20/84

Dear Michael,

Last day with my students, except for one hour tomorrow when they come for their report cards. I don't know whether it is the strain of testing, or my state of mind and body, but yesterday and today I have felt exhausted by the time I get home from work. Last night I planted the last of my bulbs, giving them an extra little pat saying, "You won't get any more attention until I get back from seeing Michael." I am holding off mowing my lawn until Monday after I go upstate to see my father on the weekend. Gotta gather information about fishing, you know!

It seems strange to be driving to Cleveland. Eric asked me to deliver his trunk if I were going out there this summer, so I'm making that leap. I stopped at the garage and made an appointment for next Tuesday—muffler, alignment, new tires. I'll get it all taken care of, as I plan on doing some traveling this summer.

I can't ever recall this kind of need to see you and to talk to you. I have been feeling particularly vulnerable these last few weeks. I have unfinished business about Milo that I never dealt with because it was a matter of survival at the time. I stuffed my feelings about him to such an extent that it was almost as if he had never been in my life. When I went to Arizona there were many distractions, the new wife, the sights, and little time with him personally, so I continued to feel detached. This time it was on a one-to-one level, and I can no longer keep those feelings locked away. I presume there was some of that going on for him, too. I feel fortunate to have had a chance to convey to him my love and appreciation of the person he has become. But now I have this bunch of feelings to deal with. I need to sort them out with you.

Soon, Love,
Verge

7/24/84

Dear Michael,

HI HOOT,

HOPE YOUR FISHING HAS IMPROVED. SEE YOU SOON. I'M WORKING ON RULES FOR THE FISHING CONTEST.

LOVE, GIN

(Sorry, I had to give her space or she would never have left me in peace.)

It was like imps jumped out of my post box today shouting, "Surprise!" I actually gasped. I had the distinct feeling you were standing there grinning your fool head off. You must have sent the package and cards while I was still in Cleveland, for them to arrive on my birthday. I can't guess when you had time.

After opening the present, Gin and I had to grin at each other. Unless you are catching guppies, those itsy bitsy fishhooks will never do. They're not for the kind of fish we are going to be after. Gin went around the house dangling those little do-dads saying, "Awwwww, Hoot, these are soooo cute!" She also kept asking me what one was supposed to do with the dough balls. Wuz you supposed to throw them into the water like chum, getting the fish to gather so you could net 'em? Or maybe if a fish ate enough of them it'd float to the top like a bobber, from the gas created. Well, she is still puzzling it out, and every once in a while she runs in with a new one, "Maybe they're just plain poison and kill fish on the spot, like those South American Indians get fish with poison darts." I don't dare tell her they're to put on the hook; she would make herself sick laughing.

Tonight for my birthday, I invited Elle, Herb, and the snowplowing neighbor and his wife over for ice cream and cake. I made sponge cake like the one we had in Cleveland, only I mixed raspberries and peaches to go on top. It went great with the Rocky Road ice cream I got special for Hoot. We sat around the outdoor table, talking until dark.

When you asked me how I felt doing dumb things that I just want to do, without the repression of Eric's control or anyone else's, I didn't answer you very well because I wanted to think about that concept. It had never been stated so concisely before. There are things I find joy in doing today, that I would not have dreamed of doing even a year ago. Inviting the neighbors for dessert gave me a big happy boost. We are basically lonely people, and we all enjoyed the evening's companionship. Reaching out just a little—letting myself be just a little vulnerable—has huge rewards. I wouldn't have dreamed of willingly celebrating my birthday in such a way ever before. It would have been such a weakness to even admit I wanted to celebrate such a childish thing as that. Yet, in my secret place, my Gin would be crying a little because nobody noticed her natal day. Thank you for making my birthday special,

Verge

7/28/84

My Verge,

Hoot came to me, day before yesterday, looking serious with his head down. "Oh, oh," I thought, "those two have been at it again. It's probably over those dumb old fishing contest rules." That wasn't it, though.

Hoot said, "Gin has been writing out in the open things like 'Love, Gin', and 'Hoot and Gin'."

"So?" I asked, "Does that make you mad?"

"That's just it," he said, "It doesn't. A while ago, I would have been mad if she did that. I even told her not to write that stuff and for sure not to say it out loud. What if some of the guys heard it or found out? "

"I see what you mean."

"The thing that bothers me now is that I like to see it written out, and to hear her say it. Is there something wrong with me?"

I said, "Yeah, there is, and when it gets you, it gets you good. But there is nothing like it. It's like you never can get enough. Sort of the way I keep saying anything, just so she will answer me and I can hear her voice. The music of her voice and the way she says things just knock me out."

"Me, too, like when I say 'Wellll, Gin,' just so she will say, 'Woool, Hoot!'"

"We search for new ways to tell each other about how much bigger our love gets, and she wraps it up in one simple phrase, 'I love you just as you are you.' Nothing to add or subtract."

"Yeah, I know. I don't care what any of those guys say. I wish Verge and Gin lived here with us."

"Yeah," I said, as Hoot stumbled out of the room, carrying his fishing pole.

Thanks for telling me about your birthday party and how it felt. You made me feel good, telling me, and telling me how you can do dumb things now, if you want to. I think that is important. I am also glad the cards and gift did just what I intended—sort of added to the cake and ice cream party. Good luck with the Board of Ed.

I love you just the way you are you, too.

Michael

7/30/84

Dear Michael,

I went to the Board of Education on Thursday, and everything was closed, as were all the schools. Elle told me there was an art teacher position at the high school, posted when she called in early July. When school got out at the end of June, there were no openings posted, so I left my phone number and the number in Cleveland at the Board of

Education, with the request to be notified if there was an opening, so I could make a formal application. As you know, I was not notified. For now, all I can do is send a formal back-up letter of application and wait.

I loved your Michael and Hoot letter. I didn't know if I should let Gin see it or not. It seemed an awful personal tale about Hoot. I think I will save it for some day when she is in a raving snit about him. She does them to herself, you know. Nothing Hoot does brings them on. It's when she thinks he is mad, or hurt, or upset, and he won't tell her why that she gets all carried away, making up in her head why he is acting as he is. Usually, she decides it is something she has done and then she comes all down on herself or Hoot, and Hoot hasn't even said a word. After watching her, I've decided you have to tell me what you want me to know, or how you feel, and I have to do the same for you. We should not play that fathom-what-is-in-each-other's-head game. We should not expect the other one knows, just because we are so close and usually do know.

Tonight the cicadas are sizzling in full force, telling me that out there is my summer love and we are going to get us some cicada madness soon. Sizzle on, you little buggers! Gin and I are enclosing some proper hooks for catching real fish. We do have a small request that you let us each use one. Only one. If we lose it we are on our own. Gin is still busy making up new contest rules every day.

Love,<br>
Verge

Hey Hoot,

I just happened to find a book at the library today called, *The Complete Guide to Lake Fishing.* Course, I don't need it myself, but I took it out to see if the person who wrote it knows what he is talking about. I could bring it with me and maybe you would like to read it while I'm out catching the big ones! Only kidding. And, no, you can't sit on me for that one.

LOVE, GIN

7/30/84

My Sweet Verge,

As I told you briefly on the phone, the conversation between Doreen and me opened up out of nowhere. Actually the situation, being alone on vacation together and acting like brother and sister, caused me to pain over the relationship more acutely than ever. The idea, or reality, that you pointed out almost a year ago was gnawing more than ever—the one that said, you have to get some honesty in there someplace. It is unhealthy, for two people, in what is supposed to be a close relationship, to behave that way, and then not talk about it, or do anything about it, but just to go on grinding and grinding inside. I found the grinding was getting heavier as there were no other people or interruptions, like there are at home, to use as an excuse to ignore the situation.

It is such a many-faced thing, with so many nooks and crannies. There is no hostility except that which I am sure is seething below the surface in both of us. I guess I mean no apparent or open hostility. My head was awash. "What is honest? What is right, or wrong, anyway? Am I being impatient and forcing an issue that needs to be left for later?" I didn't or couldn't know. I only knew something was pushing and pushing to come out, to be said, anything to start the air flowing, for it was stifling. I called on H. P. and all the imps I could muster, to somehow let me know whether to talk or not, and if an opening came, to have the courage to grab it. If nothing came, to know enough to shut up. Your voice kept echoing, "Don't say what you don't mean." (And my head added, "Don't do what you don't mean.")

By Tuesday, the need to get something said became painful; not necessarily to resolve anything, just to acknowledge out loud that all is not right. I went up to the second floor to sit on the sun deck. Doreen was coming up later, and I decided that if some opening did not occur, I would know that it just wasn't time. (Back to imposing my own conditions.)

Maybe my senses were sharpened to recognize, or maybe my imagination was ready to put a label on anything, but shortly after Doreen came up, she said something that related to her and me, and my ears picked straight up. I just knew that was it. It had some special quality, a feeling, and I acted before I could even think. It was almost like it was taken out of my hands. I don't even remember what Doreen said. I said something like "I feel uneasy about our relationship—uneasy about behaving like brother and sister." (Some several months earlier I told her I didn't have any interest in sex—that I didn't know why, but at that time I didn't. That was even before last summer.) The notion flashed into my head, and just as quickly flashed out of my mouth that I was indifferent about it; that I was uneasy, but indifferent to whether it got solved or not. I was also uneasy about the indifference. That snapped Doreen straight up, and the conversation continued off and on 'til dinnertime.

I don't know how to label it, tentative maybe, cautious, afraid? Both exploring. A lot of it is hazy. Nothing was solved, but the fresh air felt good. I said I would take steps toward my health, but I did not know what direction that would take me. If I sought counseling, or therapy, I wouldn't know if the growth and changes I have experienced would take me in another direction, for after all, we both seem to have gone off in different directions as it is. We agreed, and definitely agreed that it was scary. What I said was the truth for the time and place, and the way I felt. I didn't mention you or us. I did not think that was necessary then. I believe as you told me once, "It is important to settle our lives, so if we then want to, we can walk to each other rather than run from something."

Later, we had a drive and went to dinner. The next morning Doreen told me she had gotten very angry that night, but she had worked it out alone. There were no great solutions, or anything, but I had to sort it out with you. Thank you for listening. Time has run out. If you are confused I know you will ask me. Soon we can talk eyeball to eyeball.

Michael

8/14/84

Dear Michael,

Tonight I am mentally exhausted. I didn't sleep very well last night as I was projecting about the job. This morning I went to the Board of Education and was informed that the art position was filled. I hadn't allowed myself to expect the job, due to past history; nevertheless, I felt betrayed and rejected. After the initial reaction, though, I was fairly calm. I could hear your voice in my ear telling me Program. Mostly I resent the cavalier treatment. I can accept not being qualified, but not being granted the courtesy of an interview galls me. There is a nag at the back of my brain saying, with a newly appointed high school principal who intends to shape up the school, and my hotshot department head, I might do well keeping out of the fray and continuing to prepare for the eventuality of a move or a new career direction. I did speak to the union president, but he said he couldn't do much until he was sent the Board minutes stating who was appointed to the position. Does every piece of life have to be such a struggle?

Then, this afternoon, Elle told me that the two fellows who rent across the street from her were saying they had talked to my landlord about buying my house. He told them I only had a year's lease. Something tells me I better get into today and stick there. I'm beginning to feel hurt, angry, and unsure, and I know none of those feelings are going to get me anywhere. Tonight I'm going to a new Al-Anon meeting. I think I better keep adding some on for a while. Even little thoughts of losing this house get me scared. I feel especially vulnerable right now, still torn apart from you. Half of my psyche is off wandering somewhere.

Verge

8/16/84

My Sweet Verge,

Many times, just by behaving the way we do together, we are reaching out and guiding each other through bushes, over fences, around puddles, hand in hand as we talk. The way we talked and talked about ourselves last week is an example. It helps us to know ourselves as well as each other. We even have developed a delightful process of inventing situations and conditions with Hoot and Gin that we use for our development and growth. What an easy feeling to be in your company and how reassuring to know that we have discovered the way to resolve times when it is possible to not be so easy. Even that discovery had a special feeling.

You laughed when we talked on the phone about your job, saying that you didn't want to hear that Program crap. I took it in the joking manner it was said, but somewhere in the back of my head a buzzer sounded. I knew you were hurt and disappointed even though you sounded brave and coping. Your letter confirms that. I want to reach out and hold your hand real tight and look into your brown eyes so you can see I understand how lonely and cold it can be out there. When you walk, I'll hold on tight and walk, too. That house thing surely came out of the wildy blue! What a stunner that must have been! You could let word of the ghosties leak out.

For solace, I came and got you from the noise and dust of the new roof they are putting on your house, and took you to the Bluff. It was like you said about photos of us, though, the indefinable something was missing. Your presence was hazy, unlike other times when it felt pretty much real. Maybe we have gotten too close to ever have anything that involves being apart be very real anymore.

Michael

8/16/84

Dear Love, My Michael,

Signs and portents. I have joined elemental man in the watching for, belief in, and puzzling over signs and portents. Tonight, at deep dusk, I got out of my car with my house keys clutched in hand. When I went to put the key in the door, instead, in my hand was the blue secret-decoder that Hoot gave Gin. Simple coincidence? Not if you are a signs and portents reader. My instant reaction was, "Oh, Hoot!" I treasure those close up pats I perceive when such things happen. It helps to keep the lonelies at bay.

Last night I went to a theatre meeting. My hesitancy in joining another group has been the notorious pastime of drinking, so prevalent in the groups I have known. Didn't I meet a fellow traveler there whose job, mentioned in passing, is working with alcohol and drug abusing kids? Signs and portents, or just a big ear out for opportunity? Maybe losing out on the high school job is a gift, and I am meant to keep preparing for some other occupation.

If nothing else, following signs and portents seems to make order out of the chaos of life. If I can only decipher the pattern, or figure the action indicated, maybe all of it will make sense sometime. My aching for your presence first led me to this belief, fragile as it still is. The very impertinence of believing that some God, Gods, or Impish power looks upon this grain of sand, me, and cares, is hard to trust. If I can keep blind and deaf to those doubts and inspect my progress, it comes easier to believe, and it does have a comfort to it. All my previous life before us, as we know us now, I refused to believe that we were more than bits of chaff blown on the wind with chance being the only fate. There is too much of us that cannot be answered by pure chance and coincidence. If I can believe the mystery of that, it is easier to believe the mystery of signs and portents.

No Indian ever more closely observed his surroundings for signals from the Great Spirit, no cave man ever drew pictures more faithfully to gain favor from the powers that be, and no sheep entrails, wine dregs, or tea leaves have been more carefully inspected for omens. No scarlet leaf spirals but it is Hoot teasing Gin about school starting soon. No coffee is spilled that is not Michael jostling my arm to make his presence known. No rain just rains and no star just falls. Everything touches my life through the filter of signs and portents.

This morning on the phone, you asked if I had made any attempt to put our latest time together into words. My saying no was not an indication of disinterest, only that I am still mulling it over. I usually sweep an important experience such as we just had to the back of my brain, and, other than herding any stray bits back there, too, I leave it in its raw state for a while until it starts generating pieces of thought that I collect in some other place (often in letters to you). Eventually, streams of insight begin to pour out. You have said on various occasions that I give you a lot of insight. Sometimes I find myself astonished at what I am saying or writing, because it comes out in entire hunks from a source of which I am not conscious. It's not as if I had taken bit-by-bit, and pondered, or reconstructed, or consciously done any work on the thinking about it, at all. I used to picture practically everyone else working at the serious hard labor of thinking, so therefore my thoughts seemed less weighty or less meaningful. Now, because I suspect you might think this way also, I begin to accept that although my style of thinking is a grasshopper making music, instead of an ant toiling away, maybe it's still valid. If the snows come and freeze my toes and hunger shrinks my belly, though, it will be a sign that the whole idea is hogwash.

One overriding thought about our interaction, during the last time together, is how courageous we were. I keep looking at several aspects of what happened during that time and it makes me want to pat us both for being so brave. We found new sides of our selves to expose, and explore, and poke, gently. We even allowed our vulnerabilities to get hurt in front of each other and allowed our psyches to admit that hurt. We let that hurt be seen without the pretense of not being hurt, and then told the other why we hurt. It took courage to allow that to happen. The cause was not intentional, but when it happened we rode it together and worked it out. It is a fairy tale to think hurt does not happen between people who love each other as we do. It was a serendipitous test of our communication. What joy to find it works!

In retrospect I can see a progressive build up to that test, although it felt like a first time experience: last fall, your hurt about leaving the house across the lake and all the good times we had had there that you couldn't verbalize for six months; your hurt this spring when you perceived that I had disparaged your handling of the canoe, that took a few weeks to talk about; and last week your hurt when you felt I was pushing and rushing you when you were trying to fix your fishing pole. Your anger came out sideways for a couple of hours until you were able to tell me how you felt and why. We didn't crumble when you told me you were angry, and we found that the telling cleared the air, dispelling the hurt feelings we both had, by then. Courageous. There were other courageous things, too. You told me of your feelings about growing up with your father's alcoholism and later his descent into Alzheimer's. I told you of being molested as a child. By searching painful places together, those hidden from self and others, we helped each other get perspective on carefully forgotten issues. We had the courage to take time to look at our life. We had courage enough to allow each other to see personal failings (doing things we were rusty at or unskilled, like fishing and speaking French) and even exposed our apprehension and fears (swimming in unplumbed depths and thunderstorms). When our time was up, we had the courage to leave each other again. As I am writing this, I am looking at us through the wrong end of a telescope, and I feel very tender about those two courageous people.

Verge

8/18/84

Dear Verge,

I especially like these pictures of you I am mailing. You have that look I was trying to tell you about. A special something peeking out of those pretty eyes, a tilt to the head, an angle of the chin, a promise of self-assurance which I find very exciting. It came to me, as I was sitting on our Bluff that the grown up is beginning to take over. We have been boosting each other along and now the Verge of you is overtaking the adolescent Gin. It is very, very attractive.

I have just finished reading your signs and portents letter. It delights me, the way you fit our signs to elemental man's signs and interpretations. A phrase I used to like the sound of and clung to was: "If there is any God or Gods, they look on us with little more than indifference." We, I was assured, were all out here to be blown in the wind. The gutsiest and the strongest held on the tightest, dug in a toehold, and made it from one end of life to the other without too many lumps or bruises. I thought that huddling together as a group didn't help much, for the winds were strong, and no one knew more than anyone else. Head down. Buck up.

Hope for the best. Amen. Never to be admitted was that booze was my hiding place and my personal guardian angel for those extra rough spots.

You said "elemental man." I liked that, because when I stopped drinking and didn't have anything to hide under, and the people in The Program were relying on a Higher Power, seemingly doing all right, I was outside looking in and feeling like I was back to basics with no toehold. It got so I either had to face the life I was going to try to live or go back to the old one. Duking it out alone was getting tougher and tougher. I read in some of the books that all I had to do was be willing to give H. P. a try. You recommended some reading that gave me some new ways to look at spirituality that could fit my head. Finally, it was be willing to try, or hurt and be confused too bad to stand up against. I tried, and it didn't hurt; the pain turned gentle and did not crush me. Eventually it didn't matter any more whether it was Universal Truth, or the Great Spirit, or positive thinking—it worked, was kind, bore me up and carried me along when I let it. It was far better than being a bruise all the time.

You marveled at our having the courage to allow hurty things to happen on "our time". That grabbed my attention. We could have swept anything that interfered or rankled under the carpet for later on, or for never, because our time was limited, and we were going to make the best of it. But we have reached the stage where ignoring it would be ignoring life. It is the time in our life where we prune, and weed, and align, and if something doesn't work we rearrange or adjust the fitting of ourselves together, so no startles can exist to shatter the beauty built on that foundation. Surprises make life more interesting, but startles could be ruinous. Certainly we needed courage as we approached the proving ground, for possibly we couldn't face or reconcile the complex personality traits emerging, as we lived in extended proximity. Without running, we did as we have been doing all this time; we stood together and faced ourselves.

I have to treat that experience, the way you do, put it on the back burner and let the wafting steam carry the pieces of thoughts and ideas to me. I dig that notion of thinking. You helped me understand the idea of creative thought coming from within, from the total person and the total experience flowing out. Not until then, did that sort of thinking, which I can do if I let do, start to take on validity. Bottling up, holding back, inhibiting oneself because of fear or lack of assurance is stunting. We nurture all these healthy pieces of ourselves, the way you bring a roaring fire out of a humble smolder. Gently, patiently you guide it, 'til, poof—a flame! Then you add a few little sticks there and eventually a big chunk here, then, look—a miracle! That works for me, too. One thing springs from another until sometimes I can't write fast enough to capture it all.

You steady on validate a way of life for me, when you are with me sharing your life style, or sharing it in letters. You put into words and bring to actual life ways of looking at and doing everyday things that I thought were strange private parts of me. I thought anyone else would think them strange. They seemed too insignificant to share with anyone or ask about, so I carried them through life, alone, wondering if anyone else does them or thinks that way. You bring even those little things out into the light and it makes my life less lonely. I love you just exactly the way you are.

Michael

8/21/84

Dearest Michael,

I told you early on about knowing before an event transpires that it is going to be very important in my life. As it is happening I can see, as if I am observing at a distance, that it is a life's crossroad in progress. Our time at the camp in Quebec was one of those events, and I am left with the feeling that our life will vibrate and reverberate for a goodly time from things begun there.

Thank you for talking about how Eric influenced your life, and for encouraging me to talk about him. I feel a new sort of compassion, as I think of him back when we were all beginning. I see clearly now that he was as vulnerable as we were, just a human feeling his way along an unknown path like the rest of us, only more determined that no one would know. He was writing his notes as he went along, hoping none of us would call him on anything. By perfecting his derisive attitude and sharp tongue, he made pretty well sure no one would. I think he was also unsure and scared at times. All of us supporting his own myth must have left him very lonely out there; God forbid he should show his clay feet. Having this new perspective of him helps to let me give up the notion he deliberately did anything to hurt me. By talking to you about that hurty stuff I could feel the hurt slipping away. I can forgive because I can see that he was perhaps more lost than either of us. Internalizing that understanding has taken his power away from my life. He didn't stop me from talking; I stopped communicating because I believed that nothing

I could say was wise enough, or funny enough, or interesting enough for his ears. If he treated me as half-bright, he did not have a whole lot to go on to think otherwise. I began to think of myself as half-bright.

Thank you for the opportunity at the camp to read over some of my old letters. They helped me to believe my brain works pretty good (if we discount continued short term memory loss). Daily I find the same in your letters. They make me laugh, they make me think, and they hold me spellbound. Fortunately, we did not end up as Eric clones, despite his magnetism, but in our silent ways we benefited from exposure to him on many levels, not the least of which, we learned to express ourselves vividly.

We spent that whole rainy day of our vacation talking about Eric and your father and the state of our state. The next day you got angry with me because I was trying to hurry you to go fishing and you were trying to fix your fish pole. You said I was being a controller. You were silent and brooding for most of the afternoon. Earlier in the morning when you had put on your bathing suit, you were already inviting a negative response from me. I am wondering if some of that behavior used to give you permission to go and drink? Later you told me you felt like running away. That day scared me a lot. For a few moments of panic, I, too, felt like running away. What if all our days became like that? Maybe we had finally found the place where we would begin to think less of each other. Maybe it was a 24-year-old fantasy and we had killed it.

Then a calm of sorts came. I was able to keep the panic out of my brain and to see your hurt for what it was, to believe if I could wait long enough it would work out. I put my trust in our honesty with each other working. It did. It made me feel good when you said, instead of running away you talked to me and told me what you were feeling about being pressured. I believe that is a major growth step for you.

You have mentioned counseling a few times. I think you are at a place where, if you were willing and able to level with one, a counselor would be impartial and separate enough from your problems to give you a fresh perspective and a few more options. Increasingly, I see two men. I see a strung taut at home man who holds everything in, a grit your teeth and do it because it is right and because you have to, sort of man. Reserved is putting it mildly, more like cold. And I see a grabbing-at-life, exuberant, expressive, loving, out-giving man. I do not think you have a serious mental problem, Michael, so I am forced to think one of those men is a lie. The more you grow, and change, and accept the new you, it seems the more tightly you hang onto that other image, as if should you let it go, everything will go smash. The more you grow away from that man, the tenser you seem to get about it. I love you, Michael, and I am very concerned about that increased tension. Somehow you have to integrate those two men. You have to be honest enough to yourself, to Doreen, to your kids, to me, and to whomever it takes to get those two into one. A tall order as they say in the Program! Where do you start? Why not give a counselor a shot? In the back of your head you know that honesty is part of the problem, because you said on the phone, "Maybe the first thing I have to do is figure out who is Hoot and who is Michael."

I love you,
Verge

8/27/84

My Verge,

I want to hurry to tell you in writing that your letter didn't set me off on that pity party. It had been coming on for some days before. Your letter told me things I was supposed to hear—told me the way things are, but I just didn't want to hear them. When I did, I decided to gather them to myself as slings and arrows rather than the love and caring that they were.

Actually, what I had been doing was forgetting that, like it or not, I have to go pretty closely by The Program, or I start losing hold. One of The Program slogans is, "A Day At a Time." I had started the old habit of flying in many directions, both on the ground and in my head. I was steadily getting more and more confused, and so, more touchy. By the time your letter came, I was ready for any excuse to self-destruct. I have to remember that patience and "One Step At a Time" are the only way it works for me. When I rush things or take on too much, I crumble. Because I go slow doesn't mean I am not working on changing. Experience has taught me that I must go at my own pace.

You were right in your letter. A lot of my behavior is dry drunk stuff. Man, the longer I am sober and work on getting better, the more I find there is to work on. Pretty good for a body who thought, when he came into The Program, there wouldn't be much for him to do to get everything down pat and out of the way. Ha!

I feel better now. I took a few more tiny steps and am ready to move on some more, not forgetting good old "Easy Does It." I hate to drag you along through all this, but I know from the way I feel about you, that you want to be in on it all, good or bad. Thanks for the just-the-way-you-are gift from you to me. I cherish that.

Michael

8/31/84

Dearest Michael,

Happy Birthday Cake Day! I am here on my bed, feeling like singing a praise of my Michael. Sometimes I'm overcome like that, out of the blue, just a great surge of Michael love. I want to hug your Mommy and your Daddy for the union that created the most precious human being in my world. They did everything just right when they made you. I love them both for that.

I just reread for the umpteenth time your letter about my letter that was the occasion for your bad feeling last weekend. You said that you knew it wasn't my letter, other than symbolically, that started your bad feelings. I am overjoyed by your huge new growth in your letter. First off, you admitted you were feeling bad. Second, you realized my letter was only an excuse to tie a whole bunch of things together to feel bad about. Third, you saw my letter as an act of love as it was intended, rather than as the criticism you first mistook it for. Fourth, you recognized how to use your Program on your problem—"Easy Does It" and "One Day At a Time"—to diminish its effect. And last, you recognized a need to go at your own pace and were able to clearly state that fact to me. Sweet Love, we still have some mighty growing to do, but we begin to know how to do it in less self-destructive ways. True, you are feeling down on yourself just now, but you have taken some giant strides and you are still striding. You can't see your progress because you are still out in the middle of the lake, and when you paddle out there you are not aware of your movement unless you look back at the canoe's wake. You are making steady on progress, so stop and give yourself a pat and some hugs, and get back at it, 'cuz it is the right direction.

Whatever is the matter with Gin? She's been wandering around looking gloomy. I asked her what was wrong and she said maybe she should'na. "Should not have done what?" I asked her.

"Should'na sent that letter to Hoot," said she. "The Post Office should have a return to sender button you could push if you decided you didn't wanna after you did." She said she was skairt that Hoot wouldn't want to ever see her again because she'd told him too much about something.

"Sometimes you can get in too close to people, and then you want to run away because you don't know how they feel about you telling too much, even when it is a nice too much." That is how she explained it, but it left me confused because I thought they were pretty tight. I hope it works out. Does Hoot seem to be all right? They're so cute together I hate to see them get all flummoxed up and hurting. Michael, it is nice to know things like that don't ever happen to us, huh? Not for long.

We both are beginning to become grown ups. Unfortunately, there is that awkward adolescent period when we have to test out new ways to be, and some of them are not too graceful. We are newly allowing each other to see the depth of our vulnerabilities without the usual defenses, because we have painstakingly disassembled those walls between us. Now we are faced with nothing to use except new tools and new ideas. I have had to take a close look at that thing that sounds and feels like controlling or being bossy. It is, in reality, an overbalance on learning to say what I think and what I need. I am not graceful at it yet, but you helped me be aware of that, and now I am working on it with conscious thought. Keep telling me when I tread on your personal needs. At this point, we can't afford to beat around the bush with each other. All we've got is hanging on tight and writing lots of notes. As you said, I want to grow apace with you. I love you full up and spilling over.

Verge

9/6/84

Michael, My Love,

Where we are now feels very much like the time between us when you came that February to say you were going to stop drinking. I am glad we have that in our history to help keep our fears at bay as you start going to counseling. The thought that even our love is growing up gives growing pains. It is almost enough to make me want to tug your hand and say, "Michael, let's just stay where we are. Let's just leave everything as it is." But you know and I know, that not much is about to stay stationary once the process of growing up begins. Growing up, itself, takes you by the hand and says, "Come along, now, and stop resisting. We have things to be about."

Because we both seem to be at such a vulnerable stage, I'm glad you are coming again for reassurance and that extra infusion of faith and vitality being together gives us. I sense how hurt you are feeling, and I know that pre-leap terror as you stand on the precipice of action, future, and change. There isn't a map; all is unknown.

I found the leaping part, when it came, far less painful than the indecisive stage. During the indecisive time I was living everyone else's life—how would my change affect everyone I knew; how would they survive it? When the leap began, I was living my own life, maybe for the first time. I couldn't live anyone else's, because living mine required all my energy. I really knew, then, for the first time, that I couldn't arrange anyone else's destiny.

I found, in my freedom, I loved you even more. The more options and choices I had, the more I chose you. There is no guarantee you will experience the same. Your options and choices may lead you someplace else. I am willing to risk that, Michael. I love you enough to let you go about finding your own destiny.

Verge

9/11/84

Sweet Verge,

I will be telling you on the phone all about my visit with the head-fixing man. I appreciated what you said in your letter about being scared, and I share it. I also like your bravery, and because of it I feel I can muster up enough for myself to proceed. You are right. The important thing is to get healed up and grown up so we can live our life in a healthy way. The "ain't easy" part is not knowing where or how this will lead. Having faith that this is the best and necessary way to go is the only thing that gives me the courage to proceed. Getting straightened around and leaving the garbage behind is more desirable than standing still. (I hope.)

I have been thinking about that drive to your house. What made it so different from when I used to drive there? The lack of booze was different, of course, and going to see just you, was different, but even the return drive home wasn't too bad. I think part of it was being alone. I had the feeling that I liked being alone—enjoyed it—liked sharing the adventure with myself. I sort of had that old boyhood feeling of being away from the familiar and not wanting to go back. I could drive along and have you in my head without interruption; that made the trip less painful. I have thought it over and over, and it is true of my whole life: having you in it makes it less painful and makes the journey more fun to take. I am surprised about enjoying being alone on the trip, considering how I have been feeling about myself lately.

Michael

9/12/84

Dear Michael,

I feel encouraged for you; your encounter with the psychologist sounded most propitious. Anyone who recognizes your intelligence so swiftly and your capacity for creativity can't be all bad! What you told me about the man and the way you told me sound like you feel comfortable with him and like you can level with him and with yourself. Self-reliance is such a prideful thing. It hurts to give it up or to even relent around the edges of it.

You asked if I had ever had counseling and I said no, but those small group counseling sessions I participated in during the counselor training course were active groups where we were learning by doing. They gave me a good idea of how counseling feels.

While you are there, you could ask his opinion about your forgetfulness. I believe he will reassure you. It seems to have some correlation with your rise of anger this spring. The more disturbed you have grown, the more it seems to manifest itself in forgetfulness. That you are a child of an alcoholic is also pertinent information.

Yesterday, after just one week of getting students settled in, my art supervisor came unannounced to my last period class and took notes the whole period. Our school contract states that we are to have a pre and post observation talk with each formal observation, and although I was furious at his surprise interruption, I was able to calmly cite the contract requirements. He said that was only for a formal observation. Today I received a copy of the observation in triplicate to sign. I call that formal. The wording was mild enough, although he implied that my style was too relaxed and a more structured attitude was necessary to make art serious to the students. That was precisely what was causing one of my problems in the move to the junior high. I had been tightly structuring the classes as I had at the middle school and I met with a wall of resistance. After not getting the high school job this year, I determined to try a different approach, in a renewed effort to reach these students.

Although I do not relish making a lot of waves, the union president called today to inform me that I have an appointment tomorrow with the grievance committee to determine if I have a case about the high school job. While I am there I will ask their opinion about whether an observation in triplicate is informal. I feel my supervisor should be kept to his contractual obligations, and as I have little hope of moving, asking can't do any harm. Apparently my name is already mud with him, and it may keep him from bugging me in my room at his whim.

Verge

9/17/84

Dear Verge,

As I sat in church this morning, I thought about our conversation of a week ago when we were sitting at your kitchen table. I liked your reason for relating more to the religion of your childhood for its variations from service to service rather than a fixed ritualistic ceremony. I still can't capture the mobility of your face as you talk to me, but I hear your sweet voice, see your gestures and I feel easy. What I said still feels true; I feel comfortable going to the church I have gone to since childhood because of its familiarity rather than its content. It is a familiar place to gather with a group to commune with a Higher Power. It is fun to see how we integrate our lives in all phases and facets.

Thinking of integration and us brought me to the idea of fusion. I have heard and read that fusion is an unhealthy reason for a relationship. I am not sure what it is, but it must be when two people become so closely entwined that they rely on each other for existence and lose their individual identity. I can see where that would be unhealthy. It is the unfused part I find attractive about us—discovering the joy of learning and growing with another human who is unique. You consistently inspire me to find out more about myself so I have more to share.

Sitting there, I thought about the experience last visit, when I looked inside you. As I looked in your eyes, I remember the intensity I felt, the power of the drive to see in deeply, even to go beyond decency crashing any remaining barriers to learn your every fiber, to see the tap roots and how they pattern, to become part of you for that time so I could establish a foundation on which to place understanding the growth that is fast overtaking you. I see only the corners of that growth in your elusive, new, independent look I find so attractive and beautiful. Thanks for the you I found in your giving of it.

Michael

9/20/84

Dear Michael,

I am a sing!! The more I think of what you told me on the phone of your day with the psychologist, the more I want to burst with joy. I was projecting that when you told him about us, at the very least he would suggest that you not see me for six months, to figure out your priorities. I have tried to rehearse in my head how I would endure whatever time he suggested. I would do it willingly if he deemed it necessary for your well being, confident that separations in the past had little effect, other than to strengthen our feelings for each other. I did not relish the pain, though, because it would be like cutting off our heads and hands and ripping out our vitals to find out if we really need them, or if they are just excess baggage in our lives. Obviously you are suffering pain and need help and guidance, and it is very important to me that you do what you have to do to feel better. Telling you of my fears did not seem in anyone's best interest. Considering all my projecting, you astonished me with the information that the doctor man validated our relationship.

Even before your phone call, I was falling in love with you anew, all day. What set me off was your letter in my coming-to-work mailbox that I had missed last night because I had to go to a meeting at the high school after my classes. I felt deeply honored to be taken to church with you on Sunday. I consider that your serious meditation time—have always—and to be a part of your meditation is a solemn business that I put under the heading of major honor. Thank you for taking my thoughts on religion seriously. Having been associated with Eric who scoffs at all religious affiliations, I sometimes wonder if you can believe my attempts to regain faith by searching out what belief I still have. Actually I had a rift in faith before I met Eric, over what I perceived as prejudice in my church toward a black couple newly arrived in town—the only black couple in town. I already questioned a God who allowed unequal birthrights and bad things happening to innocent people. Although I gave up on organized religion, I hung on to some spiritual belief, and I never questioned another's right to believe. I always worried that, without any introduction to religion, Milo would be at a disadvantage when it came to understanding cultural heritage and history, as well as reams of literary allusions based on religion. I also thought that we might be depriving him of a source of comfort at some point in his life. I knew of many intelligent people who derived comfort from their religion. I suspected that if one could believe, it might be a help in troubled times. When I argued these points with Eric, they mattered a gnats naught to his conviction. So, I felt we deprived Milo of a choice and an education.

When I told you on the phone last weekend that I stayed up until 2:00 AM reading for the first time in forever, you asked how come I keep such a rigid schedule. I hadn't thought about it in a while, so I put off answering you. Back when I was first new in The Program and started to get a little saner, I began trying not to react to Eric. I set a schedule for myself: I would go to bed and shut off my light to sleep at 11:00 PM and get up at 6:00 AM and eat at regular times. Previous to that I used to get up in the middle of the night, or be gotten up, or just never go to bed, to work around Eric's increasingly erratic demands on my time to cook, to play chess, to be company. I thought I could keep him placated and away from waking Milo in the middle of the night. As you well know, nothing placates an alcoholic for long, so everything just became more erratic and I started living on the sun porch or in my bedroom to be near an exit for the crazy times. The schedule was my attempt to put some order in my life. I stuck to it rigidly.

When I moved to this house, I kept that same schedule, and I spent my time in the kitchen or the bedroom, only using the other rooms when you were here. I laughed at myself this summer when I found myself using the living room or porch for the first time since moving here, and now I'm even beginning to vary my schedule a bit. Gradually I am healing up. When I become aware of it, I am shocked. With your help, I am beginning to trust my world and to live without fear, that most oppressive of feelings, whether actual or made up in one's head. Thanks for the liberation.

Verge

9/27/84

Dear Verge,

We have brushed against the subject of religion lately, and I would like to share a sight I saw when I visited *ma mere* at the nursing home. Approaching her room, I happened to glance into the room diagonally across from hers. Sitting by the window was a very old, hunched over figure wearing a quilted long coat and headgear that reminded me of a Mogul warrior. The garb was very unattractive. Her sour expression was one of forlorn bitterness. She was truly an unholy sight. My mother told me she is a nun. I wondered what happened to the spiritual part and the serenity that it should impart? I figured the serenity wasn't there because the spiritual isn't. Do we do that to ourselves—make ourselves destruct because of bitterness? I have to say yes, because I have felt it and lived through it to some extent. Do we twist religion to suit our twisted feelings and anxieties so we can hide behind it? If so, we drag the spiritual out of it and leave a shell that spreads disease. Whole it is good; stripped it is destructive.

Another thing I was thinking about in church that Sunday was how you thanked me for not shutting you out when I hurt. I thought about that day in Canada when I did shut you out for a few hours because I was hurt. I thought, what an awful thing to do to someone close who trusts me enough to be vulnerable to my self-pitying ego trip. It was so easy to fall into the trap of closing my mind to the pain I inflicted on you, while leaving myself wide open to my own pain that soon distorted all of life. You were left outside, alone, wondering and paining over some unknown. It was a cheap shot. I am glad you have helped me to see that and to make an effort to grow beyond it. The pretty part to me is that there is a way out, and it works. I think it is better to air out the painful part, even if there is no solution and pain persists, than to wander around in the darkness and confusion of the unknown or unspoken.

I remember the first time you told me in a letter that I was your heart's husband. Then my heart missed several beats, and my head took several spins. "Does she realize what she wrote?" I asked myself as I read it over and over. "Of course she does, silly. She is well aware of all that she writes. Well, then, Wow," I said. That was long ago. I don't remember if I reacted then, or was afraid to say anything for fear of stirring up muddy water, or even if I said how I liked it later. Today our love has gotten so much bigger, the word husband is just a word compared to it, although it still carries all the connotations the society we live in gives it. So, even though we live more of what the word means today—more than most people who officially wear the title—my heart still leaps and my head still turns at the sight and thought of it applying to me.

Now I can go shave, put on my jeans and hurry off to you.

Michael

10/3/84

Dearest Michael,

What a very busy day! How very, very much I miss you. The day you left I had a pre-observation interview with my supervisor. He was polite, even friendly. We discussed my lesson plans and objectives and he mentioned different ways he could evaluate me, giving me a choice. If that had been my first encounter with him, perhaps I would never have had the misgivings I had. Maybe some of his improved attitude stems directly from not letting him intimidate me earlier. In the past it would have been just too much trouble to speak up. I would have felt like I was making more of things than I should, that I shouldn't be a pain in the neck. I probably could only have done it if I were livid with anger, which I was not.

Today's observation did not go smoothly. Unexpectedly, I was nervous. I passed over some material I intended to cover, and my timing was off (the lecture was five minutes short of the end of the period). The students were super, though, answering questions intelligently and not acting out for a change. Afterwards, my supervisor bent over backwards to compliment me on my lecture, on the knowledge the students had, and on the "artistic environment" of my room. He asked if his presence made me nervous, and I admitted that it did. He said he was sorry that we hadn't gotten our year off to a very hot start, that through his eagerness to be a strong leader and some misunderstandings, he had made some mistakes. He said he hoped we could go on from there with a fresh start. It seems that setting limits gains respect.

The saga of the house continues. As you know, my landlord gave notice that he must sell it by the end of the month, when my lease is up and asked if I was interested. I called my dad and asked him to think of all the things I would need to know if I were buying a house. He and his wife are coming down on Saturday. Then, I called my landlord for an extension until next week to decide what I want to do. He said OK, but there were people interested. He said he would prefer to sell the house to me, but he was not at liberty to vary much on the price.

Yesterday I called the teacher's retirement agency to find out how much money I have that I can access. They are sending me all the information, but it takes four to six weeks to get the money. The outcome is in the hands of the imps. At times I decide imps have no place in a grown-up world, but repeatedly I've have been forced to swallow my grown-upness and go back to imp belief, despite myself. Somebody, something, some force out there loves us, Michael.

Verge

10/5/84

My Verge,

What to do with this rock bottom, bone-chilling, frog-toe-cold loneliness, this all out missing you? I don't know what to tell my skin, or what to tell my prickling hairs, or what to tell my brain which waits for more fodder from you to process, and chew, and distribute throughout my body.

I will never stop being amazed at the mysteriousness of humans, at least this human. There was a time when I firmly believed there was no joy, nor could there be, in living a life without the enhancement of mind alterers. The mundane living experienced by square human beings was too dull and gray to be endured. At least the promise of a high somewhere, sometime down the road, was necessary to endure the every day in, day out chore of living. Yet, here I am ready to tell you that the joy of knowing the real you, and the joy of experiencing growing up by way of great pain and struggle, is more exciting and rewarding than any high or promise of one.

Specifically, I have been thinking of us walking along that coaxial path, surrounded by woods, when we were last together. You were talking about that "upset day" in Canada and how the anger worked out in sex form. I am glad you brought that up and talked so frankly about it, so we could examine it together. It opened a new road for me to explore about myself. It could have remained hidden to my eye as I look at myself, but now I can clearly see what happened, and the potential for harm, if I am not aware of it. I can actually feel the growing as I work that over in my mind. I am grateful for your courage to bring up the thoughts you had, so we could explore them together in the sunlight. The joy of us, and how we are together, is all that is necessary for a whole life high.

Michael

10/8/84

Dearest Michael,

Isn't it beautiful—loving someone even more when they become bone naked without any pretense or illusion? We just stand around hoping the other will cast off another shred of flesh to expose more bone. As we travel along, I am amazed to find anything left to cast off, although I am aware that my life was full of shams—mostly pretending to be stronger physically and emotionally than I actually was. Out of pride, and especially because I wanted to maintain the façade that ours was a normal household, for our son, I single-handedly took on the running of the house, including doing jobs, through sheer desperation, that I had no expertise in such as repairing broken windows and holes punched in the walls. Secretly, my self-image was of a child person who wished someone would come along and take care of all those problems, but I hid that weakness behind the sham that I could do everything all by myself. I suspected you sometimes were also at a loss, playing big, strong poppa can do it all, but out of collusion perhaps, we never called each other on it. Self-reliance ended up being the last sham between us, for it is terrifically hard to admit childish weakness.

Only in the last few months have I come to understand that exposing weakness and imperfection might be a strength. It seems to go in conjunction with learning to like myself despite my flaws and foibles; and learning to accept your loving me in that naked state. In turn I can allow you to have flaws that I don't call something else and like you even more.

Somewhere in this process, I find I have lost that ache to be taken care of—to have someone magically appear and make decisions for me. I have particularly become aware of this since I have been faced with deciding what to do about the house. Dad and his wife mostly affirmed my idea that I could buy it. They gave me some practical considerations like taxes and insurance and lawyers. I wanted Dad's opinion, I wanted your opinion, but I feel they are input and not deciding factors.

Dad suggested I make an offer and see what my landlord says. I did that this evening. He sounded less than impressed, saying the other person offered more. We left it that the woman will come to see the house tomorrow night and he will give me a chance to change my bid if she is still interested. He sounds like a person who is in trouble, somehow more anxious to move this property off his shoulders than a person might normally be. He says he needs to have a contractual agreement signed right away. He also said if I do not buy the house, I will have to move soon. I told him that I would need a month's notice. I can't do any preparation either to obtain money or to look for a new place until it is decided. That makes me nervous.

Yesterday Dad's wife called me into my bedroom, where they had spent the night, inquiring if she could ask a personal question. She pointed to your boyhood picture, "What a handsome boy; was that Eric when he was young?" I just said, "No," and walked away. I thought briefly, after collecting my thoughts, of saying more. I think the situation called for something kind to be said, but I couldn't jump that gap. She wasn't trying to be nosy, but I was overtaken with not wanting to give a lengthy explanation, and perversely amused to let her draw her own conclusions.

Later on, at dinner, when we were talking about my buying the house, I said something about, "...even if I want to rent it out." She, characteristically, couldn't resist saying the first thing that came to her mind, "Why would you want to rent it out?" Without conscious thought, almost wickedly, I said, " I might get married again." My meaning was that I have choices, but another part of my brain was aghast at my forwardness in voicing that thought. I gave a mental gasp, "Look at your audacity!" but I also had a flying feeling of freedom in saying those words I had never allowed myself to think before. I guess I said it forcefully, because she looked embarrassed, and said rather mumbly-like, "Well, I hadn't thought so soon..." and trailed off. That was wryly amusing, as she married my dad before her husband was dead a year.

You've sounded so happy this last week in your phone calls. There is a lilt in your voice that makes me want to check you out all over. I guess some of it is from the pills your psychologist prescribed. There is a noticeable difference. I was getting awfully scared about your heavy depression.

Verge

10/10/84

My Verge,

It is amazing how the telling makes things all right. Not just telling anyone, although that might work some, but I don't think as perfectly as with the likes of us. Maybe that is part of the reason that some people in The Program say they feel that their Fourth and Fifth Steps were not completed, and they take them over and over. I think it is a special cure that takes a human contact that encompasses heart and spirit. It doesn't necessarily have to be a love as big as ours, but it seems an understanding must take place, as opposed to casually telling someone for the sake of telling, alone.

You have done it again! You did, Verge. You made my scalp prickle and that Jell-O feeling in the pit of my stomach. You did that by telling your dad and his wife you might get married again. Ginny, my mind raced lebbenty-million miles per hour from thinking that maybe the marryin' part might include me. If I'm presuming, don't tell me right now, because it feels too good, and I'd like to hold on to it for a minute or two. I'm trying to be cool and not say things I'm not supposed to, because it is too soon and ahead of myself, but it feels good, so I'm just skirting around the suburbs.

I know you are sad to finish up your counseling class. I'm glad you chose to take it and followed it all the way through. You received all those bonuses over and above the counselor training, insights into the disease and mostly into yourself. I love the way you grow.

Believe it or not, I still, after allll this time, feel full of awe and a little afraid in the face of this no-half-truth-honesty between us. Must be all that beauty involved!

Michael

10/11/84

Dear Michael,

Tonight I feel like that little girl again, who wishes someone would rescue her. All that grown up stuff, out the window! It hurts. I got my head all centered on buying this house. I did the research, asked the questions, elicited the support, got my head on go, and now, back to zero. I suppose I learned things in the effort, but, Michael, I do not want to move. I'm tired of being tested. I fail to see what more senseless tests can prove, or teach, or anything. This time I don't think I deserved it. I think I was pretty mature about the job disappointment, and my supervisor problem, but this one really has me by the nose and it's swinging me all over the place. I just want to feel your arms around me and hear you say, "It's OK, Ginny."

I have a mental picture of us, sitting on the sun porch that winter day, with the snow laden tree limbs drooping over the house. We were so happy, seemingly enclosed in the tree, watching the birds. It has been a place of peace for both of us. I could look around for another house, but it is not that I am hot to own a place—it is that I didn't want to leave here. I know I am in the middle of a vast pity party. I can feel all those stress symptoms, just like I had last fall when I left Eric, swooping up fast as thunder. Tomorrow I will get perspective, but tonight I have to feel sad and rage some. Perhaps I don't need to be encumbered by owning property at this time in my life.

The warm up exercise at my writing course today was: "Writing Is Purposeful Because..." or "Writing Is of Little Use Because...." You can imagine what stance I took, little realizing that this very evening I would be holding onto the shreds of my equilibrium, if not sanity, by pouring out my sorrow to my lover who will read it and know how I felt when I did not win. Good night, My Love.

Verge

10/15/84

My Verge,

I do notice a much better frame of mind in my head these days. In fact, shortly after I started taking those pills regularly, I noticed a change in my thinking. It was subtle at first. I noticed that I wasn't swearing at myself, or balling up my fist at myself when I looked in the mirror, or wallowing in morose thoughts. I would stop and say to self, "You aren't thinking so negatively these days. Try to have a negative thought." I would squinch up and try, and none would come, no matter what. Then I would say, "Self, it must be the working of those pills." Self replied, "No way! It is the result of my hard work. I ain't contributing any of my success to anybody's pills. I got myself on track, along with Ginny's help." I said that, ignoring the fact that the depression hung on, came and went for weeks, in spite of anything we did. (I think you were right about that day in Ontario, the more I think of it the more I am sure depression was hanging tough that day. The beauty part is the way we handled it, and it responded to our us and dissipated.) But, it returned. I had to know it was the pills helping me. All that terrible thinking, so painful, that I hung onto anyhow, (sometimes because I wanted to and sometimes because I had to) wouldn't go away, just as it won't come back now, even when I try experimentally to get it. I told the psychologist that and he nodded and said he knew how it was, that feeling of being unique in the face of all my humanness. He said he was that way, too. He said he heard a person say in an AA lead that he suffered from terminal uniqueness.

You wrote about how you viewed your life as a series of shams. The thought occurred to me two weeks ago at the Friday meeting that my life has been a lie. In my comment I used the imagery of forging that lie link by link into a chain wrapping my body. The unbelievable part is that I could not see it, or feel its weight. I truly believed it was my ordained duty to show by the exemplary life I led, how the true way to salvation was to be achieved. I only realized the lie, in retrospect, with the newly found vision of my developing self. I know well the lonely feeling of having to keep up the strong, unshakable front for all to see, but wishing for someone to remove the huge responsibility and cuddle my tired self in large-as-the-world arms and breast. The worst thing that could happen, though, would be for that wish to be revealed by a careless slip of my guard, or lessening of determination. Unlike you, I found the paradox of showing a childlike dependence, even helplessness, to the casual world got needs met and cooperation or help, but it was always veiled in some other guise. Sometimes the veil only worked on me, but it got results. I wonder at the conflict that sort of ambivalence caused inside. I wonder if that is the reason why, at very stressful times, I found myself unconsciously thinking of Doreen as a mother figure and renewing resentments of the real mother who failed, in the past, to be there when I needed her. Naturally that feeling was kept pushed way down inside. God, don't let the world know. I would surely be squashed like a bug for falling short of my ordained duty. Roll that all into a ball, stuff the whole thing inside, and push and push it, over and over for years when it tries to ooze up, add the poison of booze as a catalyst, and—well, Babe, here I am.

I'm glad that we can talk and write and think this stuff to each other. What you tell me helps me with my own insights. You are right; it is heady, exciting stuff.

Michael

10/17/84

My Michael,

When I was in the teacher's lounge on Monday, I overheard one of the teachers talking about having an upstairs apartment for rent. I went to see it this afternoon. It has more space than I have now, and I would have instantly jumped on it if it weren't in town. She seems like a person

I would like to know better. We have always been friendly, but she is a private sort of person, as am I, and we have never gotten very deeply involved under school circumstances. Maybe this is my test to see if I can live in a city. I know sooner or later I have to wean myself away from the lake. Elle said I could leave my canoe at her place and use it whenever I want.

Tonight, I began the task of packing my books and records. I am going to indulge myself with someone else moving them, though. Moving the furniture with Dad last fall was more than either of us should have been doing. (I can even begin to contemplate the fact, Michael, that I am not super-woman.)

I am thankful I didn't scare you by being flippant with Dad's wife. I had nothing but fantasy to base that on. It was sorta fun to peek at the possibilities for a minute, but I give you back all the shields of unsaidness. I'll cherish your letter, but I won't consider it etched in stone, or gospel, or anything. Just one secret place in my heart will store it, only because it didn't frighten you or make you angry.

Your tape was so especially welcome on the day it arrived. You could not even have known how needed it would be. Don't feel bad about saying how you felt about my being a homeowner. I believe every bit of experience comes in useful at some point in our lives, sometimes in ways we never expect. I told Dad I would accept his loan until spring to help with moving. Milo's tuition is due, and I will use part of the money to finalize my divorce. I might as well tidy up my life as much as possible. I don't believe one person is ever singly unhappy in an unhappy relationship, so that will leave Eric free to his choices, too.

I love you unconditionally,<br>Verge

10/20/84

Dearest Michael, my true love and real,

The meeting tonight was on reality, as opposed to fantasy, as recognized by a recovering Al-Anon. Isn't it strange how things seem to come about in their proper sequence of time? You and I have been talking about real and tonight a meeting on that topic without my instigation.

I get the feeling that your search for self is scaring you a bit, because you have the feeling you have to construct a self. My experience was, instead, it's a matter of releasing, or unearthing that self. It was a matter of washing the windowpanes of my brain, scouring away the grime of neglect, sweeping out the cobwebs and looking inside at what had been stowed away. A matter of walking around in there, sorting out the treasures, finding things entire, unbroken, forgotten perhaps, but better than I expected or half-remembered. It had something to do with understanding that I was allowed to be any or all of those forgotten parts of myself, even the imperfect parts, the indulgent foolish parts, the whimsical parts, or the parts that strive to attain things I may never be able to attain. Each was special because it was mine, not me-as-someone-else-wants-me-to-be. The scary part was that once I tried on the real me, I neither wanted to nor could pretend again to be that superimposed person others had encouraged me to be. That is when I started running my own life and stopped allowing others to manipulate me with their various weapons of guilt.

As a result, I simultaneously had to become responsible for myself. I had to realize I had set my own trap; I had made myself unhappy. I made my life be what it was and nobody else was to blame. I don't pretend to have finished that process, but I think I have traveled along its progression and nothing would make me want to go back. It is a great joyous feeling, and I love your beginning to travel this way, too. Even its hurts are rewards in retrospect, because they make the in-charge-of-yourself feeling more precious.

Once we dare be the real persons we are, we become less vulnerable, because our attack places are diminished. When we say to the world, "We are not perfect. We have faults," feel comfortable with that, and know we are not less for it; failures cannot destroy us because we have already acknowledged their possibility. If we live by what we believe, we do not have to fear being found out. If we please ourselves, we don't have to live with an ugly knot of resentment and anger tearing us apart because we are doing what others want us to do. If we say truth, as we believe it, we do not have to live in fear of being caught in a lie. If we do not de-value ourselves, we do not have to live with self-loathing.[15]

It is a miracle to discover that real is freer than fantasy. Real is exciting and fun. Real is a commitment to develop our potential. To take the raw material of self, to refine, define, and shape it into the gift it was meant to be, is the joyous act of living life.

I think this is what you have been trying to tell me for months that you have seen happening to me. I begin to see it percolating in you and

---

15 Results of applying Step Seven: "Humbly asked Him to remove our shortcomings." Ibid.,70.

I love all the glimmers of beginnings. It makes me conscious of my own growth. It is a privilege to stand next to you while all this is going on inside, and to know you still want me there watching you.

At that meeting tonight a young woman said she had a small person inside she talks to. That made Gin perk up and I had to catch her by a pigtail or she would have gone right over there to check out that other small person. Sufferers of terminal uniqueness pretty well described us until we get together and begin comparing notes. Then we find more things are alike among us than different. Sometimes I want to hold your little boy you and tell him what a very special person he will grow to be and take away some of his hurts, but the awful paradox is that without the hurts he probably wouldn't have grown into the man I love even more with each new revelation of self. I also suspect that had you been loved in a more demonstrative way when you were a child, you would have found another reason to be the lonely boy with too much responsibility, anyway. You would have caught it from your mama, despite the hugs and kisses you didn't get, but might have. I was hugged and kissed and spoiled and still managed to be the weird, mixed–up, self-righteous, lonely child I was, anyway. I had an overblown sense of my own dignity. As a kid, if I were with friends that were getting loud and giggly after a movie, say, waiting for parents to pick us up, I would be the one to say we better quiet down. I can see now it was a device to keep prying eyes from my real me, who was doing what she pleased. Early on I got the belief I had to be the real me on the sly, because others would disapprove, yet it was so insistent it wouldn't be denied altogether.

It almost seems we deliberately kept our true selves hidden from the world and even from ourselves until now. As if by design, we waited for a time when we have pained enough, follied enough, and grown enough to earn the gift of self and consequently of life.

Thanks for sharing the real,
Verge

10/24/84

My Verge,

When I finished reading the two letters I received from you today, my first response was a thought, like a voice in the middle of me, a revelation, "The only sin I commit is the one of keeping us apart."

You are right when you say my search for self scares me some. I wasn't sure what that feeling was, but your words gave it a form and shape so I can recognize it. The thought that I have to construct one from nothing is frightening. You are right, though; I don't have to. All I have to do is discover what is in there already, dust it off, discard or save, and begin to build from there. The notion that I had to start from scratch left me bewildered because I hadn't the foggiest notion where to begin.

When you said on the phone that you would like me to decorate a room in our house if we ever live together, I could feel panic rising. Where would I start? What if Verge didn't like it? I have always hidden from requests for opinions on decorating. I admit I might have ideas, but kept them hidden so they couldn't be rejected. Consequently, I have tolerated what others have liked, a trap of my own making. I have hidden those ideas for so long, I have lost what they are and forgot how they feel. You are good for me. You have laid back the big stone, which kept a major part of me buried. You don't reach in to stir or rearrange, just help me expose and watch while I do the work, applauding and supporting and still loving me no matter what.

Michael

10/28/84

Dearest Michael,

David Viscott in his book, *The Language of Feelings16,* presents a logical case for openness and letting out one's feelings, ideas my head warred against for a decade—not because I was against the ideas *per se,* but because they became trite phrases from popular usage. Viscott proposes that unexpressed feelings of hurt and loss become anxiety which leads to anger which leads to guilt and eventually to depression in that order. To get rid of depression one has to go back through the order to original hurt and loss, identify it, and express it to the appropriate source or in some symbolic way. He proposes that once that process is done, we then can access feelings to identify where we are in the scheme of things. To paraphrase, he says if I have a backlog of anger, I look through that anger and perceive the world a hostile place. My own

[16] David Viscott, *The Language of Feelings*, (New York: Pocket Books, 1976) 32.

interpretation was that I looked at the world and saw it full of anger or hostility, which confirmed my own anger and fear and hostility.

I fear this sounds like preaching, but I hope it reassures you that the struggle you are wrestling with is worthwhile. Last summer you told me how you felt when people at the pool were challenging the young boy to dive. Now I feel that way about you. I know that sick feeling before the leap to the unknown and also the exhilaration and pure joy once the leap is taken. Of course I have a vested interest. Some day I want to live with you. I feel I can openly say that, because I now feel certain I was not the cause of your deteriorated relationship with Doreen. That was between you two. The fault lies in emotional problems you both brought to your marriage and in your already evident disease of alcoholism. Nobody is actively to blame in that situation. Our dishonesty was intended to keep from hurting anyone. That it was going to hurt everyone was beyond our ability to comprehend. You and I, and I hope the others, are just getting the skills to learn how to live life. That is the one thing each of us has to do. It is our only legacy. Not one of us can do it for the other. I don't have any guarantees, Michael, but I do have eyes. I can look and see you growing healthier and I know from my own experience that once I got healthier it swept me along; I did not control it, and it would not be denied. If I were to say to you, "Michael, you better go back there and try to repair your marriage and forget me," I'd have to be crazy because it would deny the healthiest of your relationships and the healthiest of mine. Whatever happens, I am relieved to be able to believe that I did not cause it and I cannot cure it. I can only live in a now that I can honestly reckon with. I hope for the time when you can see yourself well enough to forgive yourself for the past, with the knowledge that you had a disease from childhood that warped your thinking, that you never intended the injury and hurt your disease caused, and that you do have the right to a healthy relationship. You are right about your "sin". It is a sin against your self. Self is our only natural resource and we are obligated to nurture it so it can grow in its best climate.

Sorry, Michael, I'm fresh out of lies. I can't help you with an excuse for going away another weekend. I no longer have to lie to live, and I find it hard to come up with a good lie anymore. It is so refreshing to just tell the truth or say, "I'd rather not answer that." I lied from the time I was a child and found there were people in control of me who did not like my truths. I spent all my life lying to spare other's feelings, or to live the me I was without disturbing or being disturbed by people around me. Now I find you and I like that me, and others accept me as I am, so I don't have to lie to breathe. I pray you come to experience that freedom, too. It feels like real as opposed to fantasy. I love you real.

Verge

10/31/84

My Verge,

I couldn't help laughing out loud yesterday as I drove to the post office to mail those tapes. There on the seat next to me lay two-and-a-half hours of nothing but talk, talk, talk, and yet more stuff was flying in my head to tell you. As my thoughts scrutinized some of the contents of the tapes, I thought, if you didn't know me and hadn't grown with me, much of my tape could be construed as dependent, or whiney, or sympathy seeking. In a flash of intuition, I understood what a draining thing sucking dependence can be on the one depended upon. I tell you things because I learn from your input, and I look to you for support in a sharing-life way, but I can now understand how one could be sucked dry by the cumulative effect of being too long with an addicted dependent. I consider these intuitive flashes as a sharpening of my life senses. It feels like they are coming to me more often these days.

Now Gin, you must take this question seriously, promise? In the past year there seems to be a great abundance of flowers, both in yards and in the wild; are they breeding heartier, brighter flowers? I'm serious, has there been a concerted campaign to beautify America? Last year when you showed me wild asters, they were nice all right, but the ones I see this year are extraordinary. I find it hard to believe that a person's senses could be so dulled that the countryside could look much drabber than it really is, and then it can suddenly jump into another dimension. I have been in the Program long enough to know it can happen, but it is a weird feeling to experience it.

I had a dream last evening just before I got up to go to work, about you and me and Eric. All I remember is the feeling from the dream that we were closely tied together emotionally. I don't remember the details, but when I awoke it was with the thought that the whole relationship between you and me was because of Eric—that we were staying tight so we could be close to him. I had such a sinking feeling that I resolved never to tell you of that revealing discovery. This was all in the half sleep of waking. It was as real as a drinking dream. It wasn't until I got downstairs and in my car that I realized—of course we are together because of Eric.

What is so new about that? Haven't we always agreed he was the catalyst sent by our imps, that we moved together through him until he was shed like a chrysalis and we grew beautiful together, alone? That is the reality we have always known. The pall was lifted and I rejoiced in us.

I want to live with you, Verge. I echo your words and I put all of me in them. My head says, "Did you ever ask her if she wants to live with you, or did you just assume because you guys are so in love with each other that she would live with you? Isn't it only fair to ask her? She deserves the right to consider it, now that the reality of it becomes more a possibility." I know we don't want that any more than breathing, but Ginny, it is only polite. Will you live with me, my Verge? I would be honored. It would be the realization of a lifetime. I can't ask you to marry me, yet, it wouldn't be fair right now since things are not complete—but when they are Gin, this is advance notice to think about it. I mean it as much as I mean I love you.

Michael

11/2/84

Dear Michael,

I went to look one more time at the teacher's apartment. I am not happy that it's not in the country, the bathroom is out in the hall, and the cat will have to learn to live indoors, but it is not a bad move considering I have to, so I decided to take it.

Do you remember when I told you of the danger intrinsic in half-saying things? I grew up in a family that inferred most everything. I believe it made me a very observant artist and people watcher, but the negative side is never being sure of communications. Piecing things together takes time and the interim interpretations can wreck havoc. Case in point: You report that you tell Dr. Man that you want our relationship to come to the ultimate conclusion. Two weeks later, in a moment of ...braggadocio maybe, I tell my father's wife I might get married again sometime. You write a letter of surprised reaction to that, in what I took was a serio-humorous liking of the novelty of the idea. A couple of weeks later, as a point of emphasis to some other idea, I tell you I want to live with you—share a life with you. It was certainly not a new idea to my head. You react in an excessive way, like skyrockets had blasted off and I had said the most novel thing that had ever been said between us—something wondrously unique and unheard of.

I couldn't tell you at the time what a spin of depression that put me in. You sounded as if it had never occurred to you that we might, or could, or would think such a thought. I started kicking myself around for being presumptuous. What did you mean by 'ultimate conclusion'? Did you mean that things would blow over, demands on you would stop, and we would continue on unmolested in our fairy tale existence? It was a very bad time and I could not get my own feelings of foolishness and hurt straight enough to tell you about it. Finally I decided I had to turn it all over for a while until I could be sensible and realize that you were content and desirous only of things calming down at home. I needed to again make a choice of also being content with the joy and blessings and deceit I have, or to find some way out of the picture so you could get it together on the home front. If you couldn't leave, I certainly could understand that pain, but your marriage and our relationship are to a point where they cannot continue in the form they exist and have to be resolved some way. You could not have guessed the turmoil in my head because I was careful to keep it to myself.

Today I received the only letter that could have made my head straight. I was overcome with relief. Thank you for asking me on both counts. I am still growing up, Michael, and it shocks me at times at how sensitive I am to your chance comments. I have pretty well gotten over it with the rest of the world, but I still misinterpret some of your half-spoken meanings into hurtful stuff. I would like to live with you and I will consider the other. I love you.

Verge

11/15/84

Dear Verge,

One more big I love you for the easy, loving way you encourage me to grow the way I have to. It felt good that you could write your hurting letter about us living together and getting married, not because you were hurting, but because you could tell me. Now we both know and we can look at it and talk about it and grow together with it, no hiding, no lies, no sulking. We no longer have to beat around the bush, and hurt, and guess, and pretend. That feels good. I can hold my head a little higher and my back a little straighter. (Remember how you told me about my shoulders slumping, that it came from feeling bad, and when I felt better you told me I was straighter?)

But the lie still hangs around. Keeps the head down some still. It all sounds so simple. I would have been the first to pronounce it simple back in the days of my all-knowingness. "Why, all you have to do man, is do it!" That is true. Why is it so hard? My psychologist says it is because I am a good man, and I am concerned about the other people. I suppose that is true for producing guilt. But what about being good to us? There are lots and lots of layers covering all that. I like the feeling of peeling them off, but I know if I try to peel off more than one at a time I will botch everything. It makes me mad, Gin. I think about that, and I get mad at myself, and then I want to start beating myself up, again. I know where that leads, so when I feel it coming on these days, I nip it in the bud by thinking of what we are and remembering the movement I have already made. Now, I understand a lot better what you went through. Did you swing at yourself, too? Did you get very, very impatient?

I also feel better when I glimpse small pieces of that freedom you tell me honesty brings to your life. I want to spend all of my time with you. Soon is too far away and I want to rush headlong. The loving of you brings all the sparkles and all those flowers and colors into my life. I attribute a lot of my heightened perceptions to our relationship.

Your Michael

11/18/84

Dearest Michael,

My lawyer's secretary called to say I have to go Tuesday to sign the divorce papers. He said Eric has to be served the papers. I told him that Eric has moved and is living in Cleveland with Julie. He asked if she would give them to him and sign an affidavit that she had witnessed his receipt of the papers. I said I didn't know

Slowly the apartment is beginning to take on some semblance of home. Each day I move some of my identity out of the house and each day a bit of my pleasure in the house and grounds becomes suspended—I won't say dies, for the old pleasures are still in my head. It is the process of detachment. Now I come to the house and I no longer feel "home"; it is just a place that once was important to me. It must be a defense mechanism, for the same thing happened at the lake house.

In a more emotional and personal way, it was the same process I went through leaving Eric. Gradually, as my person withdrew from him, he lost the power of a familiar being and became a stranger. It would sometimes feel peculiar to know his intimate, personal habits and yet not know him at all. A lot of the strange can be attributed to the disease, but still it felt weird to have lived with someone for over 20 years and to feel I neither knew him, nor, by that time, even wanted to.

You asked if I beat myself up over the struggle to leave him. You have to know I did. You listened to my agonizing and must have more than a hundred letters filled with I have to's, but how can I's, what if's. Every time I thought I was on the edge of telling him, I would panic. What would he do? How could I bear the responsibility of destroying a person? There was the awful unknown of what reprisal I would suffer. How could I give up being his savior, his mother, and his crutch? Would he starve to death, commit suicide, commit a crime, or disgrace me at work with some act of retribution? There was fear and terrible guilt. I had to admit I was going to break a commitment I had made and deface my pride. No one in my family ever divorced anyone; what would Milo and his aunt think?

I found the thing growing within me was bigger, more willful and more powerful than any of that. My growing self-esteem said I had a right to a decent life free of fear, free to search out its potential, and free to love and to be loved. When the words came out, they just did. I was ironing in the kitchen, Eric was playing perpetual chess, and it just came flying out—not gracefully or kindly—just flew without provocation. "Marc, I do not want to live with you anymore." That thought consumed my brain for months before I could speak it. There was no pleasant or euphemistic way to tell him. I had always couched unpleasant subjects in gently twisted terms so he would be buffered from the fact of a fact. That buffering was my attempt to avoid his anger. It never worked, but I never learned.

It is hard to think now, how I could have given him such power over me. What ego and pride I had, thinking I might destroy him by leaving! He grew strong enough by my leaving to find someone else to take care of him. Chances are pretty good that if someone needs a caretaker they will find one. Don't I know there are needy people out there who feel ego-inflated by taking care of someone? Martyrdom has rewards, no matter how loud the complaints. Healthy people are not comfortable in that role.

The truth that finally won out was that I no longer loved him, nor felt a commitment or trust, and I didn't want to hate him. Even in his sick condition I knew my feelings were coming through to him; I felt if I stayed with him my growing non-feeling was going to destroy him and the lie was going to destroy me. It was a dizzying experience when the words did come out, and a release. It was like a birthing process—it controlled me and was going to happen to my body whether I co-operated or not. It was what I had waited for all that time. It hurt like hell, and it wasn't going to stop or be stopped, and I was going to have a new responsibility—an independent self to nurture and to receive joy from. Here it stands today ready to hold hands with another such-like self.

Verge

11/27/84

My Verge,

I can hardly find words to express the touched-to-my-center feeling I get from reading and rereading your letter in which you gather all the pain and ghosties from that "birthing period" and relive them for my support. It reminds me once more that I am not in this alone; that there are some markers along the road, and that you are glad to share them with me. I have a big bowl of Jell-O in the middle of me from that letter. If I were a weeping man, I would say the feeling that pushes up right now could be mistaken for tears of joy for the you in me.

Doreen said she had to know if my Dr. Man was going to do any couple counseling for the sake of the marriage, because, if not, she would have to go back to her therapist for help; that she had been praying for patience, and she was getting impatient with praying. She said she had to know if our non-relationship had a chance of being healed, or if I didn't want to be married any more. She said I gave her the impression of someone who was beating up hard on himself—running to meetings, going without sleep, and such.

I said that I didn't think my doctor would want to see her because he was having a hard enough time with me, that there was a lot of dishonesty in my life, which needed to be reconciled. I was thinking fast and furiously, "Tell her now! Just a few sentences and it will be over. Just tell her. All that will be left after those few seconds will be the mopping up—logistics." The build up of the past weeks and months of struggling was pushing hard to be heard. It wanted to be out, but I couldn't move. "Tell. Tell. The baby is asleep on the couch and she won't know anyhow. Her mother is still fifteen minutes away. When she comes in there will be tears, but it will be over." Doreen walked out of the room. "She is begging to know. Tell her. ...I can't. You are only hurting her more. ...I can't." It was obvious then that the time had passed. I don't know what made it obvious, but it was a feeling. The door of opportunity slammed shut. I was overcome by a swarm of self-loathing, disgust, and panic. Daughter arrived. Too late.

"I can't even tell Ginny. She will grow to hate me. I can't tell anyone. I'll just have to fight it down, and try again next time. You will never do it. You want to—must—but you never will. Can't face up." I ate in a fog and focused my every nerve on the TV.

Seeping back into my head was you, my reality. Your hand was on my knee and you did not move or say anything. You just waited with me. Then I knew my only saving solid place was you, and sharing this with you. I needed to get it out into the fresh air, so we could explore it and find out what we want to do with it. By the time the show was over I felt encouraged (but how I wanted to talk with you and tell you) and I went upstairs, said my "thanks" and "thanks for Ginny", and got into bed.

Doreen came in some time later. I was still awake. She gathered up her night things and as she slid her pillow off the bed to take downstairs, I felt a rush of tear-wrenching sadness and grief. Sorrow for the years, for all the time shared, all the experiences, all the love that slowly drained away. Where did it go? It was a great sadness that I feel in waves even yet. It came to me, as I lay there alone, soul-deep sad, that I must grieve those years, those experiences, that love. Nothing will change what is today. I must grow forward, and they cannot be brought back, but they must be recognized, wept over, and then given their freedom to live in their place.

I know what it is to say those things, and agree to their wisdom as an outsider, but it is only in the living of them that they have meaning. You knew. You knew, and you were there with your courage gotten from your living of it, and now you hand it to me to use, giving me a leg up as you stand cheering for my growing up some more. How I love you, Gin.

Michael

**Virginia N. & Michael N.**

11/29/84

Dearest, My Michael,

My heart aches so for you in your pain. For days I've tried to find words to tell you how I understand the pain and feel sorrow, too, for Doreen. I have searched my soul as deeply as I am able, by now a pretty realistic understanding of my self and motives, and still Michael, my visceral response is the same as my head response. If there was any thought that you could grow to be the person I know, in your home, I would insist you do so, or at least ask you to give it a 100% try. I have no such stir of a question. My heart and head tell me your relationship is too depleted, too closed down, and too long without communication for that to happen. I know you nearly as well as you know yourself, surely better than anyone else on earth, and every shred of me believes the happy, open, trusting person you are with me is the real you.

Just as I have seen with you, that same guarded, distrusting, deceitful, uncommunicative person that I was in my home with Eric had nothing to do with my real me. It was a stranger who depressed and almost panicked me, because I sometimes felt I was sliding into that being permanently. Only with you could I let my guard down and be free of it. Since being free of that situation, I find I am more and more able to be the person I am with you, in my outside world. It gives me confidence that feeds itself. That is why I recognize the person you are at home is not any real part of you.

You do have a right and an obligation to live to your potential. You are a kind, gentle, loving person, and yet, no matter how you try to avoid it, there are times when life insists on itself; no matter how you try to protect others from it, it crashes out in a stark reality that people must learn to deal with in their own way. Sometimes they do a lot better than you expect and granted, sometimes worse, but the responsibility of living with that reality is theirs. Nothing says you have to give up the good, shared stuff—the love, the births, the raising of your family. That is a part of you that will always be, just as childhood will always be. They are phases of your life that make up the total you. You do not have to purge them. Hold them as dear as you feel.

I want to hold you and tell you things through this hard time of yours, but none of it can alleviate the pain. Just know I am with you in spirit.

Verge

12/4/84

My Woman, My Verge,

When we are not together, one second or one year, it is a state of not being whole. How long that state lasts is not important, the important part is that it exists and needs to be eliminated.

A remember came on me tonight at work. It just appeared as if a curtain opened on a set. I was sitting on a city bus as a wee tot, riding downtown to take the bus pass back to my father. Children under six rode free, so several times a week I would get on the bus with my father and get off at the next stop with the bus pass for my mother to use, then at night I would take it back to him so he could take the bus home. That particular day, I was thinking of the importance of honesty in life. I thought of how upsetting it was to me to hear radio stories in which things get all mixed up because of one untruth. People would go off in all sorts of wrong directions because of it. I hated it and felt anxious because I would know the truth, and they didn't, and I couldn't do anything about it. I remember thinking that I would always be honest. I thought how easy life would be, if you just told the truth and never allowed one lie to hinge on another so they'd get all tangled up and couldn't be straighten out.

I smiled to myself, this night, because I could visualize the location in the city, street and neighborhood, where I was when I had that thought, what the weather was like, and how I felt. I thought, "Are you sure this remembering is not your imagination, or that you are not putting something in for the sake of your life and how it is now?" I thought about it and looked closely. No, it was a real true remember. I was struck with the clarity of the recall, the insight of such a young boy, and the uncanny timing of its appearance.

Michael

12/7/84

Dearest Michael,

I enjoyed your glimpse of little boy you pondering the mysteries of truth. Makes me want to hug him and say, "Get your jammies on and I'll read you a story."

A lot of my lies were a battle to soften the blows of truth. It seemed when naked truth was around, someone had to pay. Whenever there was truth, there was blame or guilt involved. It was only in our relationship, from the very first day, where truth was just a matter of acceptance. It is a living wonder, like so many others in our relationship, that either of us had the guts to try truth. My perception up until then was that no one was capable of accepting truth without embellishment. Why I should change my whole *modus operandi* the day I opened the door to you that first time is beyond understanding in this world's terms. You and I have gone through the full range of truth to the point of brutal and never has it been too much for either of us. I am so very thankful for that fact in our life. Can you imagine if we had to struggle to unknot lies between us, too? My stomach jolts at the thought.

Even though I know it works for us, it has only been in the last few months that I have tried using "rigorous honesty" as suggested by AA in all parts of my life. It really works! Sometimes I detect a moment of surprise at my candor, and certainly it should not be used as a weapon, but it seems in the middle of this complex life people appreciate knowing where another body is coming from. I do not have to deal with so many complexities, which makes me feel better. If people are not ready for my truth, as long as I am not being intentionally cruel, then it is their problem.

I was thinking about how you told me that you could answer the searching sort of questions that your therapist asks without great pondering. I have concluded that we have done a mutual self dredging over many years, have pondered serious philosophical issues in bits and pieces and have adjusted those thoughts to match our growth over time. It did not feel like weighty ponderings as we went along because we were doing it to tell each other about our self, what we thought and how we perceived life. Through our "play" we have come to a pretty realistic self-knowledge, which gives us a firm base for making statements of belief on a vast variety of subjects. Consequently, those insightful conclusions—the ability to clearly state our thoughts—are not off the top of our heads at all. The element of trust you have with your therapist gives you the relaxed confidence to state, "This I believe; this I am." It is a case of us sneaking up on ourselves and growing wiser, all unbeknownst to us, because we were having fun revealing ourselves to each other on deeper and deeper levels.

I love the way we have tended each other and pruned and fertilized and now we have the joy of watching each other bloom. I am delighted to watch you now as you watched me last spring, and I suffer the same frustration trying to find words to describe the changes I see.

Verge

12/11/84

Dear Hoot,

I am so sorry to hear you are sick. I wish I could come and read to you or play with you. We have all those good games we made up. Verge told me that Michael said you were going to write to me and I waited and waited and I wasn't going to write to you again ever until you wrote to me, but this morning she told me you had to go to the doctor and everything, so I know you really are sick and that makes me very sad.

I thought maybe this chocolate Santa would make you feel better. I'm gonna come with Verge to see you real soon. I hope you are feeling better. I love you.

Ginny

12/16/84

Hi Gin,

Thanks a lot for the chocolate Santa Claus. That was very nice of you to try to cheer me up. I don't eat chocolate, but I thought of a starving boy someplace, and ate it for him. OK? Don't be sad anymore. I am not sick now. Thanks again.

Hoot

# PART III

# Honesty Resolved

Virginia N. & Michael N.

January 1, 1985

Dear Hoot,

Here I am back with Verge in Newburgh and I wish I had decided to stay with you. But, Hoot, you go to the high school with all boys and I would have to go someplace else 'cuz somebody told me I would never "pass as a boy", namely you know who!

Verge kept asking me really hard to answer questions all the way home, and I couldn't pretend to not hear them. I kept turning on the radio, but Pennsylvania does funny things to radios, like not having anything on at times when you really wish there would be. I kept asking to stop which only made Verge ask more questions about embarrassing stuff.

Love, Ginny

Dearest Michael,

Ginny said I could put my letter in with hers if you and I didn't read Hoot's letter. As I told you on the phone, I spent the day thinking over the year. Our growth during the last twelve months seems independent of our will—despite ourselves. I have used the analogy of a baby being born several times this year, and I am forced into it again because, other than a planted seed, I can't think of a better description of recovery, once begun, being unstoppable no matter what one's mood might be to slow down the process. Short of termination, nothing hinders the progression, nor slows it, and others had best just stand aside because it will not cease and desist. No will can stop it. Once acceptance comes it can only be seen as a generating force that must live its own life whatever the perspective around it.

And so, Michael, a salute to us in this New Year, 1985! May we treat new beginnings with the gratitude they deserve for giving us a chance to become the best people our potential allows. May we treat with respect and compassion any who do not understand, and may we have the patience to give them time to come to understanding. May we never lose sight of the purity of our love and respect for one another and continue to treat it kindly as the gift it is.

Verge

1/3/85

Dear Gin,

Finally I am writing the promised letter. It is hard for me to figure out what happened to us since we...you know. Since then I think different about you. You look different to me, too. Like it's the very first time I ever saw you. Like you just appeared from some enchanted forest, or like the good queen comes out of the bubble in *The Wizard of Oz.* I would never write this to you only I could see you looked different at me, too. Wow, Gin, we discovered some magic stuff, or something!

Remember when I first knew you, that time we slept in the sleeping bag? It felt funny to sleep with you with my jeans off, you being a girl and all. Know something? The only reason I thought it was funny was because it made me tingle, like when you hit your funny bone, when we touched. I thought that you being different down there was OK because you were little and when you grew up some more you would be the same as me, and you would like to play baseball and stuff. Little kids sure think funny stuff, huh?

Well, Gin, I liked you a lot before. We played good games together and had lots and lots of fun. No matter what we did, I always thought you were a real good kid to know and to hang around with. Even though I acted all embarrassed when you said mushy stuff, I really secretly liked it. I never knew why it made me feel funny. When we were together this time I had that kind of funny feeling only way bigger and then before we knew it we were all crazy.

Gin, would you ever think of letting me be your go steady boyfriend? You don't have to, but if you would, could you let me know so I can let out this big puff of air that is stuck inside me?

Your Hoot

My Verge,

I am glad we hang around together, albeit we don't hang around together enough. One of the many big reasons is because I can actually feel the growing up going on then. I can see both of us growing up. I remember thinking as I watched our biological kids growing up, what a powerful force that drive to get grown is. The biggest portion of their energy seemed poured into it. "I wanna do it myself!" or "Why can't I do...?" (this or that, usually something way beyond their ability, but they were convinced they could if only we let them try), striving to be like adults, but hiding behind a mask of indifference or even contempt. I would watch them and think, "If they only knew, they wouldn't be in such a rush; they would put it off and enjoy the child stuff."

I remember once when my eldest was eight; I was saying the last goodnight, after our song and tuck-in routine, when he looked up at me and said, " I don't wanna grow up." I felt crushed by the sadness in his voice. I thought, "He has found out the secret of adulthood pain and wants to avoid it." I felt helpless in the face of the relentless force moving him along. How could I protect him? Of course it turned out to be a childhood tweak that was forgotten by the next day, but I was left with the thought that grownuphood is a vale of tears and I would do what I could to forestall the onslaught of their growing up. That did not happen.

As a child, I was anxious to grow up. I wanted to be big and not so skinny, to come and go and do exciting things like have a job. It all looked glamorous in that far away world of adults. Mostly I wanted to be off on my own. Now I am once again eager to grow up—loving the feeling that urges me to keep going to find the more.

Michael

1/5/85

Dear Hoot,

Something about the way I feel now makes me want to do something special for you that makes me have to see what I can do all by myself and give it to you, just because I did it for you. I guess you probably won't understand what I mean because I don't really understand what I mean well enough to tell you. I feel all different about you, but the same, too, all to once. Oh, I guess I can never tell you what I mean, because I write it down, or even stand in front of a mirror, pretending it is you, and say it out loud, and it still doesn't sound like something that makes sense. But it makes me hop up and down and start singing out of nowhere, this how I feel.

Hoot, do you like girls that wear lipstick? Do you like perfume? Did you really mean it about being my steady boyfriend? You wouldn't ask me because you felt sorry about what we did, or something, would you? I have to know the answer to that. I can't answer you until you tell me why you wanna. I like you all right and everything, but you don't have to feel sorry for me, or anything.

Verge says I've gotta go to bed and to leave her a line for Michael, so, good night. Don't let the bedbugs bite! HAHAHAHAHAHA!

Love, Gin

Dear Michael,

Lord, will that girl ever get serious? Honey Man, I can hardly stand the breathless feeling until you decide about when you might come to see us. I can't get this apartment to feel like home until you come with your blessings.

We certainly are a couple of copycats. Our last crossed letters were a struggle to say the same thing about our growing up feelings. You compared it to watching your children grow and I talked about the unstoppable force of having a baby. We should be used to crossing ideas by now, but it's always a surprising nudge reminding us of how alike we think.

Gin is going to drive me crazy if you don't bring that boy with you soon. You don't suppose they feel about each other the way we do; do you? They are far too young to understand or feel that way, don't you think?

Verge

1/8/85

My Verge,

These are days of great disquiet and unrest.
My mind searchlights a deep, dark sky
To light it up all at once, but conceding,
Darts from star to star, faster and faster,
Out of thousands and thousands of lonely ones.

Each, out of context, flashes a brilliant signal,
Larger and stronger than ever it was born to have.
Each anxiously hurries to have its own life,
To be its own reward. As I flash past them,
I struggle against the self created life, and the draw

Those forces, no longer existent, exert. That does not
Make the struggle any less, nor the searching calm.

As I told you on the phone, this wrote itself. It is an attempt of my mind and spirit to tell you about the speeded up quality of my thoughts and feelings as the reality of terminating my relationship with Doreen draws nearer. She talks of wanting to get things settled between us, and the more she makes that known, the more I am resolved to stay face to face with her until I do. Last night, after dinner, Daughter said she was going over to her sister's to work out. The baby was staying overnight at the sitter's house. I suppose that would have been the time for talking, but there, on the brink, I felt that old fear pour back in, stronger than ever—stronger because of the imminence. I don't want to back away. There is no question in my mind. All of my energy strains in that direction; I have my toes curled over the side of the pool. I am at the point of actually putting my head down to dive and my gut churns at the prospect. No one can do it for me. I don't want to back away. I don't want to have to go through all the pain of preparing again. My mind rushes over everything that ever was between Doreen and me, and those things want to be more than they are, or be what they never were, as if to hold me back. (Hence the poem.)

I decided to get ready for the AA Meeting and if I were supposed to stay, something would happen to make me stay. (That sounds like a cop-out even as I write it, but it was the only way I could handle it.) I went to the meeting, but I can feel another step closer, in spite, or because of it all.

Michael

1/13/85

Dear Michael,

My heart hurts for you and Doreen tonight. You sounded so sad. It brought back the pain I felt when I told Eric that I couldn't live with him anymore. I remember the remorse I felt for ending a relationship that I should have been able to make work. Even though I knew we were destroying each other with anger, non-communication, and contempt, it still felt like I was bailing out on a commitment I had made. He was my first love, and at one time I loved him equally with you. I don't think anything feels as conflicted as a love that has withered away. And, to top it off, I did not have to, on the same day, collectively tell four children and their spouses face to face, that we were separating. It was bad enough telling one son and his aunt, at a distance after I was able to collect my wits about me.

I am glad your sponsor has been through this and was there for you when you needed him. I found I had to walk through the pain alone to get to the other side, but it helped to have people to talk to who understood. I found meetings helped me immeasurably. Of course you know a drink will not make any of this better, so get to as many meetings as possible. I am glad that you were going to one tonight with your sponsor. How fortunate that he is able to offer you a place to stay until you can find a place of your own. Will you have to move before next weekend? I wish I could hold you in my arms and comfort you, but your sponsor is the one you need most right now. You are in my prayers. I love you.

Verge

1/25/85

My very own Ginny,

Remember what I said about it not being so bad going away this time, because we are freer to be together? Wrong! It is just as hard only more so, 'cuz I love you way, way more. It got that much bigger in such a rush it almost knocked us both over. The traveling away from you always brings on depressed feelings, but this time I fooled them by spending the two-hour wait in Newark airport keeping my nose in my book. Later, though, gazing out the window of the plane at all the clouds below, my head insisted on dwelling on the transience of life and how fast it flies by, and how several lifetimes will never be enough for us. It made me sad for a time until I got a handle on the old "one step at a time" pattern of living. By the time the plane landed I was OK. I was busy with all those other day at a time things that, if I let stray too far, would send me into another descent. My sponsor was there to meet me, and he pulled me back into the right way. Thanks for him. In spite of his many troubles, he is always there for me when I let him know I need help.

I like the way it feels to kneel with you to say thanks.

Michael

1/26/85

Dearest Michael,

When I spoke to you this morning you sounded so blue that a crazy place in my head made me want to call you back and say, "Go back to her. Patch it up. This all hurts too much. You and I can survive on our plane of denial—we've done it for this long." But life is not just about getting through—surviving. Not for anyone. It doesn't have to be and I don't think it was ever meant to be. I don't know how many times I almost gave in to that panic, pain, and guilt to "take pity" on Eric. I had no guarantee of anything else ahead, and at least his need made me feel of some use to the world, but those were warped, crazy, trapped feelings. They had nothing to do with caring for him or caring for myself—more to do with playing god. Each of us already had a God.

You can't help Doreen with her pain, either. She, too, is going through withdrawal, but the chances are good that a time will come when she thanks you for having the courage to break off an unrewarding relationship, forcing her to take some action about her own life. That doesn't help right now—nothing will except time. It is a blessing that your children remain civil despite their hurt. You and Doreen raised loving, caring babies and they are showing their mettle in this hurtful time.

I wish I could be there to help you set up your apartment, but mainly I am excited to observe what you do, exercising your own taste and choice, however limited you might be with furnishings. I'm glad your sponsor is helping you through the rough places of being alone, by being an intermediate step. Once you get used to it, being alone is not all that lonely. If you want to walk around with your clothes off you may. Nobody inspects your mail, your tapes, or any writings you might leave about. You can read anything you please at any hour of the day or night, with no one to question your taste or to pass judgment. You can cook any concoction you want with no one but you to like it. You can talk out loud to yourself, or laugh, or cry and no one raises an eyebrow. You don't need to keep any secrets from yourself, so it is a good place to practice "rigorous honesty".[17] Please know my arms are hugging you and when you need to be private, I'll kick stones out here and wait.

Verge

---

17 "They [those who do not recover] are naturally incapable of grasping and developing a manner of living that demands rigorous honesty." *Alcoholics Anonymous*, (New York:

2/1/85

Dear Verge,

A note, a note, I must write my love a note so she will know which road I am on and can meet me along the way. We will surely be sad if we miss each other. We will not know what to do. We must hug and hug each other and never let go.

This note is all about I love you and yelling to you where I am. On the way home from work yesterday I was filled with such a strong suicidal urge that I made up my mind I could no longer endure the heavy pain and I was going to my apartment to end it. I was driving over the statue bridge (the one we stopped on last summer to look at the transportation gods) and something pushed me to cry out to any Higher Power there might be, "Please help me! I can not stand this pain."

I still marvel and am grateful for the very gentle lifting of the oppressive urges and mental anguish I was experiencing. No lights. No thunder. Not even a sudden easing. Just a gentle, gradual easing that seems to continue even yet, so that I feel better, stronger and more sure of myself, and my course of action and life than ever before.

Who would ever think that I would be writing (or talking) seriously about such stuff? But in time of hurt or need, if we dare to just try to see if there is a spot of faith, and dare to experience it, and then, if we find it works, or at least it makes us feel better, there must be something going for it. Then I look a little more seriously at it each time and feel better about it each time. How did I ever question in the face of the miracle of us? That is a first class miracle without doubt. We have said that all along. I love you beyond more.

Michael

2/3/85

Dear Michael,

I am sitting here like a teen-ager, cursing a piece of miserable plastic that WONT RING! Do us a favor and don't tell me casually you will call me tomorrow "probably in the afternoon." I can't handle it. What is

Alcoholics Anonymous World Services, Inc., 2001) 58.

wrong with me? Don't we ever get better? Fears and insecurities come up like thunder.

I don't know what I am worried about. Your state of pain worries me because I cannot help you, but there is some other personal craziness involved, like am I really good enough for you or something like that. I have never missed you like this in my life. Before, there was always that barrier—you had to live your life and we were only part of that; the rest had to be separate. I never fully allowed myself to think of living with you on a day-to-day basis. Now I have, and now I do not know what to do with all the feelings that have been undammed. I know it is too soon to allow myself all this anticipation, because you are going to need time to free yourself from yourself and to extricate yourself from your longtime relationship. You are handling things. You are moving with the flow and taking care of what needs to be done. I'm the one driving myself crazy at the moment. It is like I've got to snatch this up NOW, before I lose it, because I am so scared of losing it. All the while I'm perfectly aware that there is no way I could behave that would turn you away any faster. I hope to heaven it is a dry drunk and will pass soon. At least I am aware that this is not sane thinking, and it just points out how close we are to our sick thinking even in sobriety.

You and I are even tied together by the people we have loved in our life—Eric, Doreen, our kids, and the friends we have communally shared. I knew you, too, were suffering when I moved away from Eric. I was leaving your long time best friend (even if your relationship had deteriorated because of the disease), and leaving the house where so many happy memories resided. I was going to be a free agent making new contacts that could lead to where? No one could predict. I knew you had pain and trepidation, but I was so immersed in my own pain and guilt feelings, or if I were with you, ecstasy of being connected, that I never gave you much recognition of your pain.

This has been a scary time for me. One side is bubbling over with joy, and the other has been terrified that it all will hurt you more than you can bear, and somehow you will think less of our relationship for causing pain for you and others. I feel my whole life has been pointed toward this place in time, and now it is suspended in a breathless balance. I hurt from holding my breath. I have finally developed a self that says it is worthy of good things, and it is not willing to settle for less. I want to match up with the good, pure, true motivator in my life, namely you, and I sit knowing I am powerless and not in control of that. I have to be patient and let time unfold, as it will. And I rage, Michael. I'm scared, and

I hurt. I realize that is how you felt at that uncharted time in my life, so I have compassion for you and for myself. I dig out all the tools I have been given and work on trust and gratitude.

I love you so,
Verge

2/8/85

My Verge,

Thanks a lot for telling me so I know which stones to kick and where the muddy spots are. We always catch up to each other eventually.

When you were in the process of breaking the ties to Eric and to your home of long standing, how did you feel about yourself? Did you feel adrift because you were now alone and not connected to a group, not a family person, not a wife? Did that sudden change of status change your thoughts about yourself, change your reactions to others, at least in your head if not physically? Did flashes or even lingering thoughts of being single come to you; involuntary thoughts that being single implies many new, or long forgotten behaviors now available to you? Did they give you pause or even the hint of temptation? I suppose what is happening is what my therapist mentioned about the pressure valve that has been holding in stuff for so long, being released, resulting in a hodge-podge of feelings and thoughts. They are all so new. Sometimes I have trouble figuring out which ones to take seriously and which to laugh off. Sometimes I wonder where I really was when it came to living. I thought I was right in mid-stream, paddling, and involving, and dunking myself in being alive, but I was never surrounded by such intensity and diversity of feelings as now, with the exception of being with you, but our life has always been separate from regular life.

Back then, no matter what Doreen said about my not having feelings, she couldn't convince me it was true, because I thought I felt things. I felt perfectly alive (denial hard at work). The more she said that, the more determined I was to hide them from her. I pushed down any iceberg tip of feeling that started to noogle out in front of her or other people close to me, sometimes out of resentment, sometimes out of spite, always to hide and to protect vulnerable me. It felt good to be able to let you see; you treated them kindly, and more, you shared them in the same way. It felt good not to have resentments or to hide from you.

Besides the heavy feelings that accompanied my moving from home and all the big changes that encompassed, there were more feelings waiting for the move across the hall from my sponsor's to my own apartment. It feels scary. Now I am alone: nobody's things to fill the void of necessities like pots and pans and furniture, nobody's presence. Yet underneath there is a little current of excitement in having my own place and a large excitement of picturing you in it.

Being very tired now, I will sleep.

Michael

2/9/85

Dear Michael,

All day I have been pondering my search for spirituality. I remember having some conversations with Eric's mother about that subject well before I married Eric. I had already lost faith in formal religion by my late teens, but I felt comfortable with an idea that our creative energy or whatever intelligence we developed in a lifetime as original thought, might be collected back at death to be released within new bodies to continue their development. A cosmic mind bank, you might call it. To me, unique giftedness seemed to be the huge flaw in a theory that we were just willy-nilly spawned without purpose or reason. Those ideas were certainly not at the forefront of my brain by the time I came to Al-Anon and AA; the disease had taken too much of my focus and energy to believe in anything. I shuddered at and was embarrassed by God talk when I came to these programs, and needed repeated assurance that even atheists were able to live with the ideas proposed by them. An unknown and unexplainable force for good in our lives has repeatedly presented itself to us since we have begun this journey of sobriety, and certainly we have seen in other fellow travelers' lives things happen that can only be called miracles. I come closer to accepting the concept of God within us. Thank you for taking my hand and walking this part of our travels together and being non-judgmental of my baby steps toward a God concept. I do not want to feel a fake about it, so I have to take it slowly. Thank you for encouraging me to kneel shoulder to shoulder with you to say our nightly prayer. Six months ago I would not have felt honest about doing that.

Michael, I apologize for giving my opinion about bed buying, a decision you were trying to make about your apartment this morning when we talked on the phone. I know that each decision I made when I was first by myself, whether simple or complex, reaffirmed who I was, what I was, and where I fit in the scheme of things. I hope I can rid myself of some of my worst flaws before they get entangled in our life together—one of them being controlling. You must help me in that and not encourage my controlling. You brush it off as if it didn't bother you, and perhaps sometimes now when you are a little confused and unsure you maybe welcome a little direction, but we both know it is detrimental to our growth (both the doing and the letting). Our joy in growth is one of the things that made us brave enough to take this major step, no matter what cost the pain, so let's do all we can to promote healthy growth.

I have finally put my finger on what has been scaring me that I could not identify. I said I was afraid of losing you. That's it. The very night I married Eric I "lost" him in that fiasco of a wedding bed. I suddenly became his mother, his sister, mother of his child, a responsibility, and a tether. I became a symbol and no longer a person. My friend and lover, the important part to me, was transformed into someone at war with symbols. We had been close friends for seven years, and suddenly he wanted to establish a life, secret from me, to declare his independence as if I were the mother he was trying to leave emotionally.

I sort of gather that you had some of that war in your marriage, too. You made the observation when a couple of your kids' friends married that you were worried abut the outcome a bit because "something happens to the relationship when some people get married." That came back to haunt me in my state of feeling insecure. Now that I know what it is, I feel easier. I trust that we will adjust to our individual needs as they arise and that we both recognize that two growing people will not stay the same through time. Even if we take a few steps back on occasion, as I seem to have been doing for a few days here, we are certainly coming to this relationship with a much more developed sense of self than we ever had to share before. So, I have just tossed out my fear and am settling in to enjoy our adventure. I love you.

Verge

2/19/85

My Verge,

Well, Ginny, you have come and now flown away on the back of that big bird. Things just happened so fast they tumbled over each other. As they were tumbling by and we were catching some to look at now and saving the rest to look at later, a little incident, at least it tried to make itself little, nearly sped by without proper fanfare. We stood face to face, and in a quiet, unceremonious way asked each other if we would marry. Certainly not a new notion, not something we hadn't wanted to ask for a long time. In fact, it was such a sought after, desired moment, that it was already written in the history ledgers that the universe would party for two eons when the event took place, whether in this epoch or some other.

Events have developed so fast for me that I have hardly realized that I had the right to ask you to be my wife. If we were strict followers of rules, I still couldn't ask you, but to leave the words unspoken any longer would be silliness. It happened in the beautiful way it should—quiet and gentle and sweet. After all the time we wished for it, it didn't need fanfare because it is a truism, an axiom, a given in the life of the universe. It happened as those constants happen, with certainty and matter-of-factly. I love how it almost happened by itself as we solemnly stood face to face. Thank you for saying yes and for asking me, too.

Your Michael

2/19/85

Dearest Michael,

I am left with so many pictures; it seems I see the world anew in a curved walk and slanty doors reflected in your gray/green/blue eyes. The imps arranged for you to have those eyes as an endless source of fascination to my artistic observation—a device to draw my attention constantly to your face, the boy with the sea-change eyes. The color changes are even more apparent to me now, because you hold your eyes more open than you used to do. They often used to be hooded—to hide behind, maybe, or perhaps it had something to do with the booze. I know I hold my own eyes more open, as I have less to hide. In the last year or two of living with Eric, I didn't dare let him see me looking at him, for I feared destroying him with all the negative feelings I felt, contempt and pity not being the least of them. I had always been an eye person, checking out people's faces to figure my response. The fear of looking at Eric was a draining experience. Some of the joy of looking into your eyes comes from the relief of not wanting to hide anything from you.

Something has happened that is new and different for me. I want to tell you of it, but I'm not sure how, for we have used all the superlatives in the past at times we felt had to be the pinnacles of our love. Now language is a poor symbol system for what I want to say. It is a small quiet thing. It is about what happens when you take something you already know and put it in your heart. I am talking about a tender feeling of commitment. I got a piece of it at Christmastime with our gift giving, but it wasn't totally real then, You were still caught up in the fantasy of living two lives, and the jump from that was a mighty leap. Then, there was the goodly space of holding my breath, for my destiny rode on your shoulders. Seeing you now that you have taken that leap to integrate yourself into one whole you, I see a miracle. You laughed at me when I told you on first sight this time that your face had lost "that look". Before, it usually took an adjustment period to ease the tense lines and smooth them away. I looked at you and I was reassured that what you are doing is right. I had been swayed by doubt that it was too precipitous a move for you. My fears were calmed. When you asked me to be your wife, I felt reality clicking into place. We were no longer two children playing at being, the best way they knew how. Time had come when we were free to make that commitment. I stood there and heard your words and heard my words—did we actually voice it or was it through transference—and I really believed.

Doubts disappeared in that short space of time: Did you wanna? Was our love strong enough? Were we brave enough to weather our children's probable problem with accepting it? Could we work out the logistics of moving and getting a new job? They all withered and lost power on your voicing, "Verge, will you be my wife?" Nothing ever felt so natural or right.

There are still hard times ahead for you. The transition may take a while, but I have no doubt about the rightness of this or the real. I am not afraid for you anymore. You are beginning to find the core of your strength and courage, and it is beautiful to stand by and watch you daily grow more confident. Michael, I love you, and yes, yes, yes!

Verge

2/22/85

My Sweet Verge,

I have been sitting here pondering my lead that I am scheduled to give this morning at the AA Meeting. In four days I will have four years of uninterrupted sobriety. I still have trouble believing that. If I could only tell those people the eloquent thoughts racing through my head at this point, I would save them all for sure. They would come flocking to the table afterwards just for a chance to receive a personal word of wisdom and perhaps a touch. Oh, Boy, the messages that sing in my head! Yes, I know, that won't be what comes out of my mouth along about 10:40 AM. We both know eloquence is not what it is all about. Ego trips don't count. How it was, how I got here and what I do now to stay sober are the meaningful message. Truth and gut level feelings are what count. So, my thoughts drift to my struggle to get a handle on feelings. Maybe the word struggle is the point. Like the program, it works better if I keep it simple. It has always been a characteristic of mine to dig around at the pieces and parts, trying to figure out how they fit and how they relate; maybe if I move this or change that they will work better, or I will feel better. If I can just understand it a little more or a little deeper, I will feel in control. Then I am lost in a jungle wondering why no one else is all mixed up by all this stuff.

Naturally, as with everything else in my life, before long my thoughts turn to us. I think of how keeping it simple applies to us. When you were here, we talked about complicating our life by adding stuff to it that isn't there, or by looking for things that have never been there in all the long time of our loving each other. I get tempted to think that keeping things simple is simple minded. The truth is, it's an honest way to look at the heart of a matter, to accept it for what it is, and to accept that it works, without probing and muddling.

I only begin to feel uneasy and questioning when I try to read things into our relationship, or look for unrelated stuff I create in my head that not only doesn't fit, it distorts and twists reality. If I keep us simple, it is not being simple-minded. It is being wise. I do know how to keep us simple because we have been doing it for years. I feel good for those thoughts and glad I relearned what I already knew. I get more excited about our future each time we are together. Since our fantasies always pale in the face of our reality, we are in for a beautiful time together.

Michael

2/23/85

Dearest Michael,

I'm glad you put into words that love shift. I've been a little afraid to tell you about the perpetual excitement—heart pounding, blood racing, unsure, shaky stomach, tense muscles, alert, aching excitement—becoming a calm, peaceful inner glow. You and I have had nearly 25 years of love-sickness, or however you wish to term that first phase of intense, mind-boggling love. That has to be a record. It was a wonderful way to feel, but this has its own wonder and joy that seems to be even more rewarding.

Part of it is being sure. I always doubted others' affection. I never doubted yours, but I did doubt that we could ever take it to its fullest conclusion. I believed I would always have to know you had a reservation to your affection, that it would always have to be a secret and if it were ever exposed you would have to, at least publicly, withdraw it. My lacking self-esteem left me feeling unworthy of anyone's full all-out love, anyway. Now I feel deserving and you are coming to the knowledge that you deserve love, too.

It feels good to be able to walk down any street, anywhere, with you and not fear that someone could point a finger or "tell" someone and turn a beautiful relationship into a dirty story. I believe we were spared that, not a moment too soon, for inevitably it would have happened and we would have both been awfully hurt by hurting other people and not being understood. You and I are both sensitive creatures and I don't know how maimed we might have been by that kind of exposure.

I never worried much about being "respectable". As long as what I was doing felt right to me, and I was not actively hurting someone, I didn't care what people thought. My father's family had a big thing about being respectable because they grew up children of the town drunk. I found that something to rebel against. But, Michael, I want to be respectable for you. I do not want to be a hurtful force in your life, so I have my own reasons for wanting to be honorable. That is how I feel now, honorable. I do not fear being exposed, and that gives me peace.

I know it will take a while before you and I will be totally comfortable in that area, but nobody can rightfully be devastated by our relationship, now. If any choose to be, it will be a matter of wrestling with themselves. I do not mean that in a gloating way, just that we were headed on a course of self-destruction, no matter that it felt like self-preservation to us, and now we are not. We love each other unconditionally, and that is the most beautiful gift two humans can give each other.

Verge

2/26/85

My Sweet Verge,

I gotcha! I captured you on paper. You can't back out now. You writ by your own hand that you would. You said, "Yes," in writing, and that you wanna, and you will, and I can, and it is OK if I will, and you know I wanna, and everything. I loved your letter. I believe with the benefit of hindsight and the experience of all those imps in our life, that the first time we saw each other was the culmination of two forces that were aimed at each other long ago.

The forces looked at each other and they saw! Then they began the painfully slow move toward their destiny. For that moment all the Imps of the Universe hushed in reverent appreciation before they went about the making of another beauty.

When we stood, face to face, and gently told each other that we would take each other, not to hold but to share, we could feel the busy Imps pause again in the cosmos, as we became a part of One Force. I love you, My Verge,

Michael

2/26/85

My Michael,

All weekend unbidden scenes of us living together kept coming like Shakespearian apparitions, only not filled with doom… salubrious ones. There were scenes of introducing you to my father and laughing at the mental picture of you politely wrestling with the mind of my stepmother. She may drive you crazy, but I think you will like my father. I know I have always been a source of helpless worry to him. I think it will comfort him to know you are in my life, with our mutual love and respect for each other. Scenes of sitting in my cousin's kitchen (the one I considered my sister) laughing with her, and she liking you very much and saying to herself, "Girl finally got herself a good man!" There were scenes of cross-country skiing together and showing you the wonder of being the first to track new snow, cooking meals together and deciding the division of labor, spending the summer together and coordinating my sleep time with a night worker.

The only scenes that got a little tricky were ones dealing with our children and our ex-spouses. Those I have to deal with as they come, because I cannot pre-suppose their reaction to us as a couple. I've decided to leave them to God and trust help will be forthcoming from that source to aid in the generation of understanding. Realistically, not one of them could suppose that you and I would become less friendly after the separation. Even though it is not a present issue, at least a subconscious contending with that fact must be percolating. When we meet it, we will deal with it. Although it is not easy to talk about, I am sure you have some feelings about that and when we see each other again I think we should have some honest dialogue about it. We cannot do anything about anyone's reaction to us, but we can help each other understand how we feel to avoid big surprises between us. Our chief strength lies in our honesty and mutual support. I never knew I could love anyone as I do you.

Verge

2/27/85

My Verge,

I feel as though I have settled into my nest. I have done little else since you left than hang the kitchen clock smack in the middle of the kitchen wall over the table and set Eric's painting of the view from under the Cleveland bridges under the mirror in the TV room (called that in name only as I have no TV). Oh, I have washed dishes faithfully, carried the garbage to the catacombs, made my bed, and did some laundry—survival stuff. But, new stuff? None. I must have hit the very same wall those marathon runners say they hit at twenty miles. Steady going, that's me. When I have a spare minute I look at all those grimy windows, and the unpainted walls, and I think, "No time to start all that. I would just gather things together and I would have to quit." So each day I rub my hands together and say to self, "Lots of good work to get done here to make this place a light and airy nest—later."

In the meantime, I have gathered my little world around the wide counter between the kitchen and the small area in the adjoining room that is bathed in the light of the lamp. Beyond that, who knows? People just don't go out there. There is that narrow corridor that leads into the bedroom that is a safe harbor, and the bedroom itself, and the bathroom, but that would be desertville, too, if nature didn't force me.

My sponsor warns against closeting myself in one part of my apartment, and hermetizing myself, but it is not like that at all. It is just that there ain't nothing out there but radiators. Once I start to paint and do windows, I'll get so attached to those spaces you won't be able to get me out into civilization again. Any furniture that comes will be so unwelcome I will hang it out the window. Then if anyone comes to visit I can say, "Just step out that curved window and have a seat." I can shout and visit from my very cozy comfy corner here on this bare red floor I have grown to love and cherish.

In seriousness, it is fun to watch something as simple and unfurnished as this apartment become a home, at least in the feel of it. When special ghosties are added to the place, the rest is just a backdrop to love, feelings, and joy. Just the way we are, Ginny. The world has become our backdrop; so haunting a small apartment is nothing.

Michael

3/1/85

Dear Hoot,

Verge has become such a selfish person lately she won't even let me add a note to the bottom of her letters or nothing. I don't know what's wrong with her. She keeps telling me to go away and to not bother her while she is writing to Michael. The rest of the time she just moons around until I could give her a kick. When I ask what is wrong she says that nothing is wrong, everything is right, she just misses Michael. A couple of times I tried to tell her that I miss Hoot, too, and I'm lonely and I surely would like to have some of her attention, but I had the feeling I didn't get through. Does Michael act funny, too? He always seems to have time for me. He even made me learn to like being a girl. It sure is fun to be a girl to your boy. It makes me feel like my chicken seems to feel on the first day she is let out of her winter coop and gets to peck spring worms. She acts all crazy-like and runs around, then pecks like mad for a while, then runs around some more and sings a special funny chicken song. Hoot, you make me feel like singing chicken songs.

Anyway, those cookies in the package are my mother's special molasses cookies. I have a feeling she likes you a lot now that we know she has put her special bone curse on you. I will be surprised if you don't find a bone in the cookies. I always thought her curse was a gently teasing blessing, and if that is true, she certainly blesses you. Verge says you are coming with Michael next Saturday. Hurry up!

Love, Gin

PS: M. When I was little I would be the only one that would find a bone in my soup and complain about it loudly. She got exasperated with my complaints one time and said, "I hope, when you get married, your husband will always find a bone in his soup and complain like you do." That is why you always find a bone in everything I cook.

V.

3/6/85

Dear Gin,

Thanks a lot, Gin for the nice long letter. I was sure glad to get it. I was beginning to feel like you said Verge feels—all glumpy—because I miss seeing and hearing you. You shouldn't be too hard on Verge when she feels that way, because I know how that feels and it ain't nice and friendly, and you don't feel like explaining things or being cheerful just to cheer up someone else. I'm real glad, though, that you got hold of yourself and wrote your own letter just to me. Doesn't it make you feel all grown, to do your own stuff instead of depending on Verge for everything?

As much as I like you and miss you, do not, DON'T, sing any chicken songs! I mean they are nice and everything, but, NO, Gin, NO! The world ain't ready. I ain't ready for newly let out spring chicken worm and scurry, worm and scurry, chicken songs. I can see you getting ready to say, "Oh, yeah, well watch me!" Well, Gin, go ahead, but keep it in Newburgh. Pluck, pluck all you want to in Newburgh, Gin. That's all. I like you and everything—but, no chicken songs. I hope to see you real soon.

Love, Hoot

PS: I feel honored that your mother likes me enough to put her bone curse on me.

3/15/85

Dear Michael,

Each time we are together, I discover our love has a brand new landscape. As I knelt to say my prayer tonight, the picture of us kneeling shoulder to shoulder embraced through our prayers overwhelmed me. You said, " Little did I ever think I could let someone know I was praying, let alone watch me." When you said that, I was thinking how preposterous it would have seemed to me six months earlier to think I would be feeling comfortable and honest praying, much less shoulder to shoulder with someone. It is hard to believe how much we have grown, especially spiritually, since last summer. All manner of experiences that seemed unacceptable when they happened have proven to be a clear path in a beneficial direction, with the perspective of time to see their unfolding. That feels like a revelation, a major shift. I don't mean to turn us into a myth of our own making, but at times I feel we are allowed a glimpse now and then of another dimension of being. I cannot shake the growing notion that reality may be multi-dimensional. The more I allow myself to calmly let life reveal itself without fighting it with logic and scorn, the stronger the conviction comes that there is a beneficent power in charge who will show us the way if we ask for guidance. We already know that our thoughts travel beyond our concrete form, because that has been graphically demonstrated to us in dated letters containing crossed thoughts. We have believed for years that we can send our essence to each other, that we can feel the other's presence. With proof of the one dimension, and conviction of the other, how much of a stretch is it to belief in a God?[18]

Now it is time to sleep. I kiss your lips, and as you roll on your side I tuck my knees in under your bottom, and rest my cheek against your back. That comfort is like one of the dreams I had of what it would feel like to be married, but reality did not match the dream. Now, we have

---

[18] An example of our growing understanding of Step Eleven: "Sought though prayer and meditation to improve our conscious contact with God as we understood Him, praying only for knowledge of His will for us and the power to carry that out." Alcoholics Anonymous, *Twelve Steps and Twelve Traditions*, 96.

been granted a second chance to find that dreams are not necessarily unreal, just sometimes out of sync with time.

Verge

3/19/85

Dearest Michael,

I do not believe I could ever have been led back to spiritual matters without The Program exposing me time after time to miraculous things. Even a year ago, to speak seriously of a Higher Power's intercession in my life would have been embarrassing. I would have cringed to have anyone I knew hear me spout such fairy-tale nonsense. Today I am willing and eager to believe in another plane of life that my senses are not attuned to perceiving. Events have too uncanny a way of falling into place, to not believe there is an order to it all.

A year ago when people made sounds like this, I did not sneer at them, but I felt it was a belief created by a need for comfort, a cop out for the less hardy types, a means of coping. I told you last week that I am thankful for those people in The Program who hang in with the God talk. As many times as I made disclaimers, no one was ever rude to me or suggested I was anything but right for me at the time. The talk is usually stated in such a quiet, firm, non-proselytizing way that one begins to believe at least in their belief. As one unexplainable thing after another begins to happen in my own life, I begin to concede that it might be the work of a Higher Power, in spite of myself, out of frustration that there is no other name to call it. Remember how we had to joke about it at first to even say, "Higher Power"? The beauty part that overwhelms me is growing step by step with you in this trust and belief in a force outside ourselves.

When we were together last week, you told me how you feel a growing compassion for the other fellow travelers. I, too, have been revising my feelings about various ones in our immediate relationships. I'm still in a process of letting go of hurt and resentment toward Eric. It is strange to actually feel that shift, although it has been a very slow process—when I think it must be finished, I find another incident sweeping up, unbidden, all painful and fresh. It will stay around until I look at it and work through the feelings it evokes. Specifically, the most recent one was Eric in a blackout throwing a half-gallon of wine through the window over Milo's head and saying later he knew it wasn't going to hit him. I had previously told Eric I wouldn't go to the movies with him unless he had a nap, because he was stiff. He came out of his bedroom fifteen minutes later and I could tell down the hall there was nobody behind his eyes. That is the most terrifying feeling when you are in the middle of an alcoholic relationship—when there is nobody home behind the eyes. After the bottle throwing, he dumped me out of my chair saying awful things and went back to bed ignoring the trickles of blood all over his son. Milo and I held each other crying in terror. As I picked shards of glass out of his face and body, each one was a dagger in my mother heart. It was then he planted a seed, saying, "Mom, if you keep on drinking like you do, you will be as bad off as Dad is." I was astounded by his words because it was the first time anyone called me on my own problem. Wasn't I the responsible parent?

I know it was then Milo decided to go far away from home, because a couple of days later he told us he was going to college in Arizona, giving up his New York State scholarship. Often I've guiltily wondered if I should have left Eric for Milo's sake, if not for my own. Feeling guilty is just another form of unproductive masochism. I think I have finally forgiven myself for acts done with a warped vision, but it has been hard to forgive Eric for things he did to his son, although those very things confirm the depth of his sickness. I know how much he loves Milo, and I know he would suffer a thousand hells if he were conscious of his acts. I am not sure where that leaves Milo. I have attempted to explain blackouts to him so he can understand that his father's acts were not conscious violence, and he always replies that he has forgiven his father. For his sake I hope so, because we both know how burdensome resentments are. For myself, it took numerous open AA Meetings to truly believe blackouts and to recognize that I had had some of my own, and needed AA, too. I hope Milo has not just stuffed all of his anger.

Along with resolving my feelings about Eric, I am also coming to terms with Doreen. I feel a great compassion for her and admiration of her courage, no matter her personal hurt, for forcing the issue with you. You both could have gone on in that state of pain for the rest of your lives, and might well have done so, if she had not pressed the issue. I know the cost. I have been intimate with your pain and I empathize with hers. Perhaps she has been the most courageous of us all—being the first to recognize the disease of alcoholism we all have, and despite having the most to lose, pursuing the answers. She is the hardest for me to come to terms with as far as forgiving, her and myself, because it is painful to admit that I betrayed her friendship. After all, hadn't I taken her into my inner self and befriended her with all the openness I could muster for another female? That was my lie. In truth, I took her in and befriended her as an extension of you, which was unjust. If you loved her and if she loved you, that was enough to make her my friend. I thought I was open with her, but now I can see I never was, because I never was with anyone but you. She has true grounds for resentments about me that I had resolved in my head on the grounds that what I feel for you transcends all other relationships because of that ancient connection we have no name for. I do see human relationships in a much more compassionate way; we are all fellow travelers without notes feeling our way through.

Verge

Tuesday, 3/19/85

Hi Ginny,

I see you here in Oklahoma every bit as clear as I do in Cleveland. If this letter sounds hurried it is because it is nearly time to scurry off to catch the bus to the school. If I miss it I will have to find a rickshaw, or is it a Pawnee pony out here?

It is uncanny, the way all my memories of this place have been distilled to our short time here together. It is not that I can't recall what I did and where I went when I was here seven years ago, or two years ago when I was here alone, but those times seem unreal, while the things we did and places we went have a vivid permanence about them that feels as fresh and real as we are. I feel you right here beside me. I am not consumed beyond the ability to function, or obsessed by this love we have (it is life inducing rather than paralyzing) but it is so pervasive that it colors everything I do, with the equality of us at the center.

I love it up,
Michael

3/23/85

Dear Hootie,

Today is my younger brother's birthday. Forty one years ago today I remember coming downstairs on a frosty cold morning, pulling aside the woolen blanket hung to close off the stair-well, keeping the heat in the living quarters, and hearing my father's greeting, "Good morning! You have a new baby brother today." I remember feeling the floor grate of the furnace hot against my pajama feet and wondering, "I do? Where did I get him from?" I think I would have benefited from feeling my mommy's expanding tummy and having a few words about the impending event, but pregnancy was a hush, hush affair back then.

That night Dad took us to Grandma's house where the baby had been born. I saw my mother sitting in a rocking chair nursing my brother. I didn't feel jealous at that time—just that it was new and why did they want him. The modest exposure of her breast as she nursed was the only time I had ever seen my mother in any state of undress, and I remember thinking how pretty she looked nursing the baby.

There was plenty of jealousy when he came home and usurped my place of being the baby. My mother, a gentle person, gave me all sorts of reassuring attention so I wouldn't feel left out, but I was too sensitive for my own good and spoiled. Even with her busy schedule she always found time to take me on her lap and read to me, but I just needed more love than anyone could give, before you. She would still take me on her lap and read to me well past the time when it was comfortable for either of us—probably when my sister was being hatched and I was nine. That was when I really lost my position. My sister was so cute and compliant and loved being dressed up and having her hair curled. My mother finally got the child she craved. I do give my mother lots of credit, though, for once she was convinced I was never going to be a baby doll, she let me be the tomboy I was and made no further attempt to change me.

Today I went to the Al-Anon conference I was telling you about. I enjoyed the day. During the first discussion group on expectations, I spoke about learning to trust in having expectations again. I said that my growth in self-worth allowed me some self-expectations, and the growth of a healthy relationship also allowed me to have what I thought were healthy expectations there, too. I said I didn't think realistic expectations were bad; it is only when I impose them on others, often not even telling them what I expect yet expecting they will comply, that it becomes such an unhealthy business.

Then, I went to a discussion on Intimate Relationships. Intimacy and sex, as we know, are emotionally charged problems in alcoholic relationships. Several people admitted to hiding who they were from their spouses so as not to lose their identity through ridicule or manipulation and consequently became non-persons. One woman said intimacy was impossible because honesty was not there. Another person described that feeling of wanting to be loved so very much, yet pushing away and rejecting attempts of others to give it. Several sufferers of alcoholic impotence or frigidity bravely talked about its devastation on their relationships. I contributed that if two people have ceased feeling during the active phase of alcoholism and already have a shaky sexual relationship, then when the drinking ceases and they are bombarded by sensations they don't even have a name for, it only stands to reason that the relationship will be further distressed by frigidity or impotence until their bodies sort out what the feelings are and how to respond to them with some degree of normalcy.

The last discussion was on Inventory. I told of my experience of finding mental health with another person—growing toward it step by step—through letter writing. In an attempt to understand each other and ourselves, we did an introspective inventory over a period of years. I also said I thought an inventory was as much an ongoing thing as the program itself, because as we grow and change, our perspective changes. This year's inventory may not be the same as next year's inventory. Twice now, I have revealed what letter writing has done for my recovery and each time I have found others have also used some variation on writing, or that it struck a chord and was a hand up for someone. It is a tool I give away with love because it saved my life.

Verge

3/27/85

Dear Verge,

I have had lots of occasions in my lifetime to feel naïve. Still do. Just today, as I was standing outside on break, I was remembering various times from way back, when I felt everybody knew something and behaved as if everyone else knew, or should, and I didn't. I wondered why I didn't. I have told you about some of those times, just small things mostly, but they felt big then. That pattern seems to have followed me through life. I am sure it has much to do with my method of perceiving the world, or is a mechanism I devised to defend myself. It leaves me with a sense of resentment, but a vague one, for I am never sure who to aim it at. Even when I was little that feeling of resentment was frustrating because there really was no place to put it. That was my idle musing as I stood in the mild Oklahoma evening air, prompted by the touching story of your kid brother's birth. I got the impression that the memory is still vivid in your mind and I felt like I was standing right next to you on that warm floor register. That is another extra from our growing together; time narrows so it does not seem implausible to be sharing those memories even though we hadn't met yet.

I wish I could have been there when you reached that insight about your mother. I could feel your mind sparking as first one then another level of understanding unfolded. It would be exciting to share the discovery and feel the force of the understanding of someone so influential in your life as you fit it to the meaningful stuff of your development. It is a steady amazement how daily I feel closer to you in a way that is different than any I have ever experienced. Although I hesitate to use the word, it is almost in a mystical way.

Today I am wrapping up this course, soon to go back to Cleveland, and in less than a week you will be arriving for a glorious Easter break. I have drawn a map and enclosed special instructions for how to drive to my door. I love you and anxiously await your arrival.

Michael

3/28/85

Dearest Michael,

Michael, you let it pass. You did not bring me up short and say, "Hey, Verge, wait a minute; what did you just say?" I know you did it out of love for me and out of accepting me just the way I am, but for the very reason of that love we cannot let this pass. There is a devil within me and it pops out at all the wrong moments, especially when it knows I am wrestling with a problem, have made up my mind to act in a right way, have told myself how things must be, and then I turn around and find that spiteful creature has opened up my mouth and blurted out exactly the thing I wasn't going to say.

Case in point, the devil within me said, "Get all your family stuff done this weekend so I won't have to share you when I get there." It started earlier when I nagged you about getting your income tax done. You should have nipped me then. I did nip myself: I took myself in hand and told myself to shut up, that it was none of my business, that surely you knew all the things you had to do, and the time you have to do them in. The root of that devil is knowing I have to share you on Easter. You warned me weeks ago that your kids expected you to spend Easter with them. My head understands, and I am in agreement with you, for intellectually I know you must have time to resolve all this change with them. I also know if I quibble about it, you will have to do it anyway, and my quibbling will set us both up for a hurt we have no place for, between us. Still, that needling little devil wants to pout and say dumb stuff.

I am sorry, Michael. My head knows you must do things at your own pace, or you will be uncomfortable, and it will take even longer for you to grow through this painful period. I have to remind myself that I have had a lot longer time to weed through my feelings and the grieving process.

I am still trying very hard to grow up. Don't give up on me. At least I recognize what I am doing after it is done.[19] I am embarrassed that it had to get said before I got rid of it, because it is my problem, not yours, and I must resolve it within myself. I love you so very much that I get impatient to get to our time, even though I can see that everything is speeding along its proper course at its proper pace.

Verge

4/17/85

My Ginny,

You said that we have to be vigilant for even the tiniest things that bother us about each other, because they can sneak up out of nowhere and become big things before we know it. For instance, I was puzzling over how to adapt to your way of washing dishes. (Can you imagine? Who could care?) Then I thought, "This must be one of those little things that Ginny was talking about." I could see how it could become a big thing for no reason. So I asked myself, "How have we learned to solve this?" "Bring it to the light of day," self said. So I asked you why you do it that way. You told me why. Both of us were straightforward. Even as you were telling me I could feel the bugaboo melting away. That was the end of it. Right there, it was over and I couldn't care less how you choose to do dishes hereafter. I like the way we learn our lessons well and the gentle way it feels when they work.

Michael

---

19 Step Ten: "Continued to take personal inventory and when we were wrong promptly admitted it." Ibid.,88.

4 /19/85

Dear Michael,

I started filling in the days of my diary and got so entangled in reliving the days we just spent together that time slipped away, as our time always does. I wonder if the years will slip by as quickly, and we will end standing there holding our arms full of dreams, asking each other where could all of the time possibly have gone?

Secretly in my heart I have lived with you for years and have observed you on a "what if" basis, but it is exciting to do it straight out. "I am going to live with this man; how will I act under certain circumstances?" I want to be just right for you, but I know I have to be just me, with room to compromise, if we are going to have the equal, realistic, grown-up relationship we have worked to have. When I feel I am slipping into a passive role, I have to kick myself and say, "Whoa, this is not anything either of us want, so stop it right now."

A couple of times, it was scary to practice that with others, such as with your psychologist. A piece of me wanted to play the retiring, shy, let-Hootie-do-it person. My good sense told me that neither of you had any interest in my being that way, that it would negate all of what you and I have worked on. That also helped me to be straightforward with your sponsor and his friend. A little part of me wondered if you saw me as being too forward, but I don't think you want me to change when we are a couple, any more than I want you to. It is interesting to see us expand our world of contacts and keep our good growth present.

This is a different way, a different journey made out of both the mistakes and the lessons of the last one. We are on a path that feels right and happy. (I never knew right and happy were companion elements. I thought happy was doing what you wanted to do and right was doing what others wanted you to do.) I always thought you would be the ideal traveling companion, and I find the more uninterrupted segments of time I spend with you, the more interesting and compatible you become.

I talked to Milo this evening. He said he had tried to call me for a week and where had I been? I told him that I was in Cleveland for the spring break. He asked with whom and I told him I was with you. He said he figured that was probably where I was. He said that without any signifying. If he had any reaction, he covered it smoothly and sounded as if he accepted things straight on. I asked him about coming out with you this summer to visit, and he said he would like it if you came. The conversation just flowed naturally when I had expected it would take a lot of courage to broach the subject of us. I hope you are comfortable with that and don't feel I am jumping the gun. I love being on this journey with you.

Verge

4/20/85

My Verge,

It is a wondrous feeling to know the direction I have chosen is the right one for me and to feel that energy build to a point of positive action. The important word is know, not think, or hope, or guess—to know and to act accordingly. It is something like finding the god within us. This feeling of right and continuity is totally new to me. I mean right, not in the sense of doing what one should, or of not offending anyone, but in the sense of the right order of things, or in tune with reality. It gives me a sense of peace and sureness, an affirmation.

Now, the only danger is the impulse to dash into the streets shouting about all this to everyone within earshot, to go to Doreen's door this very middle of the night and settle everything with her, then to run to my kids' houses and rattle their fence posts to wake them, and let them share the news. God knows we have waited and waited, but I can't unwait it all in two seconds. Like you say, this all unfolds, as we are ready for it.

This has been a night of thinking about being alone. My youngest and her husband questioned me about how it felt to live alone. As I thought, I wrote some notes that prompted insight that may never have come by just letting thoughts ramble unorganized in my head. I was even inspired to write out a few notes regarding the conversation I must have with Doreen about the permanence of our separation. I don't intend to read these notes to anyone, but the writing of them helped me to develop the thoughts and even to see new directions for wording them.

If I didn't have this need to resolve further the relationship with Doreen, I would race to be with you this weekend. Alas, another offshoot of growth is facing responsibility. I can tell Hoot misses Gin, too. It is fun to watch him preparing himself for manhood. I watch him learn to not run away and hide, and hope the needed-to-be-done will disappear. The unpleasant must be faced and lived through, in order to grow, to appreciate, and to share the bigger stuff coming down the road. I attribute his changes to his relationship with Gin. I can't help but remember how I used to hide out in myself, afraid to let anyone see. I called it shyness, or worse, being distinguished. I like seeing those two open up, as they grow closer. They are a healing balm for us.

Probably just about the time you were writing your thoughts about being with me and other people, I was thinking about how we were together with others. I thought how grateful I was that we maintained our easiness and naturalness in their presence. Here and there I had tried to imagine how we would act in a session with my psychologist, and I resolved not to display us as the adoring couple—you know the soulful glances you read about, syrupy smiles and beaming delight in one another. (I don't know how I expected to control how you would act—guess I expected you would just follow suit.) When I found us in that very situation, those thoughts never entered my head. I remember feeling an arc of energy between us and thought that he could not miss the force we generate. I felt proud and happy being with you, just the way you were. That was the perfect way to be. I am glad you resisted the urges to slip back into a role we are trying to shed, although I do know what you mean by that temptation to take the old familiar way. I like the way we are together, a lot.

Michael

4/29/85

Dear Love, My Hootie,

Over the weekend, you talked about feeling seeds of honesty begin to grow and about how good it feels. Once I had some perspective of living in a different way, I couldn't believe how much time and energy I had spent in covering my tracks and worrying about being found out. (Funny how lies only took on an aspect of morality in my head if I got found out.) The book, *People of the Lie,* says in another context, if you are covering up something, then you certainly know it is unacceptable to some faction or person in your life.[20] So I guess, on some subsurface of my brain, just about every activity I engaged in since childhood was unacceptable to someone, for all the dissembling and covering up I did. It is a freeing thing to live honesty, for you no longer have to keep that

20 M Scott Peck, *People of the Lie*, (New York: Simon and Schuster, 1983).

wary eye looking over your shoulder, as you have nothing to hide, and you can give your undivided focus to forward movement.

I'm glad I was never faced with trying to unscramble the years of dishonesty with Eric. Although, in my mind, much of it was to "protect" him from the realities of life that perturbed him so, a lot of it was to "protect" me. I am sure if one wants to continue life with a spouse with whom one has practiced years of dishonesty, a major attempt would be required to sort out and rewrite the lies. " Many of us exclaimed, 'What an order! I can't go through with it.'"[21] Such an act of courage that must be! I feel compassion for you beginning to attempt that with Doreen. I can well understand your frustration when you felt you were rebuffed. I expect it would take two people committed to doing it, to make it work. I also commend you for making such a valiant effort to speak honestly with your daughter and her husband.

I was taken aback when you said that you felt I was ready to force the issue, if Doreen hadn't, by leaving you until you made a decision. It jolted my whole being, but I guess you were right. Once you start working honesty, it starts to run you. Honesty seems to beget honesty. I know I was increasingly disturbed by feeling I was at your house and in the lives of people around you, under false pretense. I felt compassion for Doreen, but I knew I could not act differently. I couldn't unlove you.

You will find honesty is rewarding, albeit a demanding master.

Verge

5/3/85

My Ginny,

This is an ordinary day, Ginny; so after we drop my daughter off at the hairdresser right next to the Deli where we often stop, let's drive to the Bluff. We have never been to the Bluff on an ordinary day. It is not a day when the sun is promising warm health, or a day when the thermometer is crouching down as low as it can so the cold won't find it, or a day when we have to say goodbye, or a day when decisions must be made, or a day when gulls have called a meeting, or a day when pretending lovers need to see how lovers really look. It is not sunny, or cold, or rainy. It is just a day with a half hour needing to be filled, while my daughter's hair gets

---

21 The response of many upon first hearing the Twelve Steps: *Alcoholics Anonymous,. 60.*

fluffed up. If we hurry we can sneak up on the Bluff, see how it looks, and be gone before it even recognizes us.

Look at that water. Gray, huh? Wonder what makes it so roiled and angry on such a day? Wow! Hold onto the door. Don't get blown away, Ginny. Something's out here and it's mad! Look at the back of our jackets ballooning out behind us. Even poor Richard Wagner is having a time keeping his sculpted cape from blowing around in front of him, blocking his view of the cars and the boys. There is a shouting match between the trees and the wind. Last summer's hot dog wrappers and last fall's leaves scurry up over the rim of the Bluff. Running fast. They don't even nod hello, as if they didn't know us. No time to speak. Gone. Headed for the shelter of the Lighthouse.

Lean into the wind. You won't fall, just lean. See how the gulls' wings stand still? They're like kites. Open your lungs. You don't even have to breathe. Smell the clean lake wind as it pushes itself right in. Even up here, lake spray sprinkles a blessing on us. Chilly. Com'on, Gin, I'll race you back.

Love,
Michael

P.S. Hoot wants to include a letter to Gin. He made me promise to leave it all folded up into this little triangle, and to tell you to give it to Gin that way. He said she taught him that fold.

M.

Dear Gin,

I just want to tell you that ever since you told me that I am Big Kid now, I feel different about you. I mean I like you and everything just like before, but it feels bigger. Can you like someone bigger? Maybe it's not bigger, but it sure is different, and I believe you, too. At first when you told me you didn't like Big Kid, I thought you were just saying that, because he was always fixing your bike and stuff. But I believe you now, and if you ask me to fix your bike I won't have to kick it first like I used to.

Well, I just thought I should tell you about liking you more, so you would know. If you think that is silly, just say so, and I'll try to stay cool. But I will still like you more. I can tell that it won't go away, not this kind of liking.

I hope you and Verge are doing OK. It sure will be nice to see you two all summer.

Hoot (Big Kid)

5/4/85

Dearest, My Michael,

Time will come, Babe, when all those stumble blocks of what-usta-be will stop popping up, pretending to be now, and you and I will get firmly planted into our own now. Eric's letter was a sentimental thank you. I would like you to read it if you want to, mostly because Eric is so tied into our life and the letter makes him a very human size, not all exalted or awe-provoking, just another human being on this search for what life might be about. I can't say the letter was exactly straight—a little manipulative, a little poor-me-ish, a little grandiose, a little disjointed, but more together than I have heard in recent memory. I felt a tiny edge of unrealistic usta-be, but I was grateful to mainly feel sympathy for another's human condition, for another fellow traveler. I found myself separated from any feeling of attachment—no guilt, no need to "save" him, nothing but relieved that he seems to have some sort of handle on his life, and not even curious as to how tenuous that handle might be. In my head I thought I was feeling that way about him, and I'm glad to say that the test of a letter slanted to encourage sentimentality proved my head right.

It feels good to gradually purge my life of retarding forces, useless baggage of fears, resentments, and guilt. It makes me feel freer to focus my attention on the business at hand, that of living my own life, connected up to you beginning to live your own life, and especially freer to continue my spiritual search.

The Father Martin lecture, I attended, was mainly on the topic of the family illness caused by living with alcoholism. It was a perfect balance of jokes and serious information. He has such charisma that his hour and a half lecture felt like 20 minutes. Apparently his *modus operandi* is to mingle with the audience before speaking. He sat beside me for a few minutes, and I felt as comfortable talking to him, as I would talk to a Program person. He smelled faintly of Ben Gay and is so down to earth and natural that he brings out those qualities in others. He probably chatted with a dozen people before the lecture; I believe the mingling keeps him humble. I have seen his film, *Chalk Talk,* which covers some of the same material, but I feel fortunate to have heard him in person.

I can't wait to see you in person.

Verge

5/15/85

My Sweet Verge,

I remember you saying more than once that you want to stick around to see how this story turns out. Of course that was when we were mired in lots of intrigue, long spaces between seeing each other, and preoccupation with the effects of the disease of alcoholism. We had little knowledge of how, or ability, to take charge of our own life or to be honest. All of those growing up things we were learning as we waited. We were doing the best we knew, as far as being honest, or kind, or civil, or moral goes, so as not to flagrantly bowl other humans over in our course that had only one direction for us. We did it as right as we knew how.

It is fun this night to muse upon the unfolding of our story. I have taken it from the past, when all of the known elements of today were a hazy, hardly-dared-to-be-hoped-for future, through the painful days when you trusted me enough to share some of the most guarded secrets in your life, to when Doreen first decided our relationship was a threat and tried to challenge it. Those things pulled on the thread that tied us from our first meeting, drawing us closer and closer. I remember well that hard pain.

Now we are moving into the time when we can realize the dreams and apply them to everyday realities. I like thinking of getting into the car and driving upstate to meet your folks and of moving inexorably toward living our life together for real, no longer playing at it. Our story is unfolding beyond any dream or hope I ever had. As usual, our reality far exceeds our dreams. I look forward to spending the next week with you applying our dreams to reality.

Love,
Michael

5/15/85

Dear Michael,

Know what Hootie? I'm sure glad we write to one another. Know why? 'Cuz if we didn't write and if you had to know me just by my actions and word of mouth, I doubt you would have been able to perceive my depth, nor would I know yours. This marvelous medium has forced us, time and again, to form thoughts that we might have been too lazy to form, if we were just talking. We have gained confidence in attacking word-of-mouth forming, after years of writing where the thoughts could be retracted by tearing up the letter. We didn't have to squirm under the scrutiny of another trying to understand, but not quite getting the point. It was a safe harbor for thought forming. We have even been able to see in black and white that our thoughts are pretty good and have had the positive feedback of each understanding the other. Our ideas flowed more freely and more confidently, as we began to believe we were pretty smart after all.

I was just thinking about various Gin-isms, and thinking how glad I am that your perception of her was tempered, by the growing you were able to observe in letters. I am glad you have other ways to observe me besides just the surface. Also I am glad you have learned to express yourself—your feelings, your memory, your mental associations so I know your depth, too. You said you didn't know love could be so open. I believe it is only because we learned to tell each other everything in our letters.

I love you,<br>
Verge

5/30/85

My Verge

I mentioned in the note I left on your pillow that it is exciting to find us approaching another dimension of our relationship, experiencing the microscopic aspects of living together. Both of us have taken care of the minutia of life, paid bills, shopped for groceries and so forth until they have just become automatic. When we have been together in the past, examining that aspect of life would just have been a waste of precious time. Incidentals would take care of themselves. We were above all that earth stuff, like money, where it comes from, who spends it on what and why, where we might live, what are priorities, what are frills? I am not implying there is a problem in those areas, just that it is novel to investigate the potentials, and it makes me feel even more intimate with you.

The prospect of this reality also signals a warning—don't take us for granted, it says. I can see where that would be easy to do. Let this slide, or shrug that off as being too small to worry about, and underneath lies the potential for the build up of smoke, then fire, then explosion. I'm glad our learning together has included lessons and exercises in talking to each other when even a hint of storm brews. I'm glad that we have found out that exposing storms to daylight dissipates them easily. Have you thought about these things? Let's talk about them the next time we are together.

~

6:15 AM: A painted sign on the door reads, "Sheriff's Office" and inside Hoot balances on an empty milk can. A July page, torn from a calendar, is tacked to the wall with the first week of numbers crossed off and a dark line circled around the 24th day, which Hoot recognizes as Gin's birthday. His bamboo fish pole leans against the door jam and an occasional worm squirms over the top of a tin can filled with dirt that is placed nearby. Hoot hums softly.

6:30 AM: The screen door of the old farmhouse slams and Gin, diminutive in the wake of such a slam, stomps out and firmly sets herself on the top porch step, puts her chin in her palm and stares straight ahead. Observing her from the shadows of the doorway, Hoot doesn't move. They sit that way for a couple of minutes until Gin finally says, "Hi, Hoot."

"Hi, Gin."

She suddenly jumps up, briskly moves to the old sycamore near the porch and retrieves her fishing pole. Hoot slowly climbs down from the milk can, reaches for his pole, stoops for the worms and strides after Gin who produces two huge donuts from some mysterious source. Hoot accepts his without question. He has known this girl too long to probe her mysteries without invitation. They walk silently, chomping their donuts oozing dark red jelly with each bite. This is not a morning for probing.

## Hoot 'n Gin

At the lake, after casting their lines into the water, Gin and Hoot sit, leaning against the base of a huge willow tree, apparently unaware of each other. Identical bobbers float lazily on the lake without a ripple. When Hoot finally speaks, Gin moves imperceptibly closer to him so just their fine arm hairs touch. "I see what you mean about sitting in that dumb old milk house. I was there at 6:00 and it felt like I was waiting for a couple of weeks."

_"Oh, I just couldn't sleep."

_"It's not that I was so glad to get home from camp, but I was itchy 'cuz I didn't get to go fishin' with you for a whole week."

_"Gin, I missed you. I felt good the minute you stomped out that door."

_"Hey, I think you got a nibble!"

_"Oh Yeah? If you know nibbles so well, how come you ain't caught a fish yet this year?"

Their exchange is not a new one and there is much more to it than the ear can hear. They sit shoulder to shoulder, touching now. Both smile but do not look at each other. Hoot reaches over and gives Gin's pole a sharp jiggle, and she gives him a play kick on the calf. He grabs her ankle and she pulls his hair. Before the dragonfly can leave the end of Gin's pole, they are rolling around on the ground laughing and fake pummeling each other. Joy is a rainbow aura around them.

Michael

5/31-6/1/85

Dearest Michael,

I lie here knowing that within the time it will take me to write this letter I will pass with you from May to June. On the phone this morning, you reminded me that in three weeks I will be with you for the summer. I can hardly believe that time is so near. It has slipped in upon me, while I was trying not to concentrate on it. I just know I will never get a proper sense of time. Can't you see Gin kicking her Mary Janes, twisting and turning, hair just flying? "Maaa! How much longer?" Then falling into a fit of despond, chin on fist, little dejected voice, "We aren't ever gonna go."

Thank you for telling me you were feeling vulnerable. When I was first alone, I used to get the vulnerables and lonelies really bad after you would visit. I still do, but they are familiar, and there is an underlying belief that they will come to an end in the foreseeable future. Also, back then, I was allowing my head martyr trips like: "If I weren't around perhaps one of our lives could be patched up and made workable." I would war up and down about that and allow dark thoughts to set in. Gratefully, I don't feel that way any more. Now I feel joy, knowing we will have a life together, after all—in this lifetime. Although that has been reached by some painful means, dignity and caring have been exercised, and there is an order to it all.

After I talked to you, I was full of the thought that I never want to forget how it felt to be lonely—no one to share a laugh, to care how the day went, no one to smile at and greet the morning. I never want to take your presence for granted. I love the way you have learned to accept the things I can give and like my giving as well as you like giving to me. That was a hard lesson for each of us to learn. It is all right to accept help. Accepting is a gift to the giver.

And thank you for introducing us to your family, for making that start before summer. I dreaded bad reactions to it. This way you have a chance to think over my coming for the whole summer. We are not committed to that yet, and if you find your children's reactions troubling, you can still say, "Hey, Verge, I need some time so let's only take part of the summer together." If you still invite me, I am glad I will have nothing to hide; I can move about freely and love you without restraint. I no longer feel like a secret. You took a huge step toward changing me from a fantasy to a reality, and I thank you for that honor. Next Saturday we will go upstate, and I will introduce you to my family. I hope you will not feel "on display" for that is not my intent. I just want you to be part of my roots.

Verge

6/3/85

My Verge,

It feels good to begin to see the pieces fall into place. That may sound strange, since I have been telling you that I am going through another one of those times of being plagued by the dreaded unnamed fears, misplaced guilt, and over active anxieties, but it is true anyway. For one thing, this experience of going through the hurty stuff isn't as hurty. For another, I feel more detached, as if I were watching it happen through a window in someone else's house. It has a maturing feel, not a hiding or running away from flavor. It gives me a chance to examine what is happening more dispassionately than the last black hole experience and lets me sort through the pieces to see which are real, which are not, and which I can use to grow on. Being able to wait feelings through allows me to examine them as they pass by. Under scrutiny they begin to lose power, and my mind lets the pain drop away. I can't put exact titles on the feelings, but they ride along with realities such as death, breaking away, facing up, and looking inside. I can't say their company is pleasant, but they add color and intensity to life and make me feel more a part of things, as if I had solved an initiation puzzle.

It is easier to truthfully face realities, such as the demands, revelations, and admissions of this week, which in the past would have been more than enough fuel to set me in a vengeful mood and cause me to pour drinks down so they wouldn't even touch the sides of my throat. Then the pities would come and I would settle in for a steady, well justified, drunk. I wouldn't get past the first few feelings before the rest were lost and I wouldn't even be aware of them. That must be a part of how we alcoholics lose out on growing up—we lose most of the growing experiences along the way.

Assuming that Doreen perceives things clearly, the kids are feeling hostile and out of sorts toward me. On Saturday I felt the tearing apart pain, in spite of my intellectualization and educated expectations. Thinking poorly of me, Papa, the ever respected and revered? A slap against good-guyism! It left me in a dark place that colored and touched all the other parts of my life. I have never felt so pervasively affected by one notion or thought. It is a different and very hard feeling. I wish it would go on by, but I know I have to feel it as it does go by.

Just as I have now become more aware of my past relationship with my parents, and have fleshed out its skeleton, I realize my grown up kids are entitled to feel and judge and conclude for themselves. I told myself over many years and beers that there was no time for laments or resentments. I was grown up, moving on, strong, alone. I accepted it all and shoved it away. I judged my parents and didn't care at all about the starkness of that judgment. The judgment was mine to make; no one could take it away from me. I enjoyed the exclusiveness and its prerogative. It was what made me an individual. So, my offspring deserve that too. The deserving comes with birth. I only hope health goes with its use. I feel it and watch it go by. I determine that my assumptions, misconceptions, and illusions won't get in the way of a healthy, growing new relationship with them. I will do what I can to foster that growth. How they travel will be their right and privilege.

I am thankful, as the long forgotten details of my growing up life push to make themselves known, that I have learned about dealing with resentments. I examine them, try to understand where the behaviors that caused them came from, how they might have had some validity for my parents, and let them go. It is good, too, that I can grieve the little boy who was never glad to go home, who didn't know how to hug his mother, and whose stomach tied in knots when his father didn't come home, or when days later he did, and mother reviled him. That little boy had to be on his own emotionally.

I'm glad to be able to look again and be enraged at that treatment, to cry over the lost little boy, to know him, then to let him go. I can let him have his life down through the ages because I can learn from him, but I don't have to carry resentments around. I can see him and his parents in the perspective of the disease and the times in which they lived. I say thanks for life.

I love you, my Verge.

Michael

June 4, 1985

Dearest, My love, Michael,

One thing I cherish most between us is our equalness. Never before in my life have I had an equal relationship. Some of that stemmed from being a female brought up in a compartmentalized society, but I really can't lay it to that, as I was always allowed a lot of leeway with supposed to's. I was fully aware that I had most of the skills that men were traditionally assigned, outside of those requiring brute force. However, I was easily convinced by anyone with verbal confidence that they were better than I at thinking, drawing, telling stories or any other intellectual pursuit. The paradox was that inside I felt independent and self-confident, but that would step aside when challenged. Early on I also developed a bad habit of people pleasing so as not to upset anyone; then in secret I could do pretty much as I pleased when no one was looking.

The point of this old stuff is that none of my relationships were equal because I did not care to take the responsibility to make them so. They served me just as well unequal, or so I thought, until I lost myself in all that inequality. If I was in the dominant role I often had more than I could handle, and in the inferior role I felt discounted. Then I met you.

I found you an equal, even in the playing of the inequality game on that first day we met. It never has been appropriate or wanted or necessary since that day to be anything but shoulder-to-shoulder, face the world equal. I think that is the keystone of our relationship, and it must be nurtured between us at all cost for a lifetime.

You asked about finances and how we shall apportion them between us when we live together—how we can get off the your money, my money kick. I think, at least for the summer, we should figure out our living expenses—rent, phone, food—and pay them 50/50. If we are honest about it, I think both of us would be a little panicked to give up knowing about our finances. We have both been in the position of having a spouse dependant on our taking care of all things financial. Although it was a burden, at least in my case, it was something I could control that gave me the attendant reward of "feeling necessary." I don't think you and I need either side of that coin in our shiny, bright, new relationship.

To ease into living and sharing together, I think it is a good idea to keep separate accounts. At first we will each have bills to pay that we bring with us, and it is a good idea to keep the responsibility of paying them off, separate. As long as we maintain separate cars I think we should be responsible for their payments and maintenance separately. None of this has to be hard and fast in case of emergencies. Entertainment could either be little gifts we give each other, or part of the mutual bill pool.

Now you write what comes to your mind. This is not a place to be sensitive. It is a gathering of thoughts on a subject. Later we can look at our options and make a decision with which we are both comfortable. Right now what I want to do is to see you. Gin says you ain't ever going to get here. I put my arm around her, give her a sympathetic hug, and say reassuring things.

Hurry,<br>
Verge

6/12/85

My Verge,

Yesterday has gone by. I drove and drove and drove away from you. Now I am settled down. My head is clear. I have looked over my shoulder enough to be sure you really aren't there. It is amazing, the things I have managed to do without you. I feel like the world has fallen apart, but I move about and do things in a fallen apart world. The magic formula is to convince myself that you are present, even if you really aren't, and that signals self that it is not necessary to curl up into a tiny ball and roll into a corner until you come back. That way I can write a letter to you and make a stab at sounding normal after only one day of recuperation.

Lots of times in the past as I got closer to someone, got to inspect their fine points, I inexplicably felt myself pulling away. Without wanting to, I felt the closeness fade and interest wane. It was a helpless feeling over which I had no control. I never thought about that with us, until we were in the midst of looking at your roots, meeting your family. I was loving your roots so much, when the realization hit me that the slipping away feeling was in reverse. The more I saw and the more microscopically I looked, the closer I felt to you and the closer I wanted to be. Did you see me start to faint? You couldn't have, because there were too many times spread out over the day, starting with sharing donuts with you at your favorite place to stop when you and Milo would go upstate. Then there was your Grandma's house and the cemetery you played in across the street, your mother's grave and meeting your favorite cousin. The day was a swirl of getting closer and looking for more. I felt the exact moment in the garden when your daddy started to let me in. Ginny, my head is still spinning. I loved it all. I'm glad you decided that we needed to see roots. I love you in such new kinds of ways; I don't even know where to start to tell you.

Michael

6/12/85

Dear Michael, My sweet man,

I have a new rush of reasons to love you, as if I needed any more to keep us fresh. I loved the way you were with my people, accepting them as my roots, that being enough cause for respect. More than that, you managed to treat each as an individual and made an individual contact with each one. (Sometimes when I am feeling "on the spot," knowing I want to or need to make a good impression, I freeze right down to the core of myself and become incapable of genuine contact. That is getting better, but it is still a problem.) Thank you for understanding that I miss

Cat. I know she is in a happy place at the farm for the summer, but she and I have been through a lot together. Most of all thank you for staying you through it all, remaining the person who gives me equilibrium.

This year seems to have been subtly, or not so subtly, designed to get me to make a decision about my work. It is the only area of my life where I am still dissatisfied and unhappy. Without the various unpleasantries of the year, it might be a harder decision to leave my job. It has been the mainstay of security through many years of upset and insecurity, and aside from the politics, I have always loved teaching. In an act of blind trust that there is a plan for my life, unknown to me, and trust that our love can survive adversity if necessary, I have gotten my head to agree to make an all out effort to find a job in Cleveland this summer. The pain of being away from you is too great to bear any longer. I've never done anything but teach. Could I handle another type of job? I have to trust that you will be behind me, until I find my niche. As an adult, I have never had the luxury of depending on someone else, and I have to learn that it is possible.

I just saw the kids going down the road hell bent for lightning with Gin on Hoot's handlebars. Gin was yelling at the top of her lungs, "No more school; no more books; No more teacher's dirty looks..."

*Hoot, Go faster! I like the wind blowin' in my hair.*

*What do you mean, you can't see nothin'? I'll tell you what you run over, if you hit somethin'.*

*What kind are we gonna get?*

*No, Hoot, it's your turn to choose! Orange Crush goes real good with hot dogs, but get what you want. Boy, sometimes when it is real hot like today I wake up thinking how good Orange Crush would taste for breakfast!*

*Are you crazy? My Mom would kill me if I mentioned pop for breakfast! I just like to think of it.*

*Com'on, Hoot, go fast again; the sweat's runnin' down my neck!*

*Look, there's usta-be Big Kid's bike in front of the store.*

*Come oon, Hoot, stop kickin' his bike before he sees you! I told you, <u>you</u> are Big Kid now.*

*'Lo. ...Hoot! Come on!*

*He only said hello. Why're you lookin' like that?'*

*Wow! Look, the hot dogs are all in a string today! Let's get six so's we can hang them out like a Dagwood sandwich going home.*

*Oh, all right. But I woulda hung on tight.*

*Feel how nice and cold the water is in the cooler. OK, Mr. Webster, we'll close it right up as soon as Hoot finds the pop he wants.*

*ORANGE CRUSH! Why, Hoot, is that the kind you wanted to get? Are you sure? Hey, don't put it back! I like Orange Crush just fine.*

*That's 50 cents, 75, Ok, Hoot, 80, 90, a dollar. Let's go! We don't want hot soda pop when the snakes are frying in the road.*

*Don't go over any bumps now, or you'll lose me for sure.*

*Ok, we'll put it all in the saddlebags. That will be a heck of a lot easier. Sure I can't wave the hot dogs?*

*Oh, all right!*

*No, I don't have to stop at the house. I've got matches and a bottle opener in my pocket.*

*Stop at the gate and I will open it. Then we can take the bike partway up the lane to the cow path.*

*Ow! Bit my tongue! You're right; it sure is awful bumpy. Lean the bike against that old maple tree and we'll walk.*

*Wheeww! Sure is <u>hot!</u> Look, your stripey shirt is all wet. Why don't you take it off?*

*Wish I could take mine off.*

*Hoot! You know I can't.*

*Course I know the way. This cow path goes right over to the quarry.*

*We have to cross this brook. ...Yeah, you can drink from it. I do all the time. Watch out for the clay!*

*Hoot, I told you to watch out for the clay, its awful slippery. You look pretty funny sitting down there.*

*No, Hoot! Let go of my foot! Stop! Stooop! Bubble, gurgle, ha ha ha ha!*

*Now, look! I've got clay all over me...in my hair. Look where my hand was on your arm. A perfect handprint. See, on your chest!*

*Yeah, one on my leg, and one for your back! Hoot, Don't put it on my shirt!*

*You look like ol' dawg when he comes out of the pond!*

*What do you mean I look like a chicken in the rain? See if I can shake my hair dry like dawg does.*

*Wool, you coulda moved! Hootie's a dri-ip! Hootie is a drip!*

*(to be continued)*

~

Time runs by when I follow this pursuit. At school this morning I was standing in the hall before class when the brother of one of my students approached me. I told you about his brother before, the little kid that surprises me with his sensitivity, a short commodity in junior high. The two of them are known as the Motley Brothers, two extra small kids in a dog eat dog world. They are picked on, called dirty, and are constantly involved in fights. Although he is not my student, he asked me to read a story he had written. During the day I read it and felt an instant kinship with him. It was very good. He is writing a novel this summer, he tells me. Both boys write computer programs for amusement and draw constantly. They are impoverished kids, but somehow, somewhere, their brains are being nourished. That is why I teach, one reward in 900, a chance to intimately touch one kid's life. I say thanks for that uplift in a year that often seemed hopeless.

Verge

6/15/85

My sweet Verge,

Going places with you is fun—any place. It reminds me of the hope I used to get, back in kid days, when I allowed myself to build expectations in my head about how an occasion would be or feel. Sometimes the real made an approach to the imagined, but either the imagined was too big or the real was too small. Even dressed up with the flourish of alcohol, festivities were just a little bit less than festive.

With you the most everyday things are fresh, and shiny, and exciting. "Let's take a trip up to see my daddy," for instance. Granted, that is not an everyday occurrence, but I could easily have set my mind on it being a chore that had to be done out of courtesy. It could have been significant only in that it took time away from us. But the very first time you mentioned that you would like to take me to meet your father, it snapped a cord in my brain; it was like an imp telling me, "This is a special thing." So I allowed myself to experience all the anticipation, the being scared, what-ifing, projecting what the experience of roaming through your roots would be like, being together in the midst of your family. None of it fell short. I was able to feel easy with people I scarcely knew, and who I should have been impressing, but I felt no pressure to do that. It was easy to feel that all was as it should be and that I belonged. I was surprised at my ability to treat each person individually and not as a blur. I have a new, even closer than I knew possible feeling for you, since going to your home.

I see more and more adult you peeking through the edges of your letters. We are emerging from our Gin and Hoot relationship, as it moves out of childhood and blends more with the grown ups, yet we can still feel the safety of slipping all the way back when we need to. It is a delight to see and feel your adult self. It is also a much larger commitment and responsibility, but very welcome—sought after, even. That is what I was beginning to see last summer at Canada time, your adult daring to set a foot out here and there. It is extremely attractive to me. The child-you enhances it, but your adult emerging fills me with more excitement than I dreamed capable of feeling. I think our going back to your home, together, paradoxically brought that wide open.

I thought I was impatient to start an every day life with you before. Now I am out of my mind with impatience, and full of hives about the delay. Your search inside yourself for feelings about a new life and a new job has not gone unnoticed. We will talk about that when you get here. Please hurry before I expire from the anticipation of our summer life together.

Michael

6/15/85

Dear Michael,

The crows are cawing up a storm down in back, so I suppose that is where the kids ended up. A while ago they went by again and I heard Gin's giggle up by the pasture gate....

~

*Shhhh, Hoot, we are almost to the quarry and sometimes there is a fox family down there. Crawl on your belly like this. Goofy! Stop pullin' my foot.*

*We're almost to the edge. Look real careful. YEOW!!!*

*Well, Hoot, it was a snake! I put my hand right on him. He was sunning on the ledge! I'm just glad it was an old black snake.*

*We can either climb down the rocks here, or go around to the other side where the path goes down.*

*Dig your fingers into the rocks and get a good hold before you move. Be careful, Hoot, or you will fall and be as flat as that frog we saw rund over in the road. Wasn't it interesting how he was flat as cardboard —toes and everything?*

*Whew! It really is hot! See where we came down? First time I did that, I was really scared. My cousin and my older brother double dared me to come down that way. They didn't think I would. When I started down, they both kept yelling at me to go back. To tell you the truth, I was too scared; it was easier to go down, 'cuz each step down meant I didn't have so far to fall, and I wasn't sure I could pull myself back up over the top.*

*Hoot, where's the hot dogs?*

*Com'on, We'll walk up the path. I forgot you couldn't carry them and climb down too.*

*I didn't know I had so much sweat in me. Let's go for a swim before we eat. If we put the pop in the water it will stay cool.*

*Neither do I. So what?*

*Do what you like; I'm gonna swim. Yeoooowwww! THIS IS COLD! It's like being inside a great big ice cube. It feels good.*

*Yea, Hoot! I knew you wanted to. No! Don't splash me or I'll hafta duck you. Doesn't it make your breath catch like when you first go outdoors in the wintertime?*

*These rocks all hot from the sun feel great. I'm starved! Lets cut some green sticks for our hot dogs.*

*No! I don't want you to find me a stick. Everybody's gotta get his own.*

*Whatcha doin', Hoot, building a wigwam?*

*Wool, that's a funny way to put sticks for a fire. I never saw such a thing.*

*At camp? They teach you stuff like that? My Uncle Wum taught me this way. Look, I got lots of matches. You light yours, and I'll light mine, and just see which one burns.*

*At least you found a pretty good hot dog stick. Mine's got a fork, so I'm gonna cook two to oncet. That way you can have a hot dog, even if your fire doesn't work.*

*Don't they smell good cookin'? I like mine black. Wow! Watch the sparks; they hurt!*

*Did they teach you to put your hot dog right into the fire like that, too? Uncle Wum says to cook on the coals, where it has burned down some. Sure, I said I like mine black, but not on fire like yours.*

*Here, want one of mine?*

*Hey, if you like your hot dog lookin' like ossified dinosaur skin, that's fine with me.*

*Ooooh, Hootie, didn't I tell you that Orange Crush was good with hot dogs?*

*Why you gotta go in such a hurry? Whaddya mean you've gotta snap beans for supper, before your mom gets home from work? That's hours yet.*

*You think it's that late?*

*Well, I am putting my clothes on! Hootie, would you wait for me? I hafta get my shoes on and put water on the fire. Get some water in the pop bottle.*

*...Hoot? You mad at me for somethin'?*

*...Your fire burned real good. Maybe I'll try it that way next time.*

*'Sall right. You were just mad 'cuz I hadda say somethin' smart about your fire, and I knew you really didn't mean to burn up your hot dog.*

*Sure, I'll come over after supper.*

Michael, I can't wait to see you. I've been rushing around cleaning the apartment and packing what I can, and tomorrow I will get my marks done for school. Next week, after I finish up with the kids, I will clean my classroom, and then I will be ready to drive to Cleveland. Are you as excited about spending a summer with me as I am with you? I can't wait to get on with our adventure.

Verge

6/18/85

My Sweet Verge,

Wooool, Ginny, my head is full up of nothing. I rattle it and look inside and probe, but it is hopeless. All I find is jellybeans, flattened frogs, AND ORANGE CRUSH! GIN! I can't stand it. I can't say anything to make this blasted time go by. My self is completely filled with the excitement of it all.

Finally! After years of wishing, we come together. Welcome, Us, to life. I embrace it; I embrace you and welcome you, Verge, my love, my life. Please be very, very safe. Drive safely, but hurry.

Michael

# PART IV

# The Promises

9/2/85 Monday

My Verge,

This is a state of confusion letter, probably a note, a head is schpinning, nerves all dumped into a bag and jumbled up letter. I don't know where I am right now. How can I? All that has meaning for me is gone away. Don't worry. I know you will worry, but don't. I just want to tell you how devastatingly empty life is this first day alone. I want to share it because the way we are, what is for one is for both of us. In the next breath I take, I want to share the immeasurable joy of us discovering we have no doubts about our making it together. But that is a truism, a fact of the ages created when all things were created. We belong together. My head wonders what we are doing apart, in the face of such an absolute, yet it nods agreement with the wisdom and good sense of exploring all avenues before we dash off.

On this first day alone, please pardon the lost Hootie who writes this, for the bleakness of going home without you there is all encompassing and bewildering. A few such days will heal that and allow the huge well of happiness that you are to me, to take over. All of me is love for you.

Your Michael

9/2/85

Dearest, My Michael,

As I jolted awake at 4:05 this morning, my instant thoughts were schemes to make money and to be with my man all to once. For one thing, I thought, I will revamp the idea I had for an art appreciation book for young children. I expanded the whole series in my head and employed Elle to do the photography. I got so enthused with the idea I nearly got up to begin work on the spot. Perhaps I could get a grant to work on such a project. To further confuse my buffeted brain of the wee morning hour, I've decided to attend the new series of chemical dependency counseling lectures. They start a week from Wednesday evening. I need to pick the good doctor's brain about places where I can volunteer, to claim some experience, and to get a letter of recommendation from him. I also decided to buy back retirement credit for the year I taught before Milo was born, to find out about Ohio teacher certification, and to go to New Paltz to check that my college file is activated.

My brain is reeling from scheming and figuring, trying to justify the need for this time I have madly set ahead of us, the while missing you with such acute pain I can hardly stand it. I know it took me a full year of being away from Eric, before I was healed enough to begin to know myself and to make good decisions. I firmly believe you need that time, too, no matter how painful it is for us.

This is a terrible scribble, but it will have to stand as a testimony of my love for you, anyway, because I have run out of time, and school waits. Feel it, smell it, crumple it into a ball and play catch with the cat, but know it says one thing, "I love you the most."

Verge

9/5/85

My Verge,

O K, it's all right now. I've convinced this body and brain that you have left. They understand it is just for 100 years or so, and after that we can stay together. They have been through a couple of day's cycle now, and they understand, accept, agree, and are calm.

Ain't we something, though? Can't help marveling at us—the way we are together. I just settle in to marveling about one thing concerning us and whole bunches of other things sprout that need marveling about. Besides the way we affect each other (that can take a whole lifetime of marveling in itself), it is fun to see the way we affect the rest of the world. We dared to look past ourselves and observed others drawing life or love from our presence. The story I told you of the whole universe celebrating our union takes on more credibility. I just bubble over with exuberance when I think of us. I have never felt so right in my life. Even in the pain of separation there is the joy and celebration of Us. Verge, I am anxious to get back to the adventure of us living together. I hate the thought of wasting even one minute more by being apart. We will make it though.

Your Michael

## Virginia N. & Michael N.

9/8/85

Dearest love, Michael,

Thank you for the courage and support you gave me by letting me involve you in the letter I just finished writing to Eric. Enclosed is a copy:

*Dear Eric,*

*Mostly I want to say thank you for the courage it must have taken for you to write me a thank you letter. In return, I would like to thank you for the many gifts you gave me, especially challenging me to think and to see many perspectives of an issue before I formed an opinion. Sometimes you gave me pretty words, and we both gave each other a pretty child.*

*I've wanted to tell you for a long time that I hold no grudges. I have come to understand that I brought as much immaturity to our relationship as you did, and that my inability to communicate (or selfish unwillingness, perhaps) complicated our problems unnecessarily. I never let you know who I was, what I felt, or what I needed. I never understood what you meant when you used to accuse me of dishonesty. I thought that was unjust. But I have also come to realize that in some vain attempt to make life nice, I never was honest about anything.*

(Paragraph on some news about mutual friends)

*Michael and Doreen, too, have been separated for several months. Sobriety left them without a cushion for their problems and each grew in a different way and apart. Michael and I went out to Phoenix this summer. Milo and his girlfriend took us on a whirlwind tour of the West Coast. Five days from Phoenix to San Diego, San Francisco, Los Angeles and Las Vega, then back to Phoenix. Somehow Milo managed to stop at the right spots long enough to have left a real flavor of what West Coast is all about. If it weren't all going to slip into the sea, that is where I would like to hang my hat. For me, Las Vegas is a one time only (and hopefully at night) city. She looked like a tired whore the next morning.*

*Michael and I have been spending a lot of time together figuring out what second chances are all about. Wish us well. We wish you well.*

*Sincerely,*
*Verge*

I knew I had to answer Eric's letter, because it got to be an incessant nag underneath everything I've done with my time since getting back here. The hardest part was that I could have written the letter without implicating you, but the nag would still have been there. Worry that he would find out casually, from a careless word or slip from one of the people whose lives we have crossed, and that old dread of bumping into him would still haunt me. Honesty gets to be particularly tricky and difficult when a truth involves another person's life. It was the one place left where I felt I was skulking around. I'm sorry I had to wrench you into the middle of it. (You could always pull the plug on your phone for six months. Both of us were projecting that he might try to contact you, and I might unsuspectingly answer the phone. Did you notice?) Nobody said we were all well yet—just working on it.[22]

I don't know if you understood that my biggest test of honesty was telling you about writing to Eric. My old self would figure it would be too painful an issue for you to handle, so I would have to keep it secret from you. I would only hint in the letter to Eric about you and me and hope no one would tell him that we were being seen together. It felt good to be free enough with you, and equal enough, to discuss the matter, to allow you to express your opinion about it, and to offer the option of being disclaimed if you wanted. I never have discussed an issue with someone, laid out all the options, and reached a mutual decision of action before. In the past I would either have my mind made up and made a token stab at allowing a modification from another person, or I would agree completely with what the other person wanted, effacing my own right to be part of the decision. The wish to consider another's part in a decision, and the desire to state my own thoughts, and then to come to a mutual ground feels (can you believe it) MATURE. I was discovering that as the whole scenario unfolded.

Now I am emotionally exhausted. I want to crawl up close, hold you tight so I feel my flesh melting into your bones, and dream-walk the night away with you.

I love you, Michael,
Verge

22 Step Nine: "Made direct amends to such people whenever possible, except when to do so would injure them or others." Alcoholics Anonymous, *Twelve Steps and Twelve Traditions., 83.*

9/10/85

My Verge,

It is amazing how you have taken this place where I was born, brought up, and have spent the majority of my life, and transformed it from a dull, dirty, uninteresting city into a pretty, lively place to be. You did that to my whole life, in fact, I won't burden you with the responsibility of being the source of life for me, we did that for each other. You took this city, shined it up and held it up to me and asked: Did I know that St. Michael's twin spires were like us? Who were the wonderful artists who created the fanciful creatures tucked into the nooks and crannies of all the old public buildings? Wasn't the lake like our ocean? Because you made me look with fresh perspective, I wanted to show you more, so we could giggle or marvel together. As you said, maybe this is how people are supposed to live. Our mutual respect and equality gives us freedom to move along unhindered by self-made obstacles and roadblocks.

I sense your relief and leap in growth since you completed your letter to Eric. I'm glad you wrote it. Thanks for including me and hooking me up to your new life in your letter. From the push I am beginning to feel to finish amends I still have left around, I can surmise your sigh of relief when it was over. I love you.

Michael

9/18/85

My Michael,

I am here early at the Wednesday night lecture series. I have just talked to the doctor who gave me the names of three people to contact for places to volunteer. Apparently he called them personally, which I thought was really nice of him. One of the people he contacted is a woman who runs an outpatient program for families of alcoholics. He said she is expecting my call, so I guess that will be my first line of attack. I would like to work with families, and I would like to have a reference like that.

I don't know what to say to encapsulate our time just spent together. The ripped parts are too raw and the missing is too bad to say much that makes sense. As usual, when we part, we never completed half of the things we intended to do. I wanted to read some of Eric's letters with you as a way for us to come to grips with him in our life. To de-mythify him if you will—to see if together, we can look at him as a mere human being with very human problems. I began to feel that happen as I started reading them over. Somehow I never could look clearly at the man. Early on, I looked at him through eyes of adoration and admiration, and later, through eyes of fear, then, resentment and contempt, but I never could look at him as a regular human being. He exuded such charisma, it never occurred to me that he might feel insecure or unsure and like no one had left him notes. As I was reading, I felt compassion and began to see him as a struggling human walking much the same path as you or I walked, only with a great show of bravado as his protective face.

Not only was I reading Eric, but also finding barely remembered self-beginnings, mostly about how he influenced me and swayed my thoughts about life. He never twisted my arm to follow him; I was a prime follower. His way was intoxicating because I could walk in his wake and reap the excitement I never would have had the guts to go after directly.

Love,
Verge

9/19/85

Dearest Michael,

When we talked on the phone, you were worrying about forgetfulness. No, I do not think you are losing your mind. I think for an extended period of time you have been under emotional strain that makes you disorientated and forgetful. Add to that the stress of parting, coupled with no sleep the night before and it is a wonder you functioned as well as you did. If you recall the last time we parted, you nearly forgot to call me because you thought I was home at your apartment. Surely that is where I belong. You are growing better by leaps and bounds. I told you that you had given up the "I forgot" syndrome over the summer. Last spring that was your every third sentence. Now you have even given up poosheling. (You know, the various releasings of air from your lips as if you were a balloon deflating.) And Hootie, I am excited about your new handle on heights. I can feel you testing your courage and finding you can stretch it further and further. I can watch you grow before my face and eyes. Usually by our time in life, if people grow or change they do it so slowly you can barely detect it happening. It may seem peculiar, but I find everything about us becoming more and more exciting.

Last night's lecture was about family treatment. The doctor said that unresolved issues in a counselor's own life will sooner or later come up as a stumbling block in a counseling session with a client; therefore a counselor should have his own support system. He said that he grew up with an alcoholic father and a compassionate, knowledgeable mother who was able to explain the facts of the disease to him, so he felt guilty whenever he found himself resenting his father's behavior. He said he was well into counseling before he found his anger at his father. He was never given a place to express that anger before, because he "understood" the problem his father had. He said he felt an awful anger that his father was never there when he needed him, made promises he couldn't keep, made dates and appointments and broke them, never went to a baseball game or a school function, and embarrassed him in front of his friends so he could never bring them home. He said the anger was awful because it had never been validated or even acknowledged.

I thought it was interesting that even in a home where someone can explain the alcoholic's bizarre behavior as a sickness, a child has a need and a right to be allowed to express his anger and disappointment and needs to be told it is all right to feel those emotions.

I just said good night to you on the phone and now I want to hold your voice in my head as I snuggle up with you.

Verge

9/20/85

My Verge,

I never thought I would eventually learn from and grow because of a mountain climbing experience. I was as sure as breathing that I would forever stay away from high places whenever and wherever they presented. I have come to believe that some, if not all, of my fear of heights is connected to immaturity. That has been borne out by the degree (however small) I have come to face that fear. With your gentle encouragement, since The Program has pointed me in the direction of growing up, I can actually go places I wouldn't even have considered before and even find myself enjoying them. That is a miracle in a Hoot's life.

When we were on Mohonk Mountain, I didn't feel embarrassed, or disgraced, or like a failure when I did turn back. I felt like a grown up person must feel when he finds himself in a position he can't handle.

Know your limits and fall back to regroup, or to find a solution, for another occasion; going through life, "one step at a time". I did not have to be perfect, or even good, right off the bat. I climbed through the labyrinth to see how far I could go and enjoy it. When we reached that point where we had to decide to continue or to leave, I weighed the fact that the fun was disappearing, against the perfectionist's notion that once you start something you must finish it. I decided that was far enough. I had learned something up until then, and to go further would be pain that would black out any more learning. Ginny, your kind patience and understanding set it straight for me. I could go back without feeling compelled to make excuses. I felt your hand on my arm, and I knew next time I would be able to go much further. Then I was able to enjoy the walk on the path and climb the tower, which I wouldn't even go near before. You make my life joyful.

Michael

9/22/85

Dearest Michael,

As I look at this stationary from the Moqui Lodge at the Grand Canyon my head swirls with thoughts. The biggest miracle of that day was watching you acclimate yourself to looking down deeper than many a one has ever looked before. It wasn't as if you were gritting your teeth and white knuckling the experience, more like letting yourself slide into the fascination of the beauty and arcing over the fear and sick of the vertigo. If I'd had my way, we never would have gone to the canyon because I thought it would be too unbearable for you; consequently, that miracle would never have happened. It was a good lesson for me: Stop trying to direct people's lives even if it is done with the best intention. I would have tried to keep you away from an experience that gave you a huge push in growth.

I was especially excited this last weekend when you were able to put that new growth to practice while we were climbing on Mohonk. I have always felt exaltation in high places and longed to share that with you, even though I, too, can feel stomach plummeting vertigo on occasion. If I concentrate on that feeling when I know it is coming on, it gets worse until my nerves jam and, paradoxically, terror urges me to jump. But if I can use that beginning feeling as a signal to concentrate on looking out at the beauty and not thinking of my immediate surroundings, I can usually keep the sickness at bay.

I think I am seeing in you what you observed in me a little over a year ago. I now feel the joy you were feeling, then, watching me, and know what an inner tickle it is to see your daily growing confidence, the surer stride, the brighter eyes, the steady sureness of your spoken thoughts and the adventurous delving into your mind. All are beautiful.

This waiting is especially hard, now that we have experienced the real day-to-day joy of sharing life, breath to breath. But you are still doing big, necessary-to-our-relationship adjustments, while we are apart, that might take a great deal longer if we were steady on in the middle of our life together. Things not dealt with have a habit of lurking or changing into harder stuff later on, so I am confident in the wisdom of this time of waiting. Just know each day I love you more for your courage and forward growth.

Verge

9/27/85

My Verge,

I am getting a lot of distance out of our mountaineering of the past few months. I can't imagine being so preoccupied with being in all those high places, when one of my main objectives in life was to turn in as opposite direction from them and run as fast and as far as I could. The message that persists is neither the mountains nor the climbing of them is important, for surely hordes of people have lived happy lives without leaving the prairie, but facing them when they do occur is the stuff by which I can measure growth.

I do that with my program, too. I try to work it one day at a time, ask for help, and seek God's will, but some days I go too fast and find myself hanging too far out where I am not ready to be. Then I have to pull back to where it is safe for now—'til I'm ready. I can't ask for total growth or serenity all at once, because I am not ready for all that. I have to grow up gradually. So, I try to go from day to day doing the best I can for that day and hope I am doing right.

I say thanks for another opportunity to get closer to life and closer to my Ginny.

Your very own Michael

10/1/85

Dearest, my gonna be husband, Michael,

Thanks for telling me how you applied your climbing experience to the "one day at a time" slogan. I was surprised when you said you felt a little shaky about taking up the EAP Counselor's request that you co-ordinate a discussion group with fellow workers. You have had substantial time in The Program, have made good growth, and have become a responsible employee, so who could be better suited? You did not elaborate on the purpose of the groups. Are they to initiate people into the AA philosophy, to act as a general support group for newly sober people, or to help people who think they might have a problem but are not sure?

I'm beginning to lose that living-in-the-present feeling I found so beautiful last summer. The happy part stays, though. I never had an open mouth smile. But, Hootie, since summer I actually catch myself using an open mouth smile. I become conscious of it when I feel my face creaking into that shape.

Something that makes me smile is the picture in my head of you carrying a red leaf and a yellow one all afternoon, as we walked in the woods. It is not so much that you were doing something I do, but that by doing it you internalized the feeling I have for such things. It is hard to put into words what stones or leaves mean to me. I could tell you endlessly about texture and color and shape, but the emotion of them is what defies explanation. It is about the uniqueness of each piece of nature. Upon close inspection, things of nature that seem the same are not. Out of a billion quadrillion stones on the beach find me two exactly alike. If two trees of the same species can produce apples, say, then why, out of fate, or mistake, or design are they each uniquely formed when exactly the same could do as well and take a lot less imagination? It seems that everything in nature is heaven (or hell) bent on uniqueness even in the middle of sameness. This is more complicated than I intended. I enjoyed watching you carry two leaves for an afternoon, because I have always done that and I never knew anyone else who did.

I miss you terribly,
Verge

10/4/85

My Sweet Verge,

Here are a few blessings I must count as I sit here and suffer with the lack of you. As I jotted down the date, it occurred to me that not too long ago this time of year would have started my excitement countdown to seeing you again, after being apart since July or August. That is where we were then and we lived with it, but now we have shifted. I am glad, in spite of the even deeper, harder hurt, that we see each other as often as we do, even if we can't be together every single minute.

I am glad we found the courage to change a painful situation to a dynamic one, even though the way was laborious. I am glad we were able to reach out to each other and to accept from each other, as we met the challenges of the risks we took. I am glad we could see clear to recognize the need and the wisdom for taking those risks. I am glad the others in our lives also saw, or at least accepted, the wisdom in the changes those risks necessitated, and had the courage to make their own changes.

I am thankful for every microsecond I spend with you—whether in your presence or in our spiritual union. I am glad for our willingness to join life, rather than relying on our own resources and combating our way through. I am glad for the chance to see and live the joy and beauty of us.

I am glad you tell me about your smile. I could see you looking even prettier, even told you about your pretty teeth, but never made the connection to your new smile. To me it was always warm and real. I am glad you are able to see those changes in yourself and to understand the way it reaches out to others. I am glad you are in my life.

Michael

10/19/85

Dearest Michael,

I am at the kitchen table smelling our pie in the making, muddling over the dinner menu and tomorrow's breakfast. I imagine your face as you will be, sitting across the table from me smiling at the pie—not entirely from greed—a lot from the fact that someone, namely me, cared enough about you to make a fat juicy pie to share. I don't believe I could feel more attached to you.

The first time I got married I didn't have time to sit around and daydream about "what will it be like," and "what will we do with our life together," and other girlish thoughts. My mind was too full of things already decided, like being pregnant and knowing I was being married for the child and not because I was significant.

I begin to feel comfortable about being an adult and having to make adult decisions. For instance, I have been pondering about what is the right thing to do to get us on the same side of the continent. During a talk with my union representative yesterday, in a matter of minutes everything came clear. You will know by the time you receive this that he said to write and ask for a professional leave of absence. He did not seem to think there would be a problem with that.

I have been so mired in "what if's" that it has kept the clear picture from coming to me. Now I see that is the right course of action. By the end of January you will have been separated for a year, which I believe is a necessary time for physical, mental and emotional head clearing for you and your family. That is semester break at school, and if I ask for a six months' leave it will give me time to research jobs out there and for you to find out if you can transfer. It also may be a controlled period of time for us to feel the burden of living on one source of income. My head says no problem there, for I have supported three people on my comparable salary, but what if one of us gets sick? I know that is a risk anyone takes, but it is a fear I have to work on and I'm trying to be up front about it.

In any case, I feel firmly committed to this line of action and out of the emotional morass of not knowing. I always know the one thing that has inspired my life—I love you intensely and I look forward to us living together.

Verge

10/22/85

My Sweet Verge,

We talked about the seven deadly sins merely being a spin off from the most deadly sin of us being apart. Remember? Well, that most deadly has a tangent—traveling through a mid October landscape alone. It is too wide in scope, too awe inspiring, too beautiful for one half of a full puzzle to be expected to handle. It was nice of the Monday morning to add a good bit of sun to its opening scene. New York State and that stretch of I 84 was prime for such a show. The browns snuggled in amongst the many shades of green, and the yellows, oranges and bright reds kept whooshing each other out of the way like prima donnas showing off. When I arrived at the mountain overlook near the end of New York, I had to whoop out loud, "Ginny!" A big old quilt of color was thrown over the mountains in all the far-flung directions.

I longed for you and I welcomed the rain when it came at Bellefonte. I hoped it would dampen the fire in my head. It made it all cozy as I relived our weekend together. By the time I passed into Ohio, the rain and the orange barrels stopped. The missing of you smoothed down so I could feel the comfortable warmth of our love. It only takes a little of that missing hurt to bring home how much more we are to each other. Before I knew it, I was home talking to you on the phone and feeling way better.

Michael

10/24/85

Dearest Michael,

It is nearly two months since we baptized each other with our tears and did a major disentangling and ripping asunder to leave the summer behind, to again walk this distance separately. Two months later, looking back at summer, I cannot make that time behave and stay two months—our summer telescopes into a small space, maybe a week, while these two months seem an eternity. This is a reverse time-warp from the days when we first met and only saw each other alone a matter of hours and altogether for two to five days every couple of years, or later during the lake years when you and the family visited for a couple of weeks each summer, it seemed like you were with me a major part of my life.

I am grateful that we have a history together. Can you think how painful it must be to find yourself in mid-life, with children, in love with a person with whom you share no intermingling of the past? We shared friends and experiences and children, and can keep our first spouses in our collective lives as part of our history, without any feeling of jealousy. We can reminisce with our children without one of us feeling left out. I think it would be painful to have a marriage partner who spent twenty-five years with another spouse and only to know about the pieces of that other life the person chose to impart. We felt jealous of each other's childhood until we devised our mixture of myth and real to insert ourselves into it.

The benefits have only just begun to surface. It is a pleasure to have shared history with your mother, your brothers, your children, and extended family. Even if some of them initially have negative feelings about our relationship because they haven't resolved their own torn or rearranged alliances, they may come to appreciate our common ground. We are not strangers who are expected to suddenly make family; we have all grown together. Milo's aunt and her husband aren't strangers to you either, and when they make reference to Eric you do not have to feel unsure. Although you just recently met my family, you have known them in letters through the years and you only had to put faces to the characters. As uncomfortable as you can be with strangers, that is the only explanation I have for how easily you fit in among them.

Verge

10/25/85

My Sweet Ginny,

It is a disquieting experience to witness the destruction of a fixture, a piece of the world that was always there and counted on to always be there. No one thinks about it, just as no one thinks about whether or not his house will be there when he comes home. Destruction happens all the time on this planet: a tree is uprooted (whoever expected to see that tree gone in a flash?); a whole cliff slides into the sea after towering over it for centuries. It is a shock and nothing is ever the same in the galaxy of a soul's life again. It was that way on a brisk autumn morning when it became obvious to this member that the beautiful wooden track was being uprooted from the roof of the YMCA. It really didn't have roots, but it has been in place so long you could swear you saw fine hairs being pulled up with the anchor posts.

Gasp! Breath stuck in my throat. An ugly disruption in the smooth clean flow of the boards, a dark scar where 30 feet of track had been! But wait! Hey wait! This is the same track on which Ginny spent the warm summer mornings running and walking and sweating and moving those crazy feet of hers, looking at the church spires she said were like Hoot and Gin. I loved it when I could look up and see her serious, getting tired, determined, smiling at me, wanting to be with me. She got the whole place humming, guys talking to me who never did before, watching her. She breathes new life into the place.

Now they want to rip the whole track out. Not a word of warning. Everyone agrees it is sacred ground. They stand silent, helpless; meaningful time ends. A notice was posted that the roof would be repaired and a new track painted on it. Also:

NOTICE
ANYONE WANTING A RELIC OF THE GIN TRACK
MUST REGISTER
AT OFFICE BETWEEN 8:00 AND 9:00 AM
ONE TIME OPPORTUNITY

Security will be on duty to help control the inevitable crowding and panic.

By the following afternoon not one grain of sawdust remains on the roof. Even swathes of roof are missing. Life will never be the same, but hundreds of households honor their relic of happy times past.

Michael

11/3/85

Dear Hootie,

Thank you for immortalizing our outdoor track. They may put in a more practical one, maybe even a less dangerous one, but will they include a catalog of names and dates and sentiments to ponder as one goes around and around? Will it be raised up so I can see our twin spires and spy on the parking lot below? Will it have variations of sound to mark the laps as I daydream in circles? I shall miss it. It became an old friend in those two months last summer, measuring the joy of testing my body and developing its capabilities. Even though that has been put on hold for the moment, I look forward to resuming that practice when I go back to Cleveland.

Twenty-three years ago tomorrow I birthed my son. Here we are, 23 years later pregnant with two more children—Hoot and Gin. The one of the body back then and the two of the brain conceived in our letters are parallel in many ways. I loved the feeling of that growing entity within my body. I felt so vital and useful. I needed to hear you tell me I was beautiful pregnant, for vanity, I suppose, but I loved my state of body.

I only hated the birthing pain because I knew it was stupid. My body wanted to be upright and the nurses and doctor kept holding me down and scolding me for trying to get up. I'm glad I had the courage to nurse Milo at a time when nursing was looked at as being somewhat primitive and not altogether nice. It was a wondrous and tender experience. Today I thank my lucky stars that he grew up healthy, because even though I seldom drank alcohol after I found I was carrying him, I did smoke like a fiend. I certainly drank during the first month of pregnancy and during his nursing time. It was not general knowledge that cigarettes and alcohol caused birth defects back then, although Eric read somewhere of concerns about alcohol and would not let me drink. (That is just a guilty sidetrack from the comparison I wanted to make.)

I can feel the outlines of our Hoot and Gin, that pregnancy of our brains, as they are kicking and bumping and growing and anxious to be released. I was never regretful or fearful when I was pregnant with Milo. I anticipated his birth with the same joy I do the release of these two. I was attuned to the baby inside myself just as we have been attuned to each other inside our brain or soul or wherever the other flies in. I intuited that Milo was a boy and we called him by name for at least three months before he was born, just as we have named our kids.

It is a little scary to flesh out our brain-children. We know the basics, their coloring, and physical characteristics, but how to describe them as intuited so it carries the message clearly to actual form. I think I have to write things about Hoot to tell about him. What is a little anticipatory right now is how clearly we agree on their descriptions. They are so very vivid in my head, but they have grown in the time we have written of them and sometimes they slip around in age as we have needed them, so it is hard to know at which stage they will emerge.

I'll just tell you a couple of things about Hoot as I see him right now. Hoot woke up one day seeing the tops of things and nothing was ever the same again. Not only that, he couldn't sing any more. Several months before, he had begun to mouth the words at choir practice, when he found he couldn't depend on the notes coming out. Twice he had noticed guys poking each other and giggling and he was pretty sure it was because of the funny sounds he made. He soon found excuses to miss practice and later told the choirmaster that his mother needed him at home to watch his younger brother.

At this rate it will take me months to describe Hoot. Maybe I ought to stick to height: 5'10", weight: 125 lbs., soon to fly.

Verge

11/3/85

My Verge,

How glorious are your insights. They add sunbeams to the already bright additions you have brought to my life. They make me wiggle with delight and discovery. You know that feeling when you have read something several times, or often heard it, and suddenly one day it leaps at you and makes ultimate sense? That is how your mind makes me feel when you tell me your fresh ideas.

The notion that we each had been peeking around at the other's childhood, secretly wanting to get in there, too, so as not to be missing out on anything, is valid. I think jealous is a good word for that feeling. Other people and other thoughts were back there that we couldn't know. When we became aware of how precious our present was it became unbearable to think of that void when we were not part of each other. We were very aware of how important all that separate life was in shaping us into what we would bring to each other. What a clever way our inner children devised to meet each other and to interweave themselves into the past rewriting our history.

That opened all of the remaining barriers to knowing each other. We took what we knew, bent it around and had learned it so well the bending became real, a new life based in fact although the facts happened in different frames of real time. Best of all, it made pushing past the stuck parts of our lives fun and we became open and accessible to ourselves and to each other. Then we could even share the buried grown-up experiences that pushed to get out and took great energy to keep hidden. We freed each other so growing up became as delightful an experience as being children together. I love being your puzzle piece.

Michael

11/15/85

My Sweet Woman,

I like this luxury of having to wonder what newsy items I have to tell you. Since we talk on the phone almost daily, see each other nearly every other week, and just talk our ears off about everything, the letters no longer have the urgency they used to. Don't get me wrong; they are every bit as precious, just not exclusive.

We decided long ago on some sun-warmed day that we would keep on writing even if we came to live together and to see each other every day. Sometimes it helps to write things even after we have said them out loud to each other. Right now I have no real important issues to rehash, rethink, empathize, or otherwise clarify, so I turn to the less urgent but no less important consideration of our courtyard.

Pelton Place settles into readiness for winter, except for the spiders. Only your arrival will make things liven up. The feeling tree waves every time I walk through Main Entrance, not in seduction, but in reassurance that you will soon be here to make it all right. Although the windows are all shuttered tightly, I detect a flutter of life behind them that says they are ready to spring open to emit joy and thanksgiving the minute you walk through the gate. Please hurry. All of Pelton needs you. Especially me. Hurry.

Michael

11/19/85

Dear Michael,

Amazing, Hootie! Do you realize that we have probably written a couple of thousand letters to each other? And how did we write them? One word at a time. Do you realize, in five years the first time I have not written to you on an almost daily basis has been during these last few months since the end of June? I have spent thousands of hours propped up in bed writing to you, as if my life depended upon it. It did. I was finding out who I was, what I thought, what I remembered, who we were, what our relationship consisted of, and making a contact mentally and spiritually with another human being. I was clutching the threads of sanity running through an insane skein of time, living a whole life in letters. It was the only reality in the midst of everything becoming a Chimera. The terror of being found out was far outweighed by the necessity of writing.

What a world we found, Michael, inside each other's head! Black and white turned to a painter's palette. As we wrote, we tapped each other's natural resources—our creativity, our humor, our love. We both grew tall and confident through our writing. We found people we didn't even know we could be, for our persons had been stuffed into dwarfed shapes that wouldn't get noticed too closely. That is why I love your letters when you tell me stories about your world and what you see. I even love when you tell me terrible lies about ferocious spiders. You make me laugh until the need to hug you nearly makes me faint.

The desire to communicate became so overwhelming that we both wrote as is suggested to any artist—daily practice, practice, practice. Although we did not write with any intent of developing that skill, serendipitously we did. As we contemplate a time when communication becomes daily talking face to face, let's not leave off writing. As you said, writing after conversations often sorts things out and forces a cleaner statement of an idea. Let's always leave that form of communication open between us. Perhaps we should consider using that energy to share our experience with others struggling with hopelessness.

I'm hurrying,
Verge

12/31/85

My Verge,

Happy New Year! Yea! Shhhh! We'll pretend to join in the Earthling New Year Celebration so as not to draw attention or make them feel bad, or inferior. They cannot conceive of the true New Year beginning on February 1, 1986. All of the Universe citizens know that and are eagerly awaiting the event. The Earth people cannot be expected to know or understand. Can't you just see the preparations for the Vector Gala? The grandest celebration of the Universe!

Don't pay Hoot any mind—he's just talking talk. We both know we take all this a day at a time—calmly, with faith and trust.

Thanks for the finest holiday time in my whole life. Thanks for the finest life in my whole life. Everything is even newer and fresher and more serene. I actually feel an even newer sense of well-being. How can that be possible? I feel confident that whatever comes down the road for us, we can face it together.

Prettiest tree, prettiest presents, yummiest eats! I love being with you. Hurry!

Michael

January 22, 1986

Dearest Michael,

Yesterday at the market my attention was drawn to a couple ahead of me. They were surely in their late 70's. I suppose they were quite ordinary looking, but they had such a kind regard for each other, such an obvious deep attachment, that they both just glowed with light and life, radiating it to those around them. She was gently joking with him about being forgetful and he was making allowances for her slowed walk. Watching the pleasure they took in walking the same space uplifted my day. I said to myself, "That must be the miracle of you and me—of Hoot and Gin." They emitted such good will and joy that even the checkout lady wasn't impatient with their getting through the procedure of signing a check. It was fun to watch them because I felt I belonged to their special race. It is like being one of the aliens planted on Earth to inculcate new hope or a higher vision.

I am ready, Michael. I couldn't get more ready. Tomorrow I will weed out my file cabinet at work and clean my room. One week from tomorrow you will come to take me away to your land. That thought makes me very happy. I want to spend the rest of my life with you.

Love,
Verge

January 25, 1986

Dear Post Box 5644,

Goodbye, old friend. You have seen us through an era and your passing marks the new freedom of receiving our mail at one address, above board, blatantly, and for the world to know should it care to stop its twirling long enough to look.

**Virginia N. & Michael N.**

More than a passage of time, your business in life has been to teach two virtual non-communicants how to reach out and identify for each other how they feel, to define their opinions, to discover selves to share, and to shape two other child selves to fill the holes between life and life—those lonely years when we each searched for our missing member without knowing what or where it was. Among your many gifts has been a confidence in the giddy flight of writing. The mechanics of putting words to paper and channeling the beating imagination in our brains into words has been a miracle of which neither Michael nor I suspected we were capable.

If we could wish you a wish, it would be that another pair of hesitant lovers on the brink of diving into life would share you. Perhaps our letter's ghosts will pat some of their rough spots, and they will be given courage to continue trying to send pieces of their flesh and bone and heart beat blood to each other.

Your gifts to us have been so incorporated they cannot be enumerate, but know we are grateful for your place in our life. Share our love with another.

Farewell,
Verge and Michael
Hoot 'n Gin

-The End-

CPSIA information can be obtained
at www.ICGtesting.com
Printed in the USA
LVHW051409050522
717952LV00003B/29

9 781958 128107